SNAP

written by **ANDY DIGGLE**

art and covers by **JOCK**

letters by **CLEM ROBINS**

additional design for the trade

by **JOCK & VINCENT KUKUA**

IMAGE COMICS, INC.

ROBERT KIRKMAN, chief operating officer
ERIK LARSEN, chief financial officer
TODD McFARLANE, president
MARC SILVESTRI, chief executive officer
JIM VALENTINO, vice-president

ERIC STEPHENSON, publisher
RON RICHARDS, director of business development
JENNIFER DE GUZMAN, director of trade book sales
KAT SALAZAR, pr & marketing coordinator
JEREMY SULLIVAN, digital rights coordinator
JAMIE PARRENO, online marketing coordinator
EMILIO BAUTISTA, sales assistant

BRANWYN BIGGLESTONE, senior accounts manager
EMILY MILLER, accounts manager
JAEMIE DUDAS, administrative assistant
TYLER SHAINLINE, events coordinator
DAVID BROTHERS, content manager
JONATHAN CHAN, production manager
DREW GILL, art director
MEREDITH WALLACE, print manager
MONICA GARCIA, senior production artist
VINCENT KUKUA, production artist
JENNA SAVAGE, production artist
ADDISON DUKE, production artist

WWW.IMAGECOMICS.COM

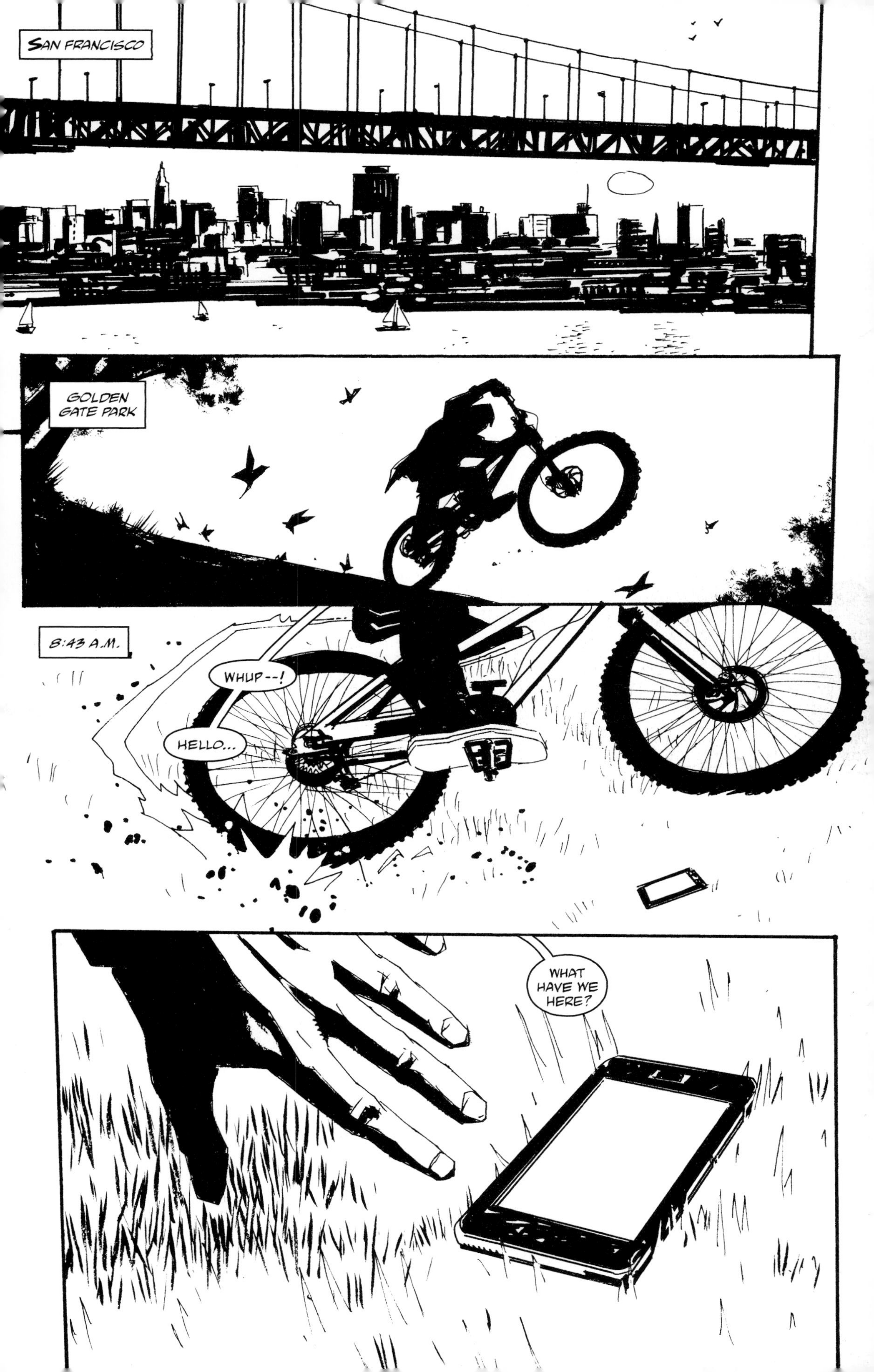
SAN FRANCISCO
GOLDEN GATE PARK
8:43 A.M.
WHUP--!
HELLO...
WHAT HAVE WE HERE?

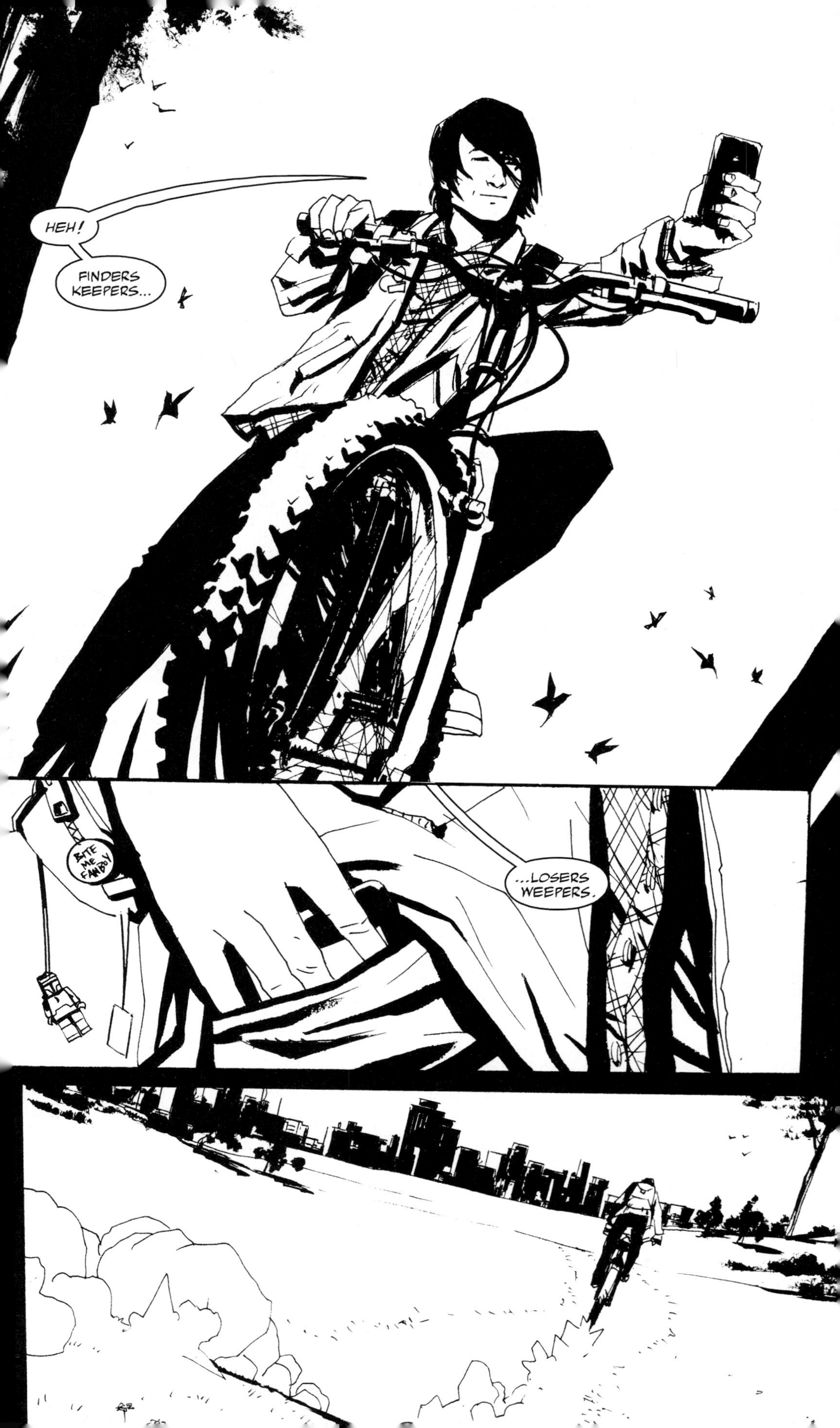
HEH!
FINDERS KEEPERS...
BITE ME FANBOY
...LOSERS WEEPERS.

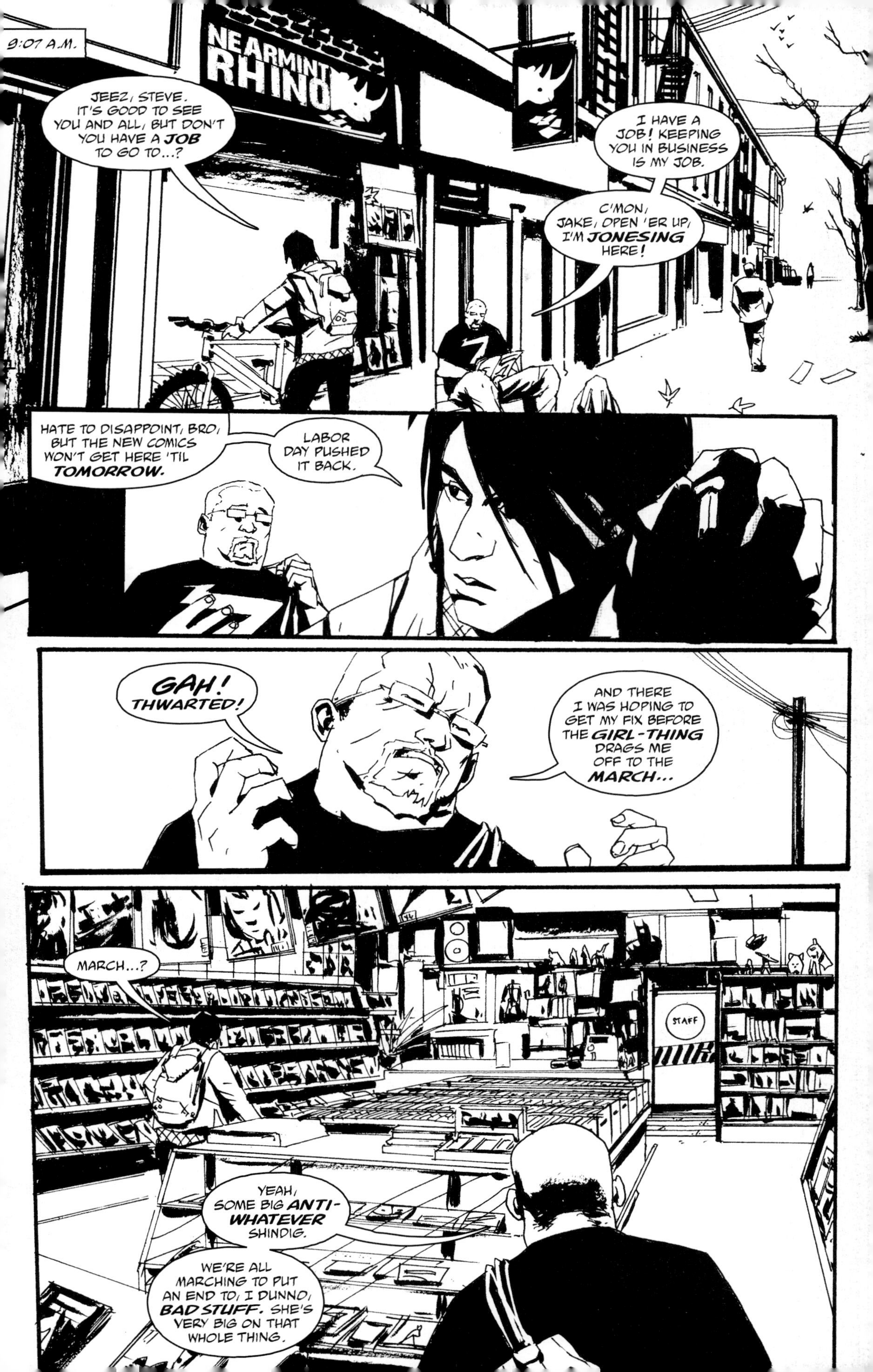
9:07 A.M.
NEARMINT RHINO
JEEZ, STEVE. IT'S GOOD TO SEE YOU AND ALL, BUT DON'T YOU HAVE A **JOB** TO GO TO...?
I HAVE A JOB! KEEPING YOU IN BUSINESS IS MY JOB.
C'MON, JAKE, OPEN 'ER UP, I'M **JONESING** HERE!
HATE TO DISAPPOINT, BRO, BUT THE NEW COMICS WON'T GET HERE 'TIL **TOMORROW.**
LABOR DAY PUSHED IT BACK.
GAH! THWARTED!
AND THERE I WAS HOPING TO GET MY FIX BEFORE THE **GIRL-THING** DRAGS ME OFF TO THE **MARCH...**
MARCH...?
STAFF
YEAH, SOME BIG **ANTI-WHATEVER** SHINDIG.
WE'RE ALL MARCHING TO PUT AN END TO, I DUNNO, **BAD STUFF.** SHE'S VERY BIG ON THAT WHOLE THING.

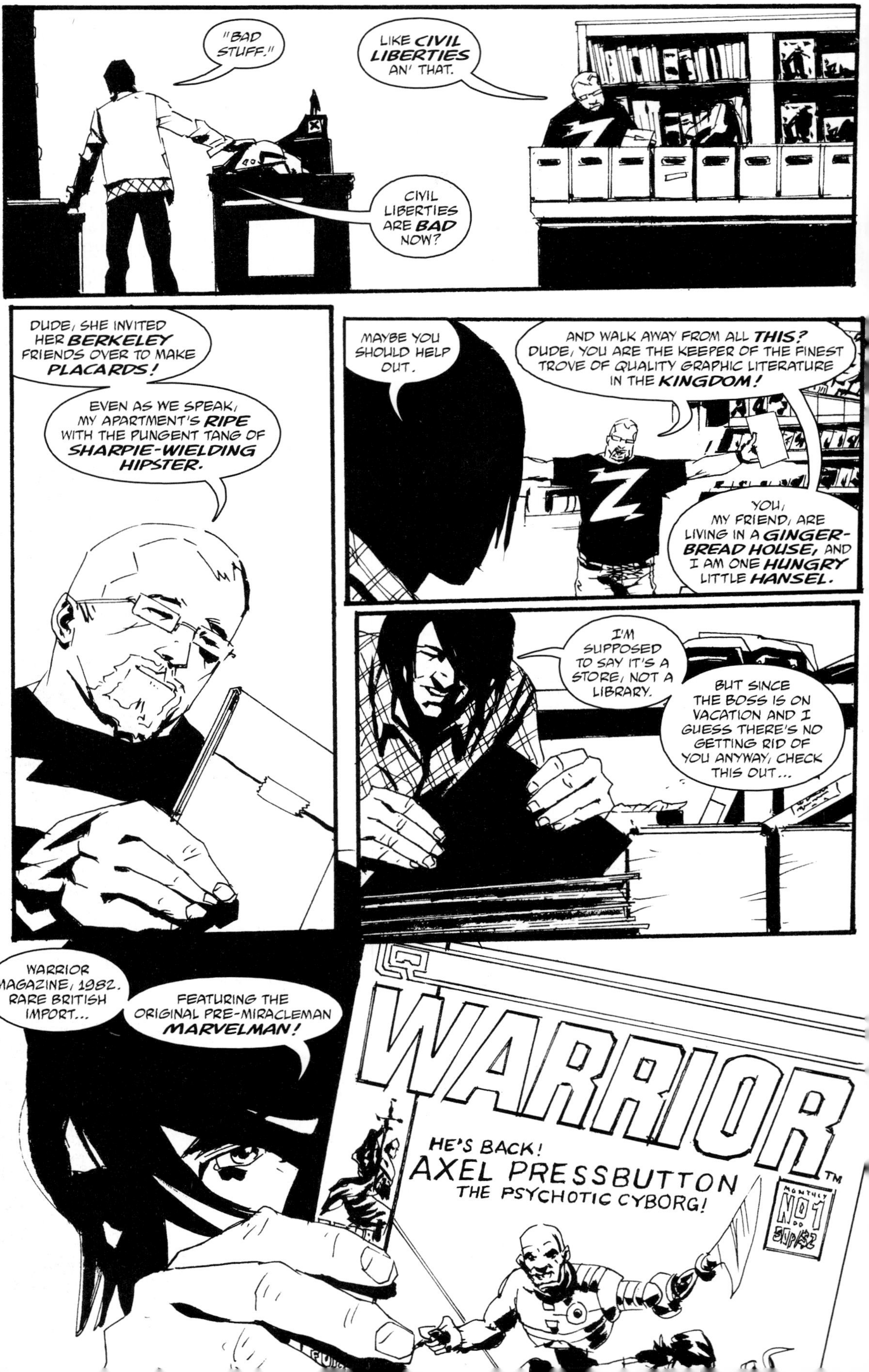
"BAD STUFF."
LIKE CIVIL LIBERTIES AN' THAT.
CIVIL LIBERTIES ARE BAD NOW?
DUDE, SHE INVITED HER BERKELEY FRIENDS OVER TO MAKE PLACARDS!
EVEN AS WE SPEAK, MY APARTMENT'S RIPE WITH THE PUNGENT TANG OF SHARPIE-WIELDING HIPSTER.
MAYBE YOU SHOULD HELP OUT.
AND WALK AWAY FROM ALL THIS? DUDE, YOU ARE THE KEEPER OF THE FINEST TROVE OF QUALITY GRAPHIC LITERATURE IN THE KINGDOM!
YOU, MY FRIEND, ARE LIVING IN A GINGER-BREAD HOUSE, AND I AM ONE HUNGRY LITTLE HANSEL.
I'M SUPPOSED TO SAY IT'S A STORE, NOT A LIBRARY.
BUT SINCE THE BOSS IS ON VACATION AND I GUESS THERE'S NO GETTING RID OF YOU ANYWAY, CHECK THIS OUT...
WARRIOR MAGAZINE, 1982. RARE BRITISH IMPORT...
FEATURING THE ORIGINAL PRE-MIRACLEMAN MARVELMAN!
WARRIOR
HE'S BACK!
AXEL PRESSBUTTON
THE PSYCHOTIC CYBORG!

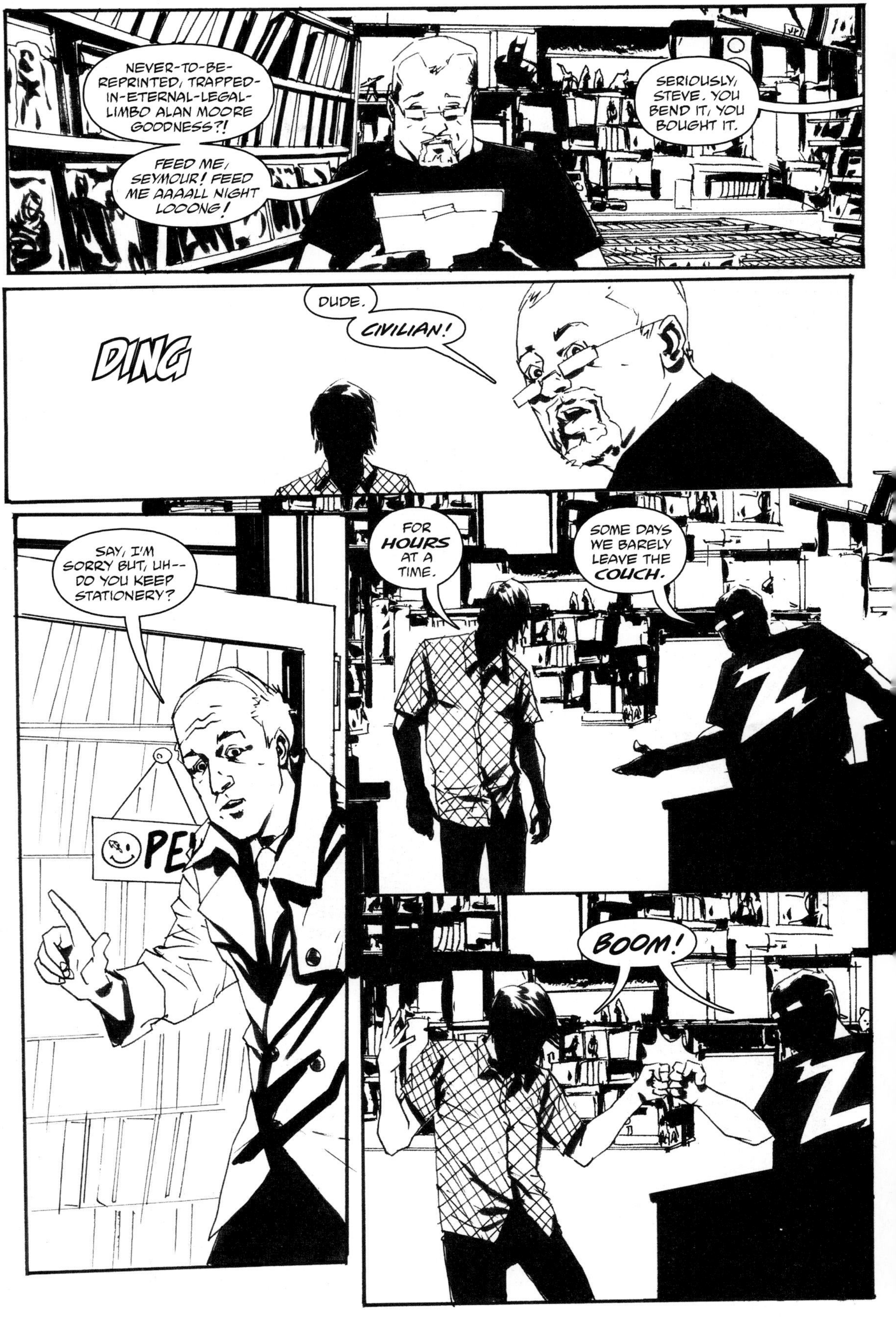
NEVER-TO-BE-REPRINTED, TRAPPED-IN-ETERNAL-LEGAL-LIMBO ALAN MOORE GOODNESS?!
FEED ME, SEYMOUR! FEED ME AAAALL NIGHT LOOONG!
SERIOUSLY, STEVE. YOU BEND IT, YOU BOUGHT IT.
DING
DUDE.
CIVILIAN!
SAY, I'M SORRY BUT, UH-- DO YOU KEEP STATIONERY?
FOR HOURS AT A TIME.
SOME DAYS WE BARELY LEAVE THE COUCH.
BOOM!

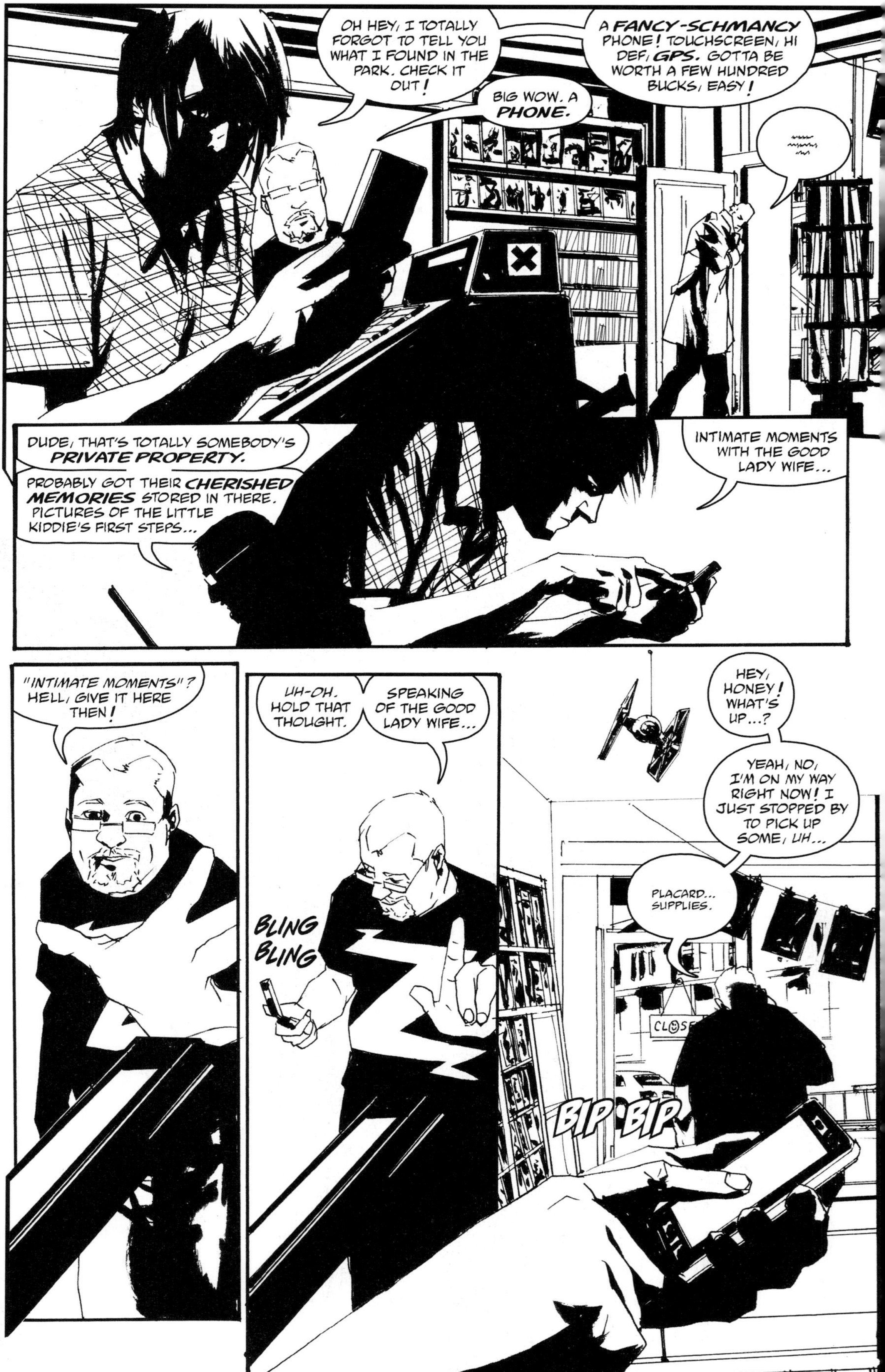
OH HEY, I TOTALLY FORGOT TO TELL YOU WHAT I FOUND IN THE PARK. CHECK IT OUT!
BIG WOW. A PHONE.
A FANCY-SCHMANCY PHONE! TOUCHSCREEN, HI DEF, GPS. GOTTA BE WORTH A FEW HUNDRED BUCKS, EASY!
DUDE, THAT'S TOTALLY SOMEBODY'S PRIVATE PROPERTY.
PROBABLY GOT THEIR CHERISHED MEMORIES STORED IN THERE. PICTURES OF THE LITTLE KIDDIE'S FIRST STEPS...
INTIMATE MOMENTS WITH THE GOOD LADY WIFE...
"INTIMATE MOMENTS"? HELL, GIVE IT HERE THEN!
UH-OH. HOLD THAT THOUGHT.
SPEAKING OF THE GOOD LADY WIFE...
BLING BLING
HEY, HONEY! WHAT'S UP...?
YEAH, NO, I'M ON MY WAY RIGHT NOW! I JUST STOPPED BY TO PICK UP SOME, UH...
PLACARD... SUPPLIES.
BIP BIP

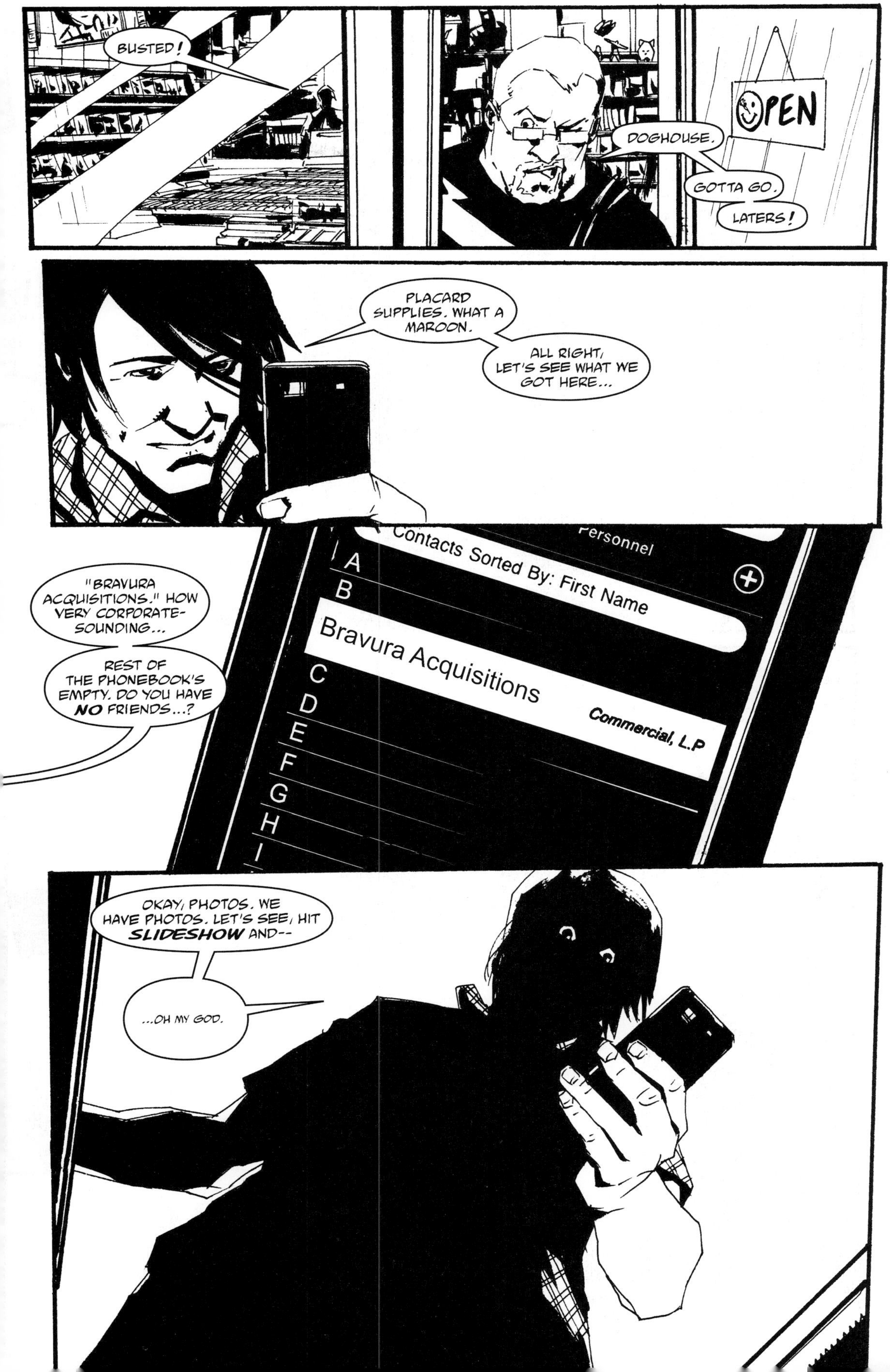
BUSTED!
DOGHOUSE.
OPEN
GOTTA GO.
LATERS!
PLACARD SUPPLIES. WHAT A MAROON.
ALL RIGHT, LET'S SEE WHAT WE GOT HERE...
"BRAVURA ACQUISITIONS." HOW VERY CORPORATE-SOUNDING...
RESt OF THE PHONEBOOK'S EMPTY. DO YOU HAVE *NO* FRIENDS...?
Personnel
Contacts Sorted By: First Name
A
B
Bravura Acquisitions
Commercial, L.P
C
D
E
F
G
H
OKAY, PHOTOS. WE HAVE PHOTOS. LET'S SEE, HIT *SLIDESHOW* AND--
...OH MY GOD.

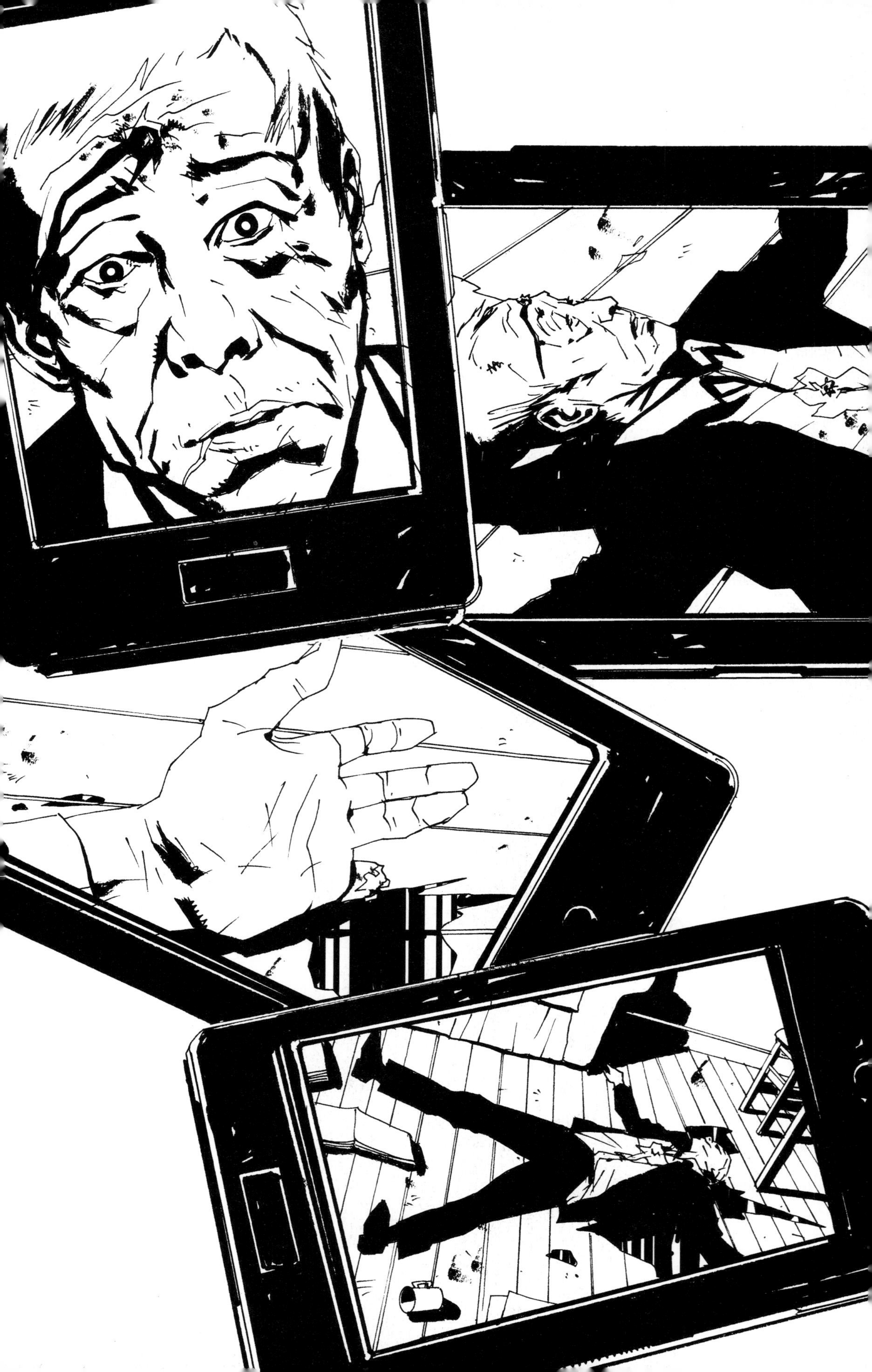

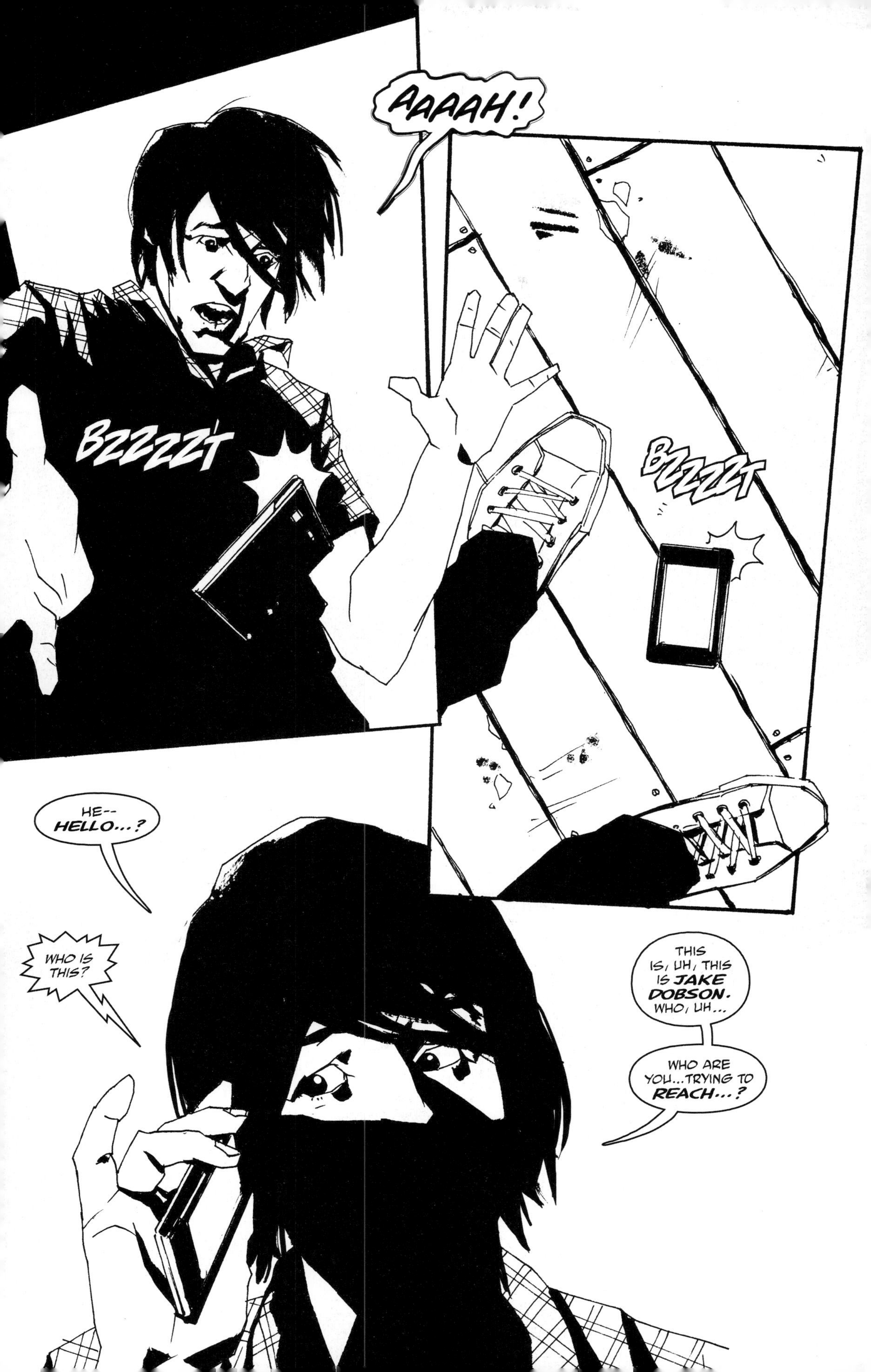
AAAAH!
BZZZZT
BZZZZT
HE-- HELLO...?
WHO IS THIS?
THIS IS, UH, THIS IS JAKE DOBSON. WHO, UH...
WHO ARE YOU...TRYING TO REACH...?

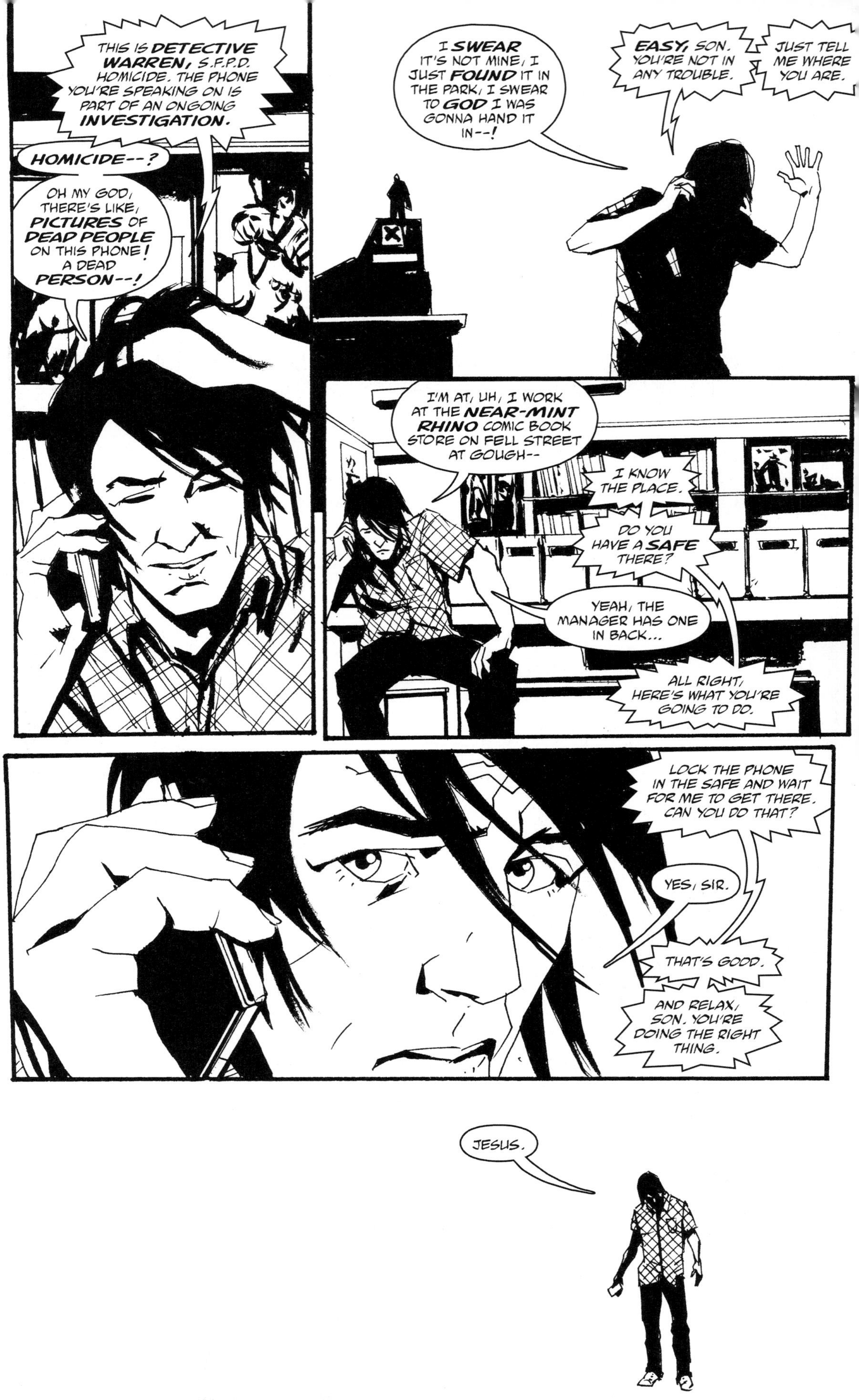
THIS IS DETECTIVE WARREN, S.F.P.D. HOMICIDE. THE PHONE YOU'RE SPEAKING ON IS PART OF AN ONGOING INVESTIGATION.
HOMICIDE--?
OH MY GOD, THERE'S LIKE, PICTURES OF DEAD PEOPLE ON THIS PHONE! A DEAD PERSON--!
I SWEAR IT'S NOT MINE, I JUST FOUND IT IN THE PARK, I SWEAR TO GOD I WAS GONNA HAND IT IN--!
EASY, SON. YOU'RE NOT IN ANY TROUBLE.
JUST TELL ME WHERE YOU ARE.
I'M AT, UH, I WORK AT THE NEAR-MINT RHINO COMIC BOOK STORE ON FELL STREET AT GOUGH--
I KNOW THE PLACE.
DO YOU HAVE A SAFE THERE?
YEAH, THE MANAGER HAS ONE IN BACK...
ALL RIGHT, HERE'S WHAT YOU'RE GOING TO DO.
LOCK THE PHONE IN THE SAFE AND WAIT FOR ME TO GET THERE. CAN YOU DO THAT?
YES, SIR.
THAT'S GOOD.
AND RELAX, SON. YOU'RE DOING THE RIGHT THING.
JESUS.

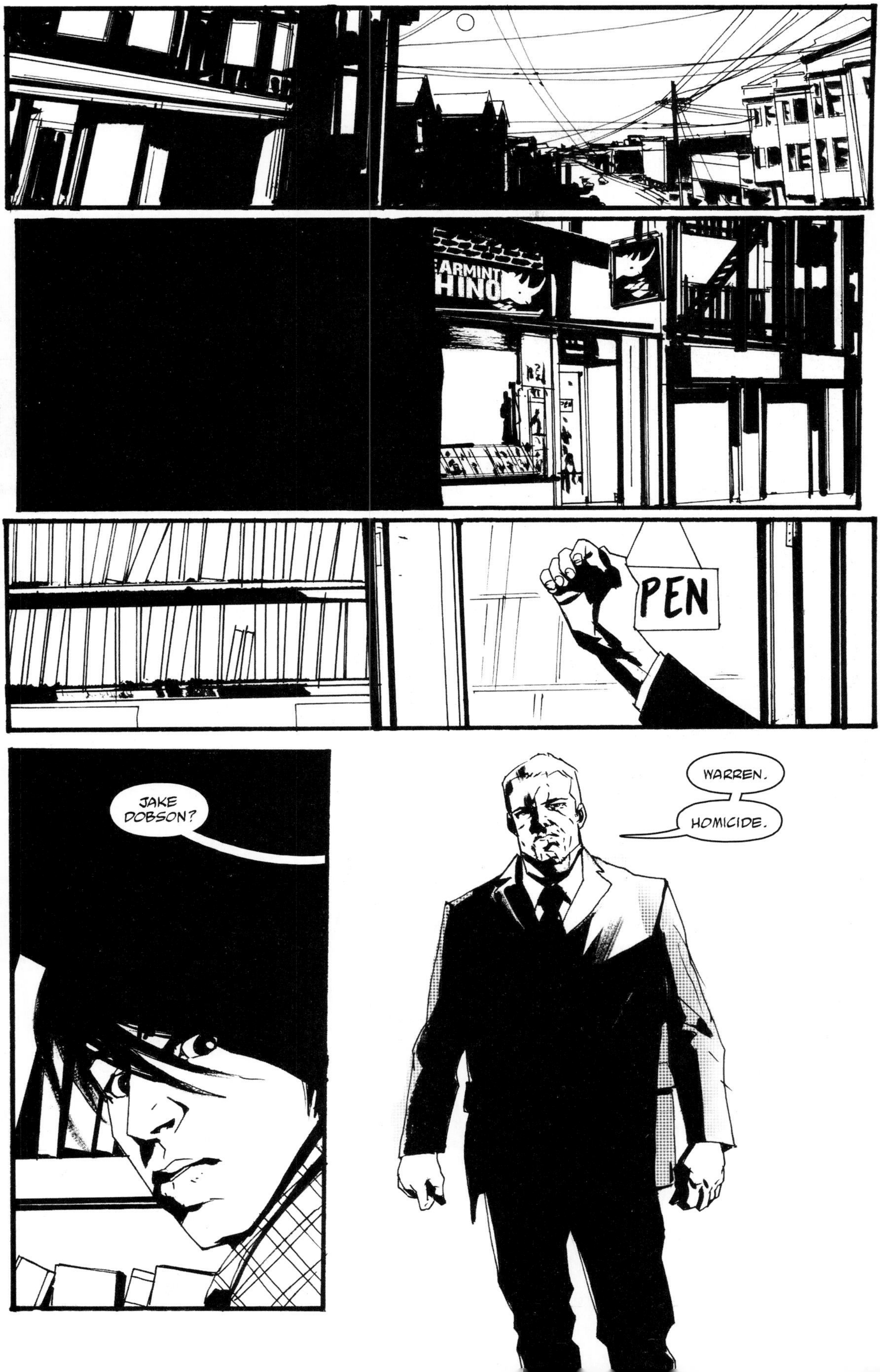
ARMINT
HINO
PEN
JAKE DOBSON?
WARREN.
HOMICIDE.

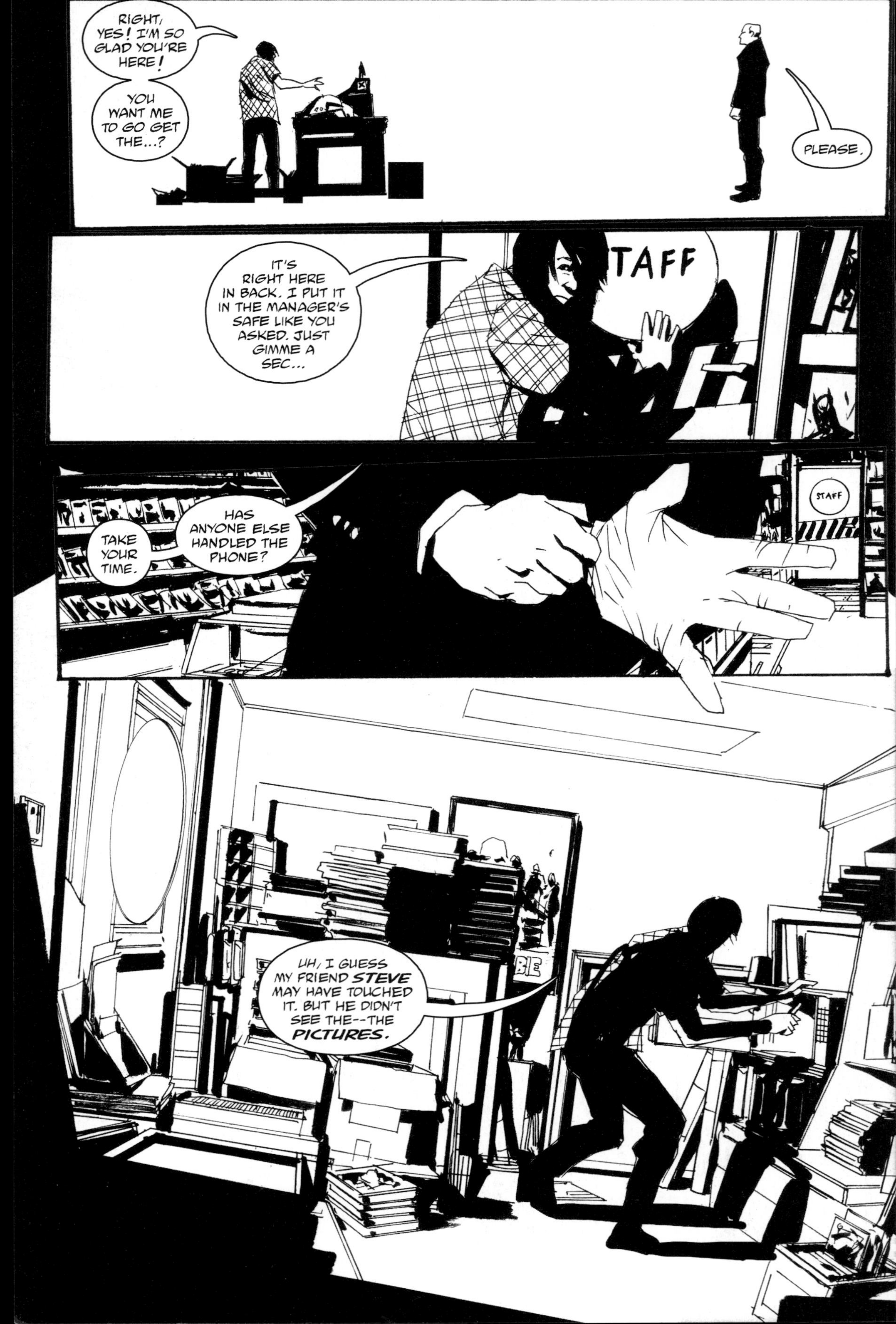
RIGHT, YES! I'M SO GLAD YOU'RE HERE!
YOU WANT ME TO GO GET THE...?
PLEASE.
IT'S RIGHT HERE IN BACK. I PUT IT IN THE MANAGER'S SAFE LIKE YOU ASKED. JUST GIMME A SEC...
STAFF
TAKE YOUR TIME.
HAS ANYONE ELSE HANDLED THE PHONE?
STAFF
UH, I GUESS MY FRIEND STEVE MAY HAVE TOUCHED IT. BUT HE DIDN'T SEE THE--THE PICTURES.

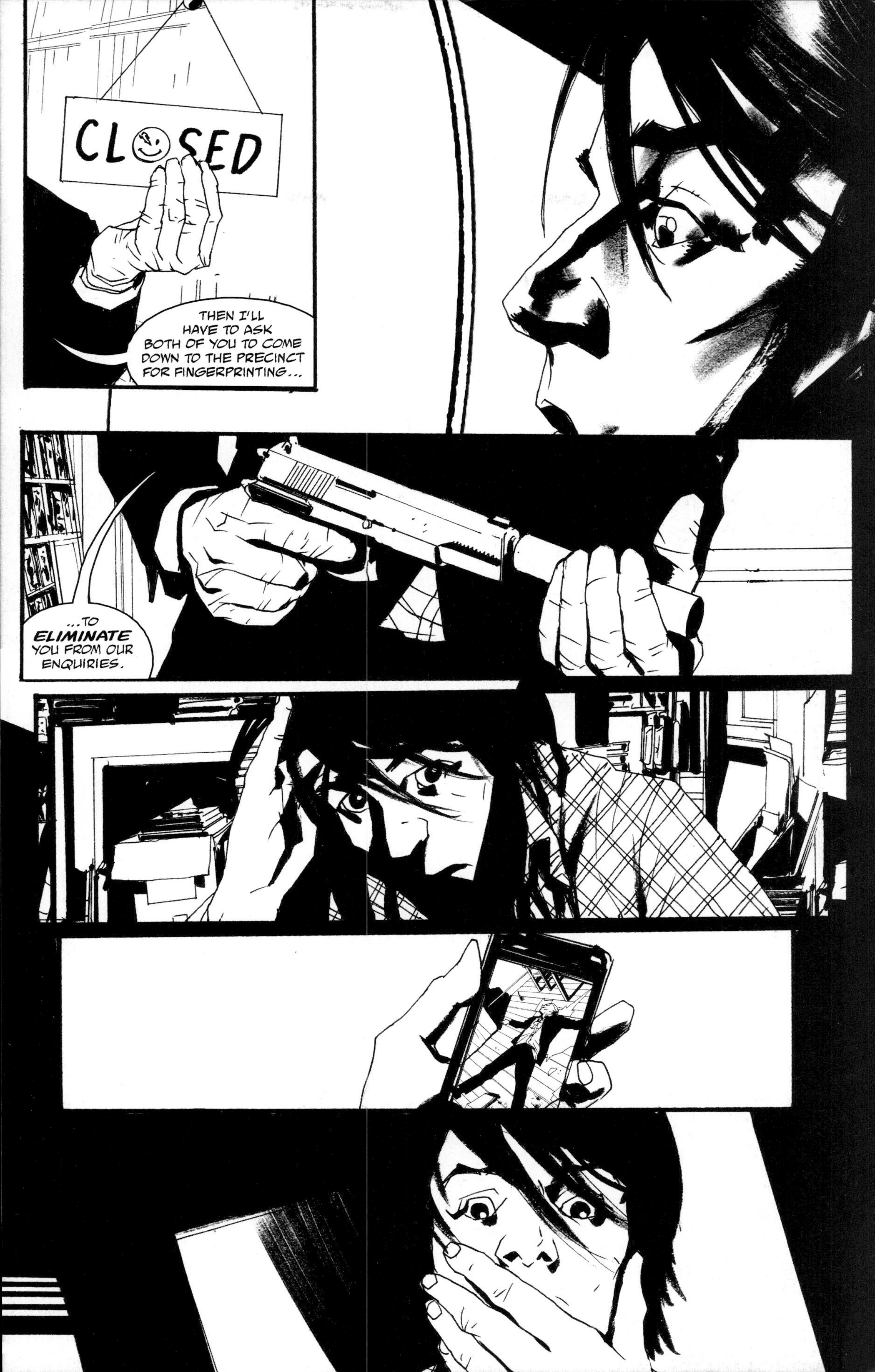
CLOSED
THEN I'LL HAVE TO ASK BOTH OF YOU TO COME DOWN TO THE PRECINCT FOR FINGERPRINTING...
...TO *ELIMINATE* YOU FROM OUR ENQUIRIES.

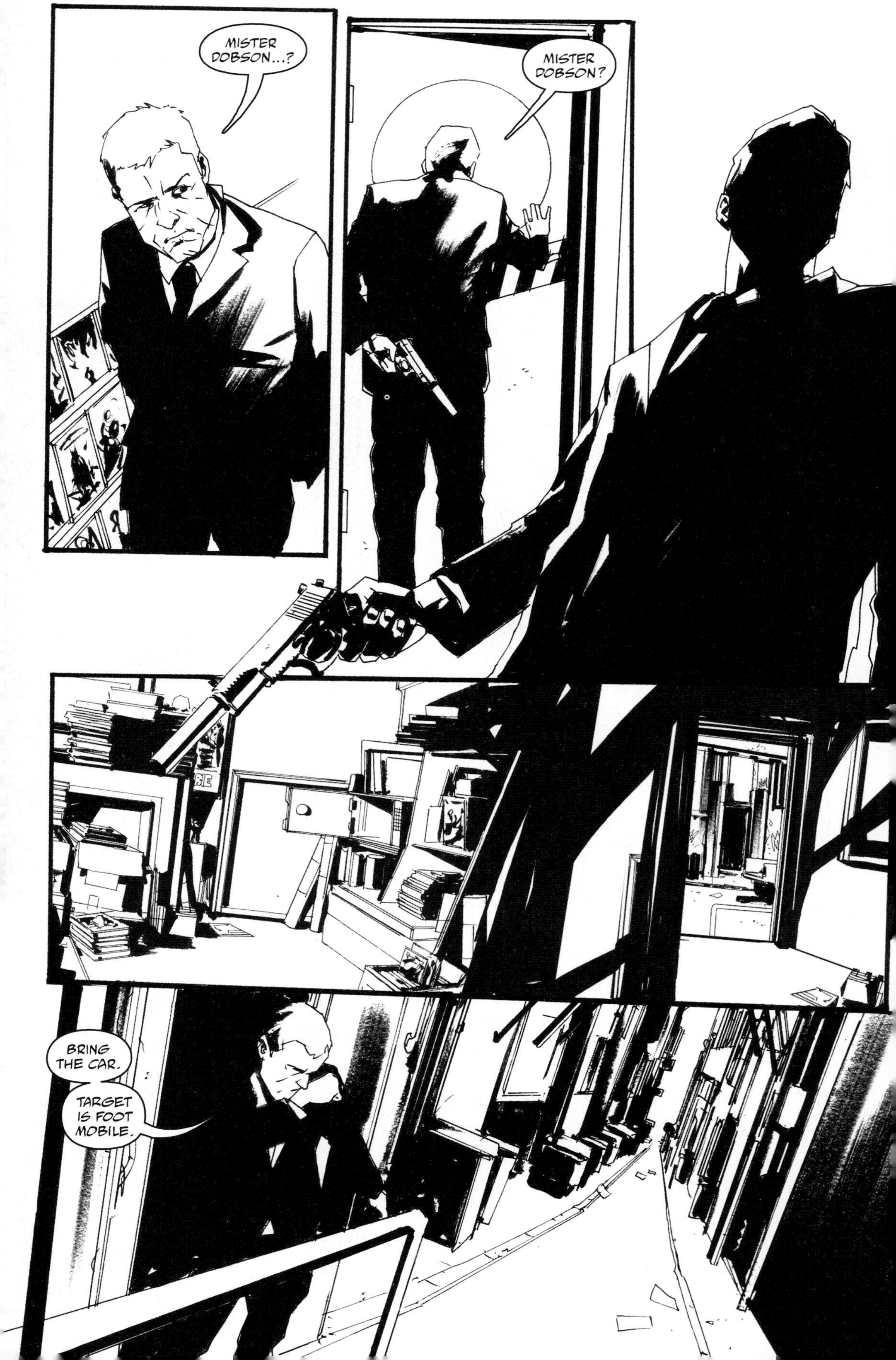
MISTER DOBSON...?
MISTER DOBSON?
BRING THE CAR.
TARGET IS FOOT MOBILE.

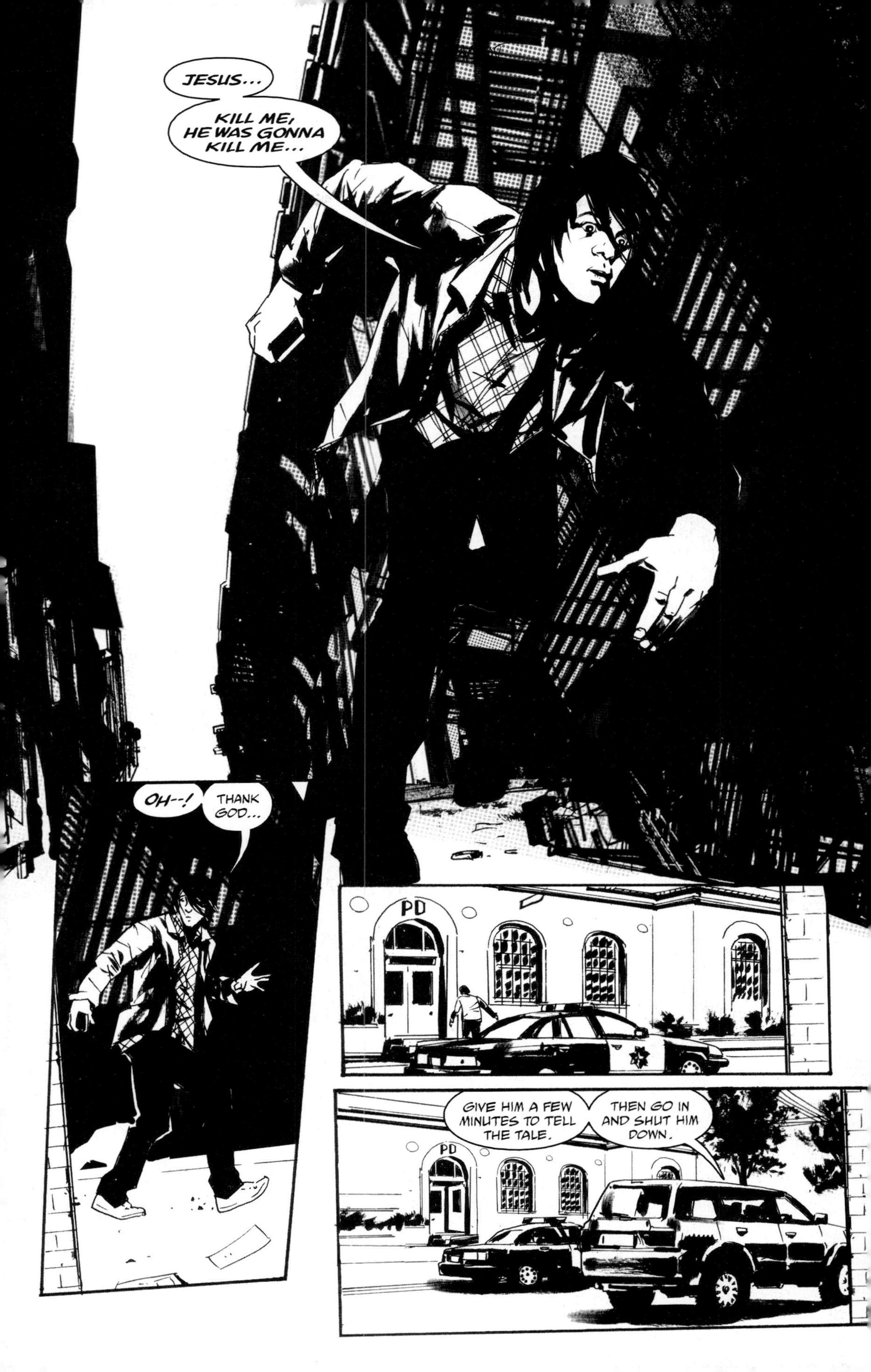
JESUS...
KILL ME, HE WAS GONNA KILL ME...
OH--!
THANK GOD...
PD
GIVE HIM A FEW MINUTES TO TELL THE TALE.
THEN GO IN AND SHUT HIM DOWN.

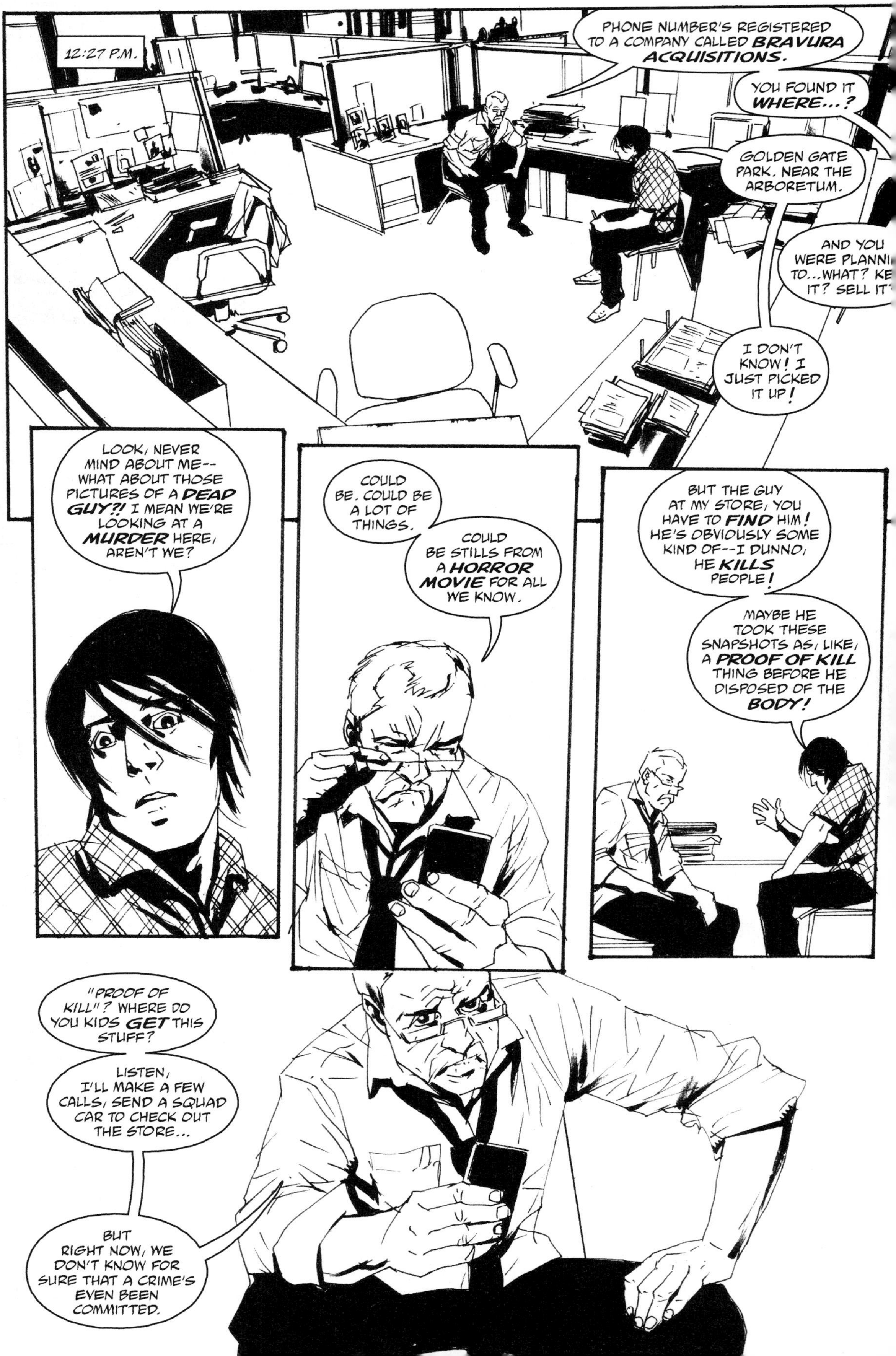
12:27 P.M.
PHONE NUMBER'S REGISTERED TO A COMPANY CALLED BRAVURA ACQUISITIONS.
YOU FOUND IT WHERE...?
GOLDEN GATE PARK. NEAR THE ARBORETUM.
AND YOU WERE PLANNI TO...WHAT? KE IT? SELL IT?
I DON'T KNOW! I JUST PICKED IT UP!
LOOK, NEVER MIND ABOUT ME-- WHAT ABOUT THOSE PICTURES OF A DEAD GUY?! I MEAN WE'RE LOOKING AT A MURDER HERE, AREN'T WE?
COULD BE. COULD BE A LOT OF THINGS.
COULD BE STILLS FROM A HORROR MOVIE FOR ALL WE KNOW.
BUT THE GUY AT MY STORE, YOU HAVE TO FIND HIM! HE'S OBVIOUSLY SOME KIND OF--I DUNNO, HE KILLS PEOPLE!
MAYBE HE TOOK THESE SNAPSHOTS AS, LIKE, A PROOF OF KILL THING BEFORE HE DISPOSED OF THE BODY!
"PROOF OF KILL"? WHERE DO YOU KIDS GET THIS STUFF?
LISTEN, I'LL MAKE A FEW CALLS, SEND A SQUAD CAR TO CHECK OUT THE STORE...
BUT RIGHT NOW, WE DON'T KNOW FOR SURE THAT A CRIME'S EVEN BEEN COMMITTED.

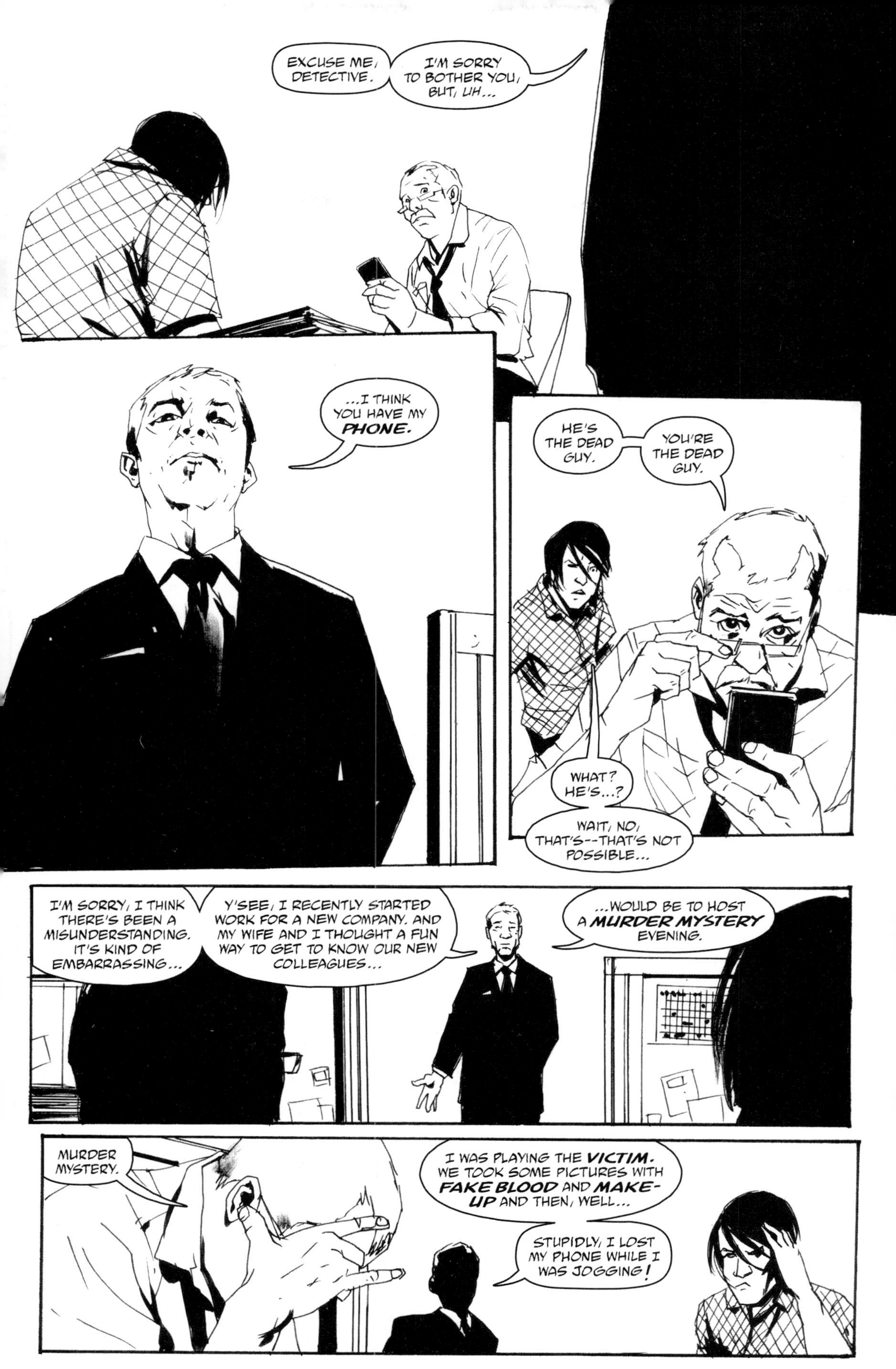
EXCUSE ME, DETECTIVE.
I'M SORRY TO BOTHER YOU, BUT, UH...
...I THINK YOU HAVE MY PHONE.
HE'S THE DEAD GUY.
YOU'RE THE DEAD GUY.
WHAT? HE'S...?
WAIT, NO, THAT'S--THAT'S NOT POSSIBLE...
I'M SORRY, I THINK THERE'S BEEN A MISUNDERSTANDING. IT'S KIND OF EMBARRASSING...
Y'SEE, I RECENTLY STARTED WORK FOR A NEW COMPANY. AND MY WIFE AND I THOUGHT A FUN WAY TO GET TO KNOW OUR NEW COLLEAGUES...
...WOULD BE TO HOST A MURDER MYSTERY EVENING.
MURDER MYSTERY.
I WAS PLAYING THE VICTIM. WE TOOK SOME PICTURES WITH FAKE BLOOD AND MAKE-UP AND THEN, WELL...
STUPIDLY, I LOST MY PHONE WHILE I WAS JOGGING!

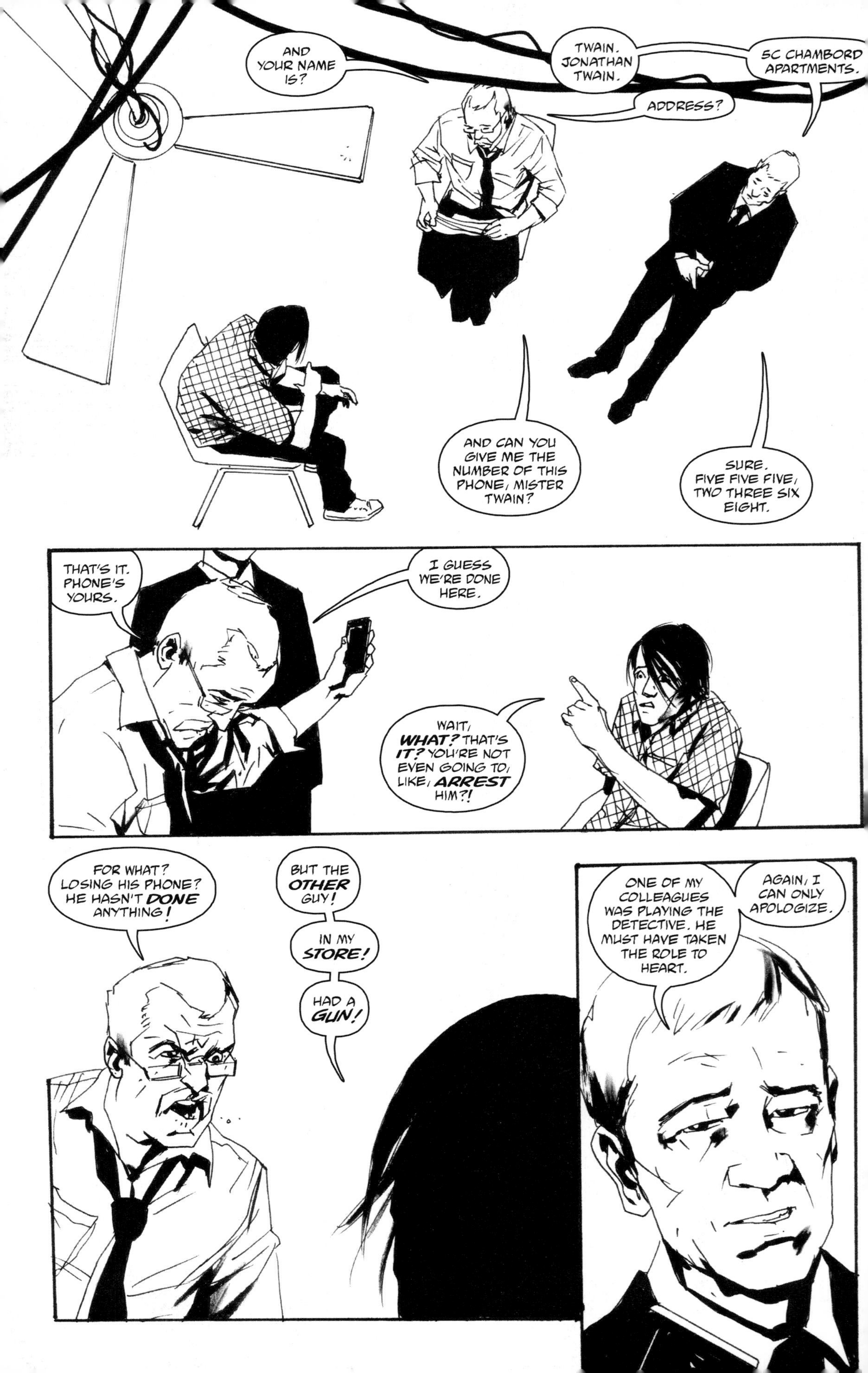
AND YOUR NAME IS?
TWAIN. JONATHAN TWAIN.
ADDRESS?
5C CHAMBORD APARTMENTS.
AND CAN YOU GIVE ME THE NUMBER OF THIS PHONE, MISTER TWAIN?
SURE. FIVE FIVE FIVE, TWO THREE SIX EIGHT.
THAT'S IT. PHONE'S YOURS.
I GUESS WE'RE DONE HERE.
WAIT, **WHAT?** THAT'S **IT?** YOU'RE NOT EVEN GOING TO, LIKE, **ARREST** HIM?!
FOR WHAT? LOSING HIS PHONE? HE HASN'T **DONE** ANYTHING!
BUT THE **OTHER** GUY!
IN MY **STORE!**
HAD A **GUN!**
ONE OF MY COLLEAGUES WAS PLAYING THE DETECTIVE. HE MUST HAVE TAKEN THE ROLE TO HEART.
AGAIN, I CAN ONLY APOLOGIZE.

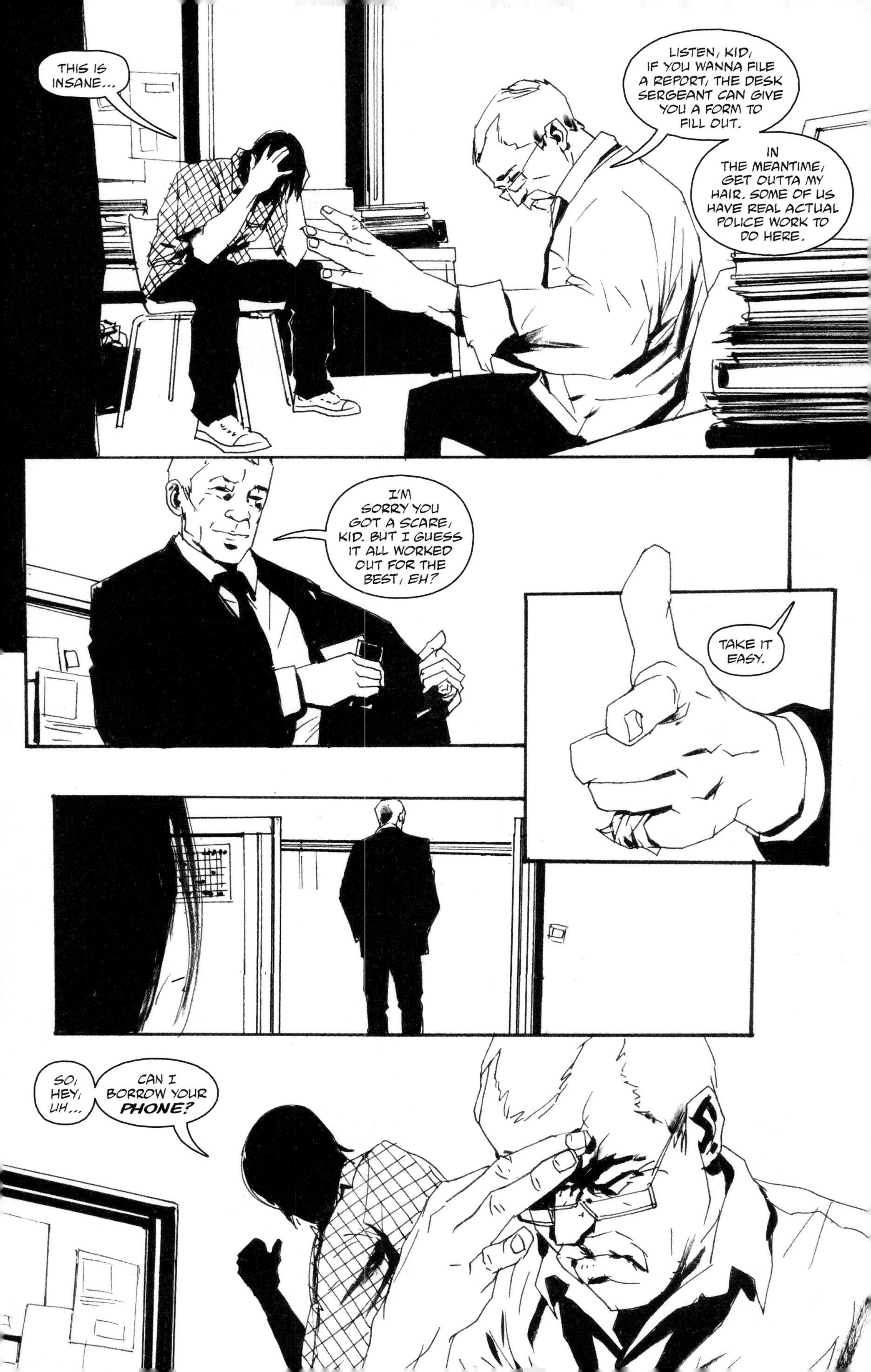

THIS IS INSANE...
LISTEN, KID, IF YOU WANNA FILE A REPORT, THE DESK SERGEANT CAN GIVE YOU A FORM TO FILL OUT.
IN THE MEANTIME, GET OUTTA MY HAIR. SOME OF US HAVE REAL ACTUAL POLICE WORK TO DO HERE.
I'M SORRY YOU GOT A SCARE, KID. BUT I GUESS IT ALL WORKED OUT FOR THE BEST, EH?
TAKE IT EASY.
SO, HEY, UH...
CAN I BORROW YOUR ***PHONE?***

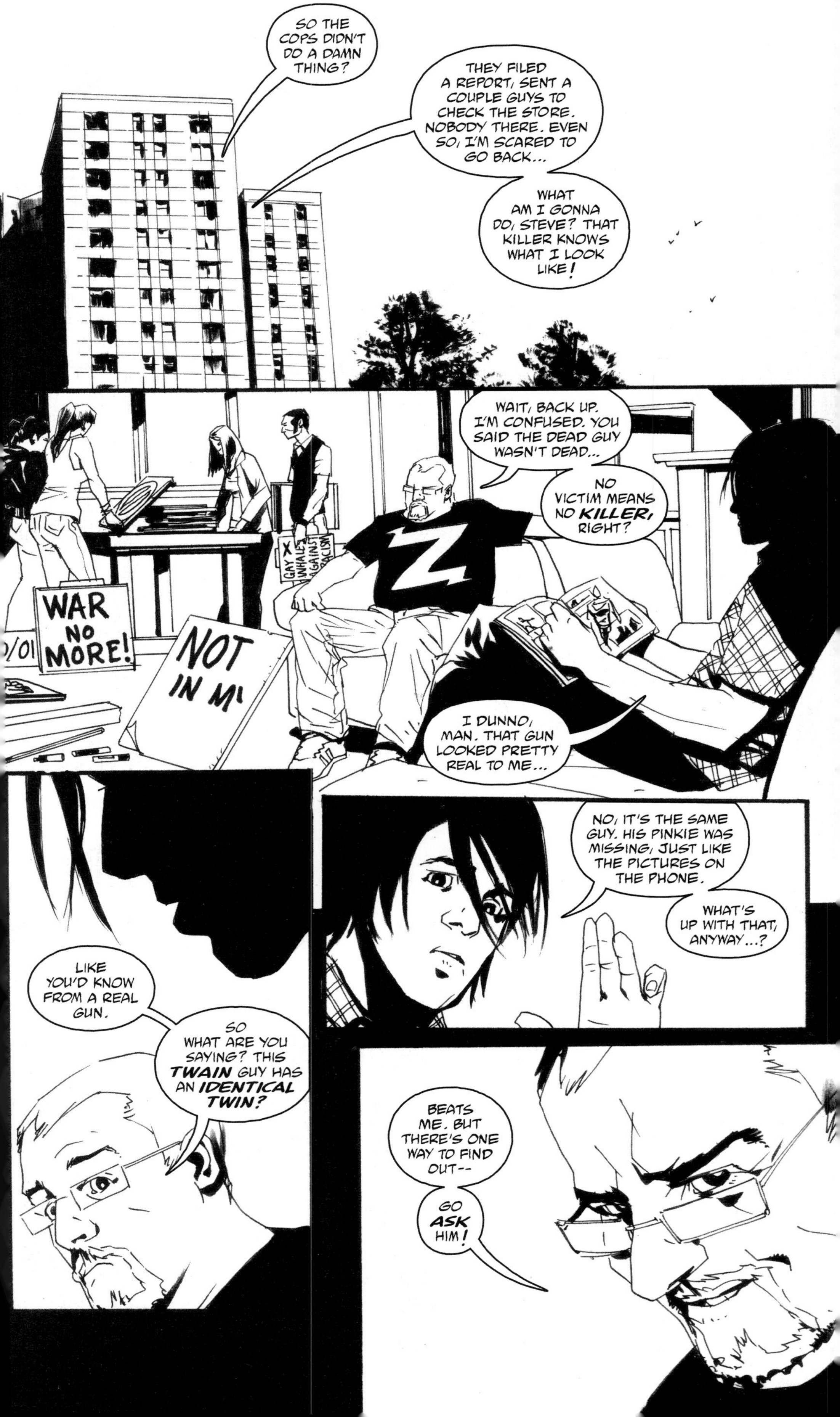
SO THE COPS DIDN'T DO A DAMN THING?
THEY FILED A REPORT, SENT A COUPLE GUYS TO CHECK THE STORE. NOBODY THERE. EVEN SO, I'M SCARED TO GO BACK...
WHAT AM I GONNA DO, STEVE? THAT KILLER KNOWS WHAT I LOOK LIKE!
WAR NO MORE!
NOT IN M'
GAY WHALES AGAINST RACISM
WAIT, BACK UP. I'M CONFUSED. YOU SAID THE DEAD GUY WASN'T DEAD...
NO VICTIM MEANS NO KILLER, RIGHT?
I DUNNO, MAN. THAT GUN LOOKED PRETTY REAL TO ME...
LIKE YOU'D KNOW FROM A REAL GUN.
NO, IT'S THE SAME GUY. HIS PINKIE WAS MISSING, JUST LIKE THE PICTURES ON THE PHONE.
WHAT'S UP WITH THAT, ANYWAY...?
SO WHAT ARE YOU SAYING? THIS TWAIN GUY HAS AN IDENTICAL TWIN?
BEATS ME. BUT THERE'S ONE WAY TO FIND OUT--
GO ASK HIM!

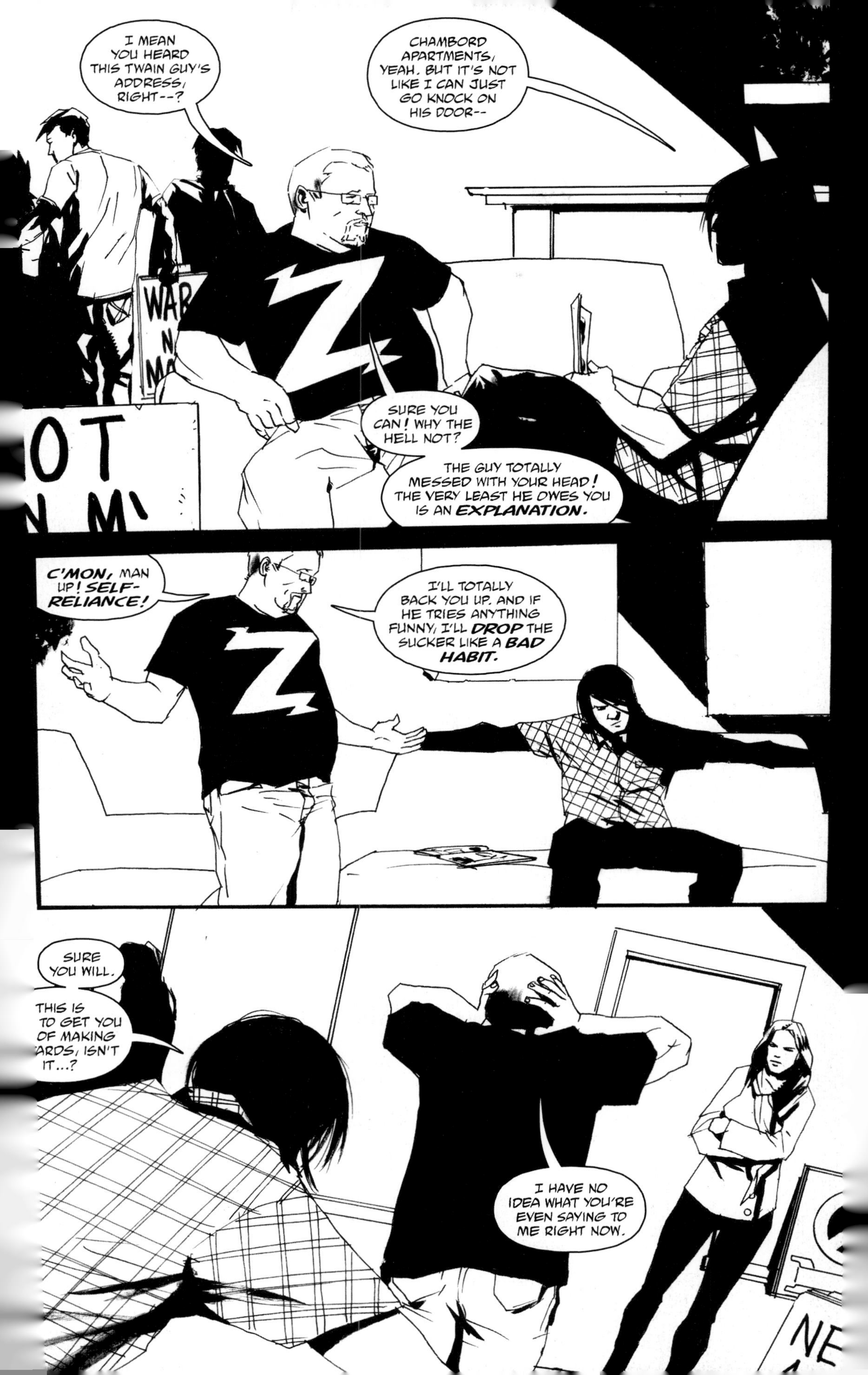
I MEAN YOU HEARD THIS TWAIN GUY'S ADDRESS, RIGHT--?
CHAMBORD APARTMENTS, YEAH. BUT IT'S NOT LIKE I CAN JUST GO KNOCK ON HIS DOOR--
SURE YOU CAN! WHY THE HELL NOT?
THE GUY TOTALLY MESSED WITH YOUR HEAD! THE VERY LEAST HE OWES YOU IS AN EXPLANATION.
C'MON, MAN UP! SELF-RELIANCE!
I'LL TOTALLY BACK YOU UP. AND IF HE TRIES ANYTHING FUNNY, I'LL DROP THE SUCKER LIKE A BAD HABIT.
SURE YOU WILL.
THIS IS TO GET YOU OF MAKING ARDS, ISN'T IT...?
I HAVE NO IDEA WHAT YOU'RE EVEN SAYING TO ME RIGHT NOW.

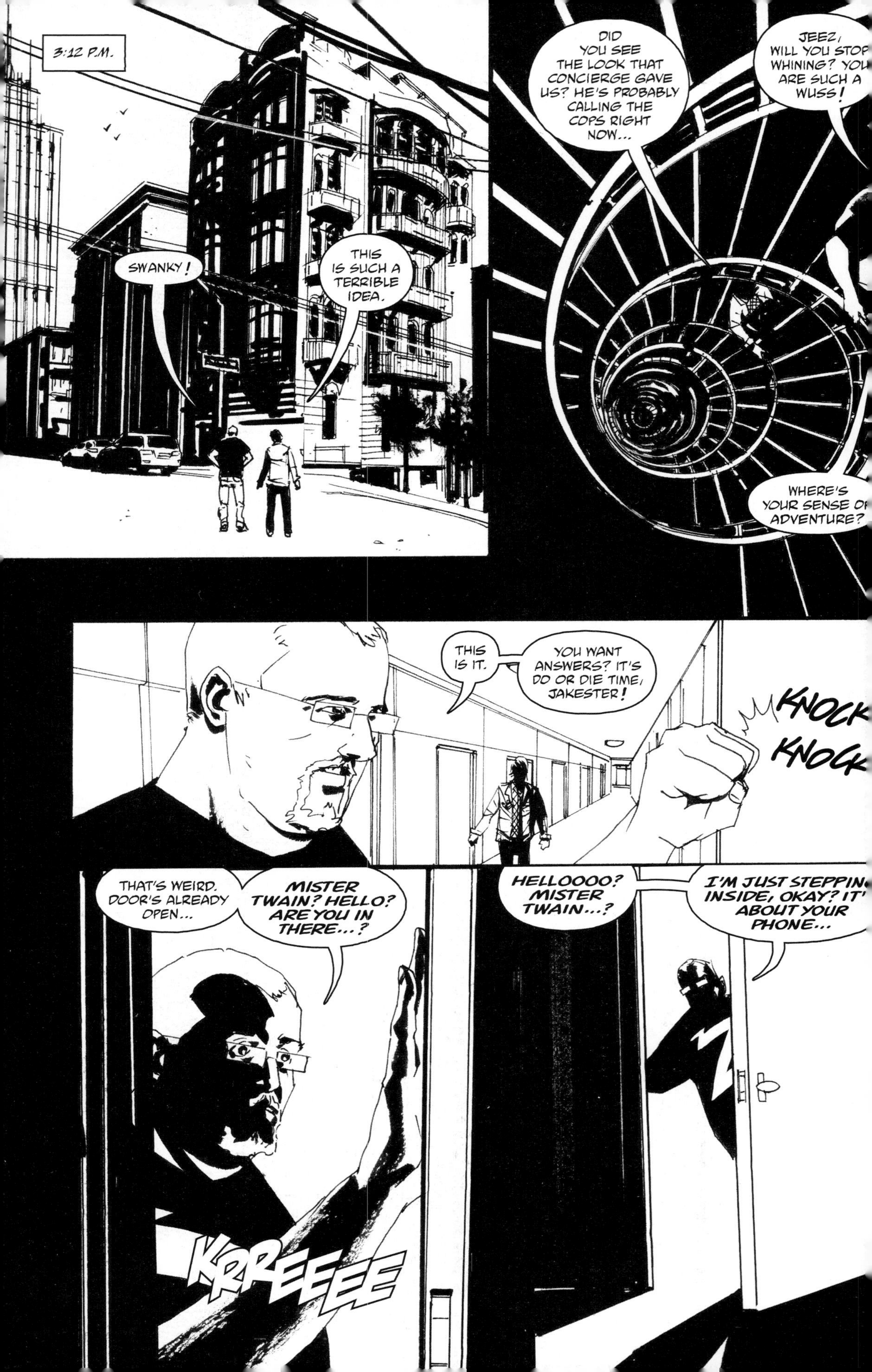
3:12 P.M.
SWANKY!
THIS IS SUCH A TERRIBLE IDEA.
DID YOU SEE THE LOOK THAT CONCIERGE GAVE US? HE'S PROBABLY CALLING THE COPS RIGHT NOW...
JEEZ, WILL YOU STOP WHINING? YOU ARE SUCH A WUSS!
WHERE'S YOUR SENSE OF ADVENTURE?
THIS IS IT.
YOU WANT ANSWERS? IT'S DO OR DIE TIME, JAKESTER!
KNOCK KNOCK
THAT'S WEIRD. DOOR'S ALREADY OPEN...
MISTER TWAIN? HELLO? ARE YOU IN THERE...?
KRREEEEE
HELLOOOO? MISTER TWAIN...?
I'M JUST STEPPING INSIDE, OKAY? IT'S ABOUT YOUR PHONE...

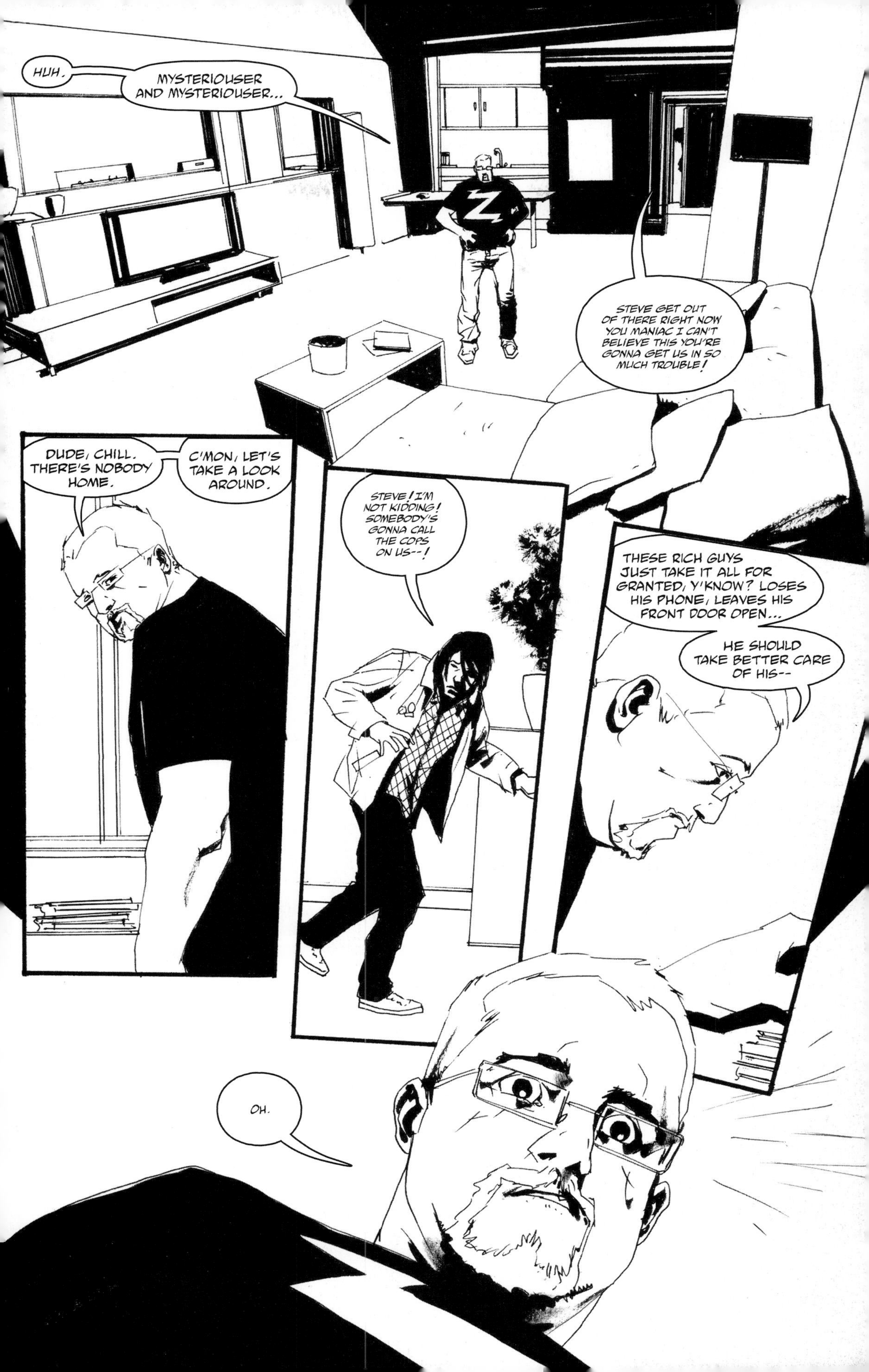
HUH.
MYSTERIOUSER AND MYSTERIOUSER...
STEVE GET OUT OF THERE RIGHT NOW YOU MANIAC I CAN'T BELIEVE THIS YOU'RE GONNA GET US IN SO MUCH TROUBLE!
DUDE, CHILL. THERE'S NOBODY HOME.
C'MON, LET'S TAKE A LOOK AROUND.
STEVE! I'M NOT KIDDING! SOMEBODY'S GONNA CALL THE COPS ON US--!
THESE RICH GUYS JUST TAKE IT ALL FOR GRANTED, Y'KNOW? LOSES HIS PHONE, LEAVES HIS FRONT DOOR OPEN...
HE SHOULD TAKE BETTER CARE OF HIS--
OH.

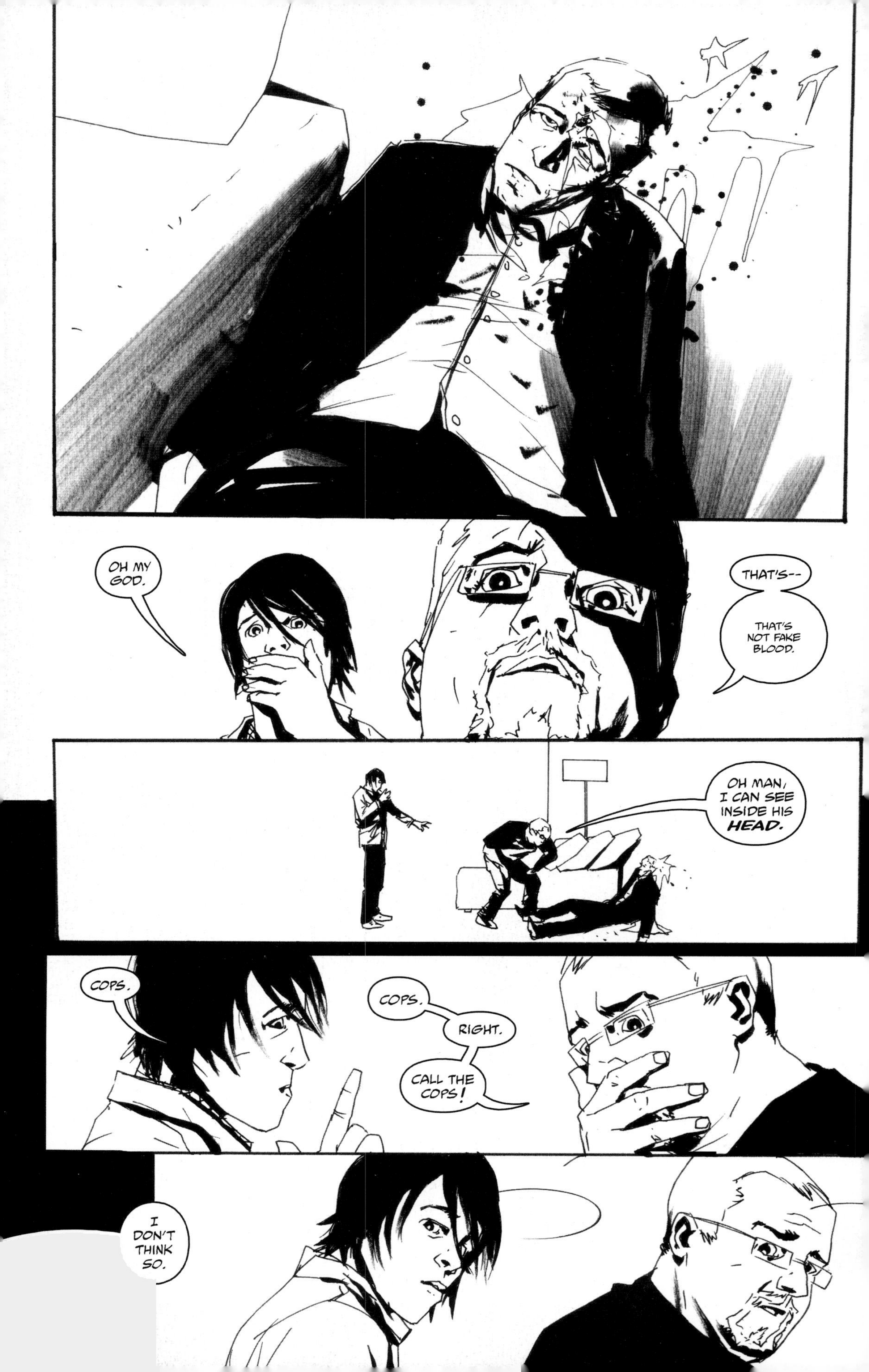
OH MY GOD.
THAT'S--
THAT'S NOT FAKE BLOOD.
OH MAN, I CAN SEE INSIDE HIS HEAD.
COPS.
COPS.
RIGHT.
CALL THE COPS!
I DON'T THINK SO.

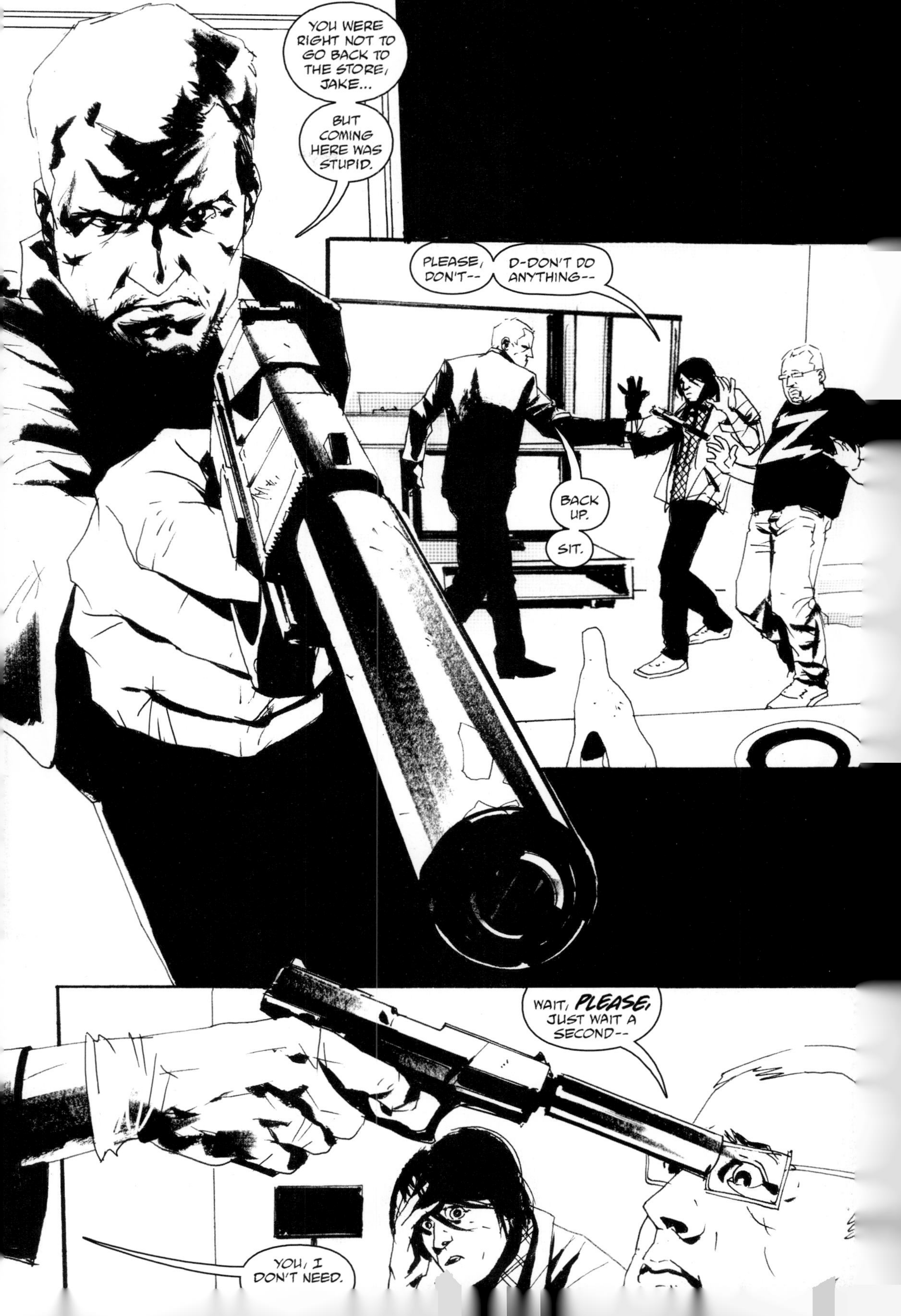
YOU WERE RIGHT NOT TO GO BACK TO THE STORE, JAKE...
BUT COMING HERE WAS STUPID.
PLEASE, DON'T--
D-DON'T DO ANYTHING--
BACK UP.
SIT.
WAIT, PLEASE, JUST WAIT A SECOND--
YOU, I DON'T NEED.

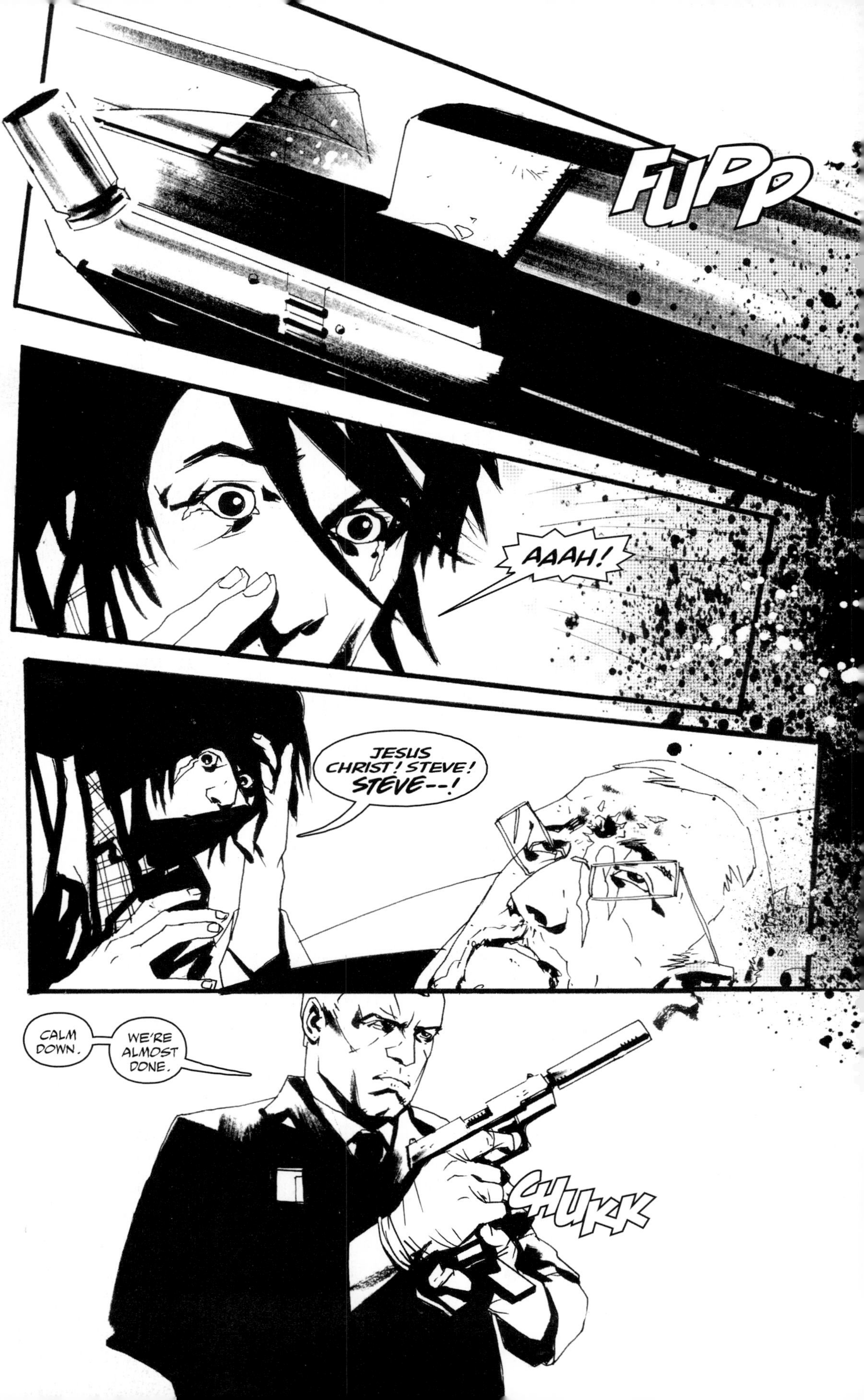
FUPP
AAAH!
JESUS CHRIST! STEVE! STEVE--!
CALM DOWN.
WE'RE ALMOST DONE.
CHUKK

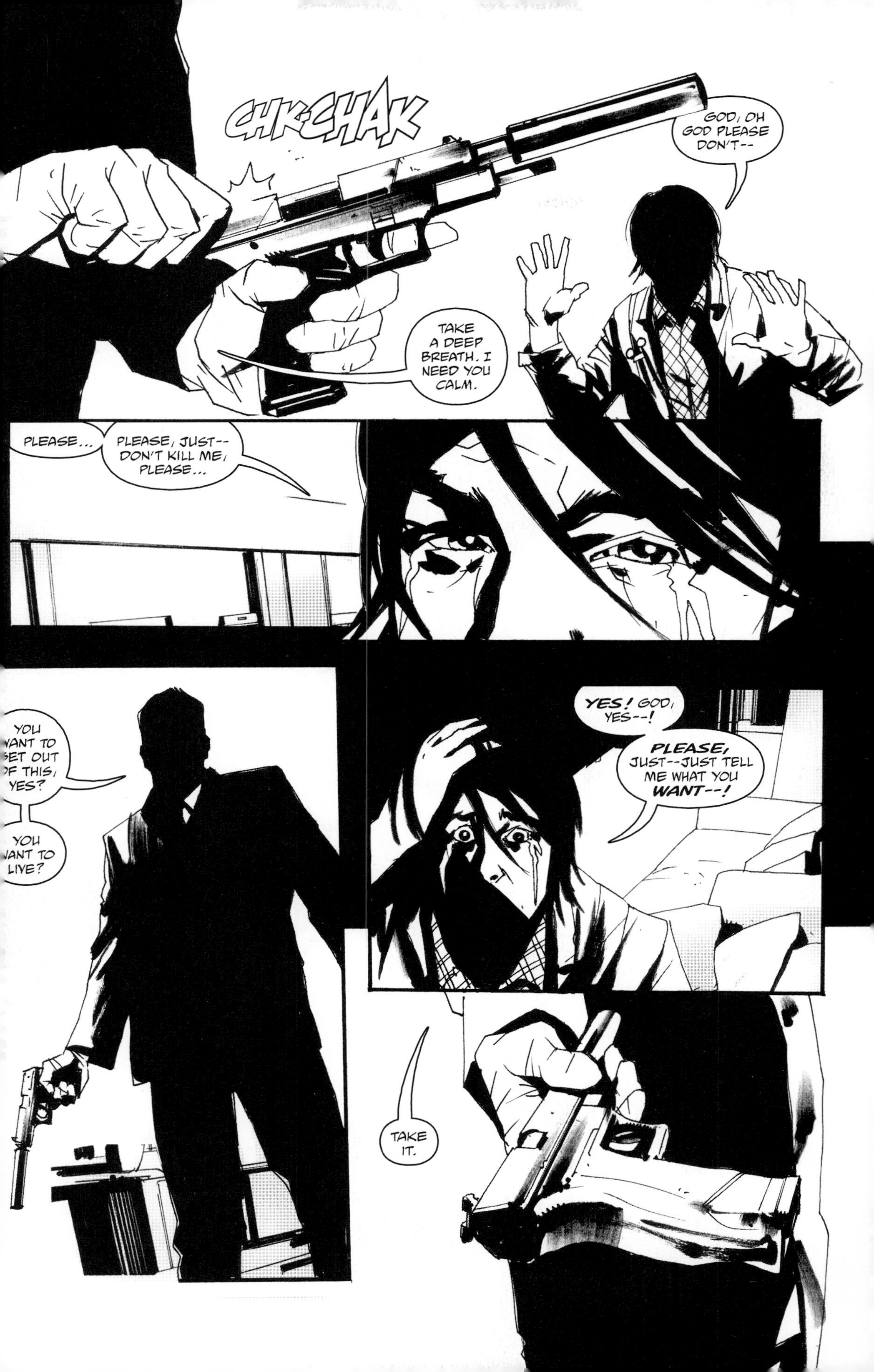
CHK-CHAK
GOD, OH GOD PLEASE DON'T--
TAKE A DEEP BREATH. I NEED YOU CALM.
PLEASE...
PLEASE, JUST-- DON'T KILL ME, PLEASE...
YOU WANT TO GET OUT OF THIS, YES?
YOU WANT TO LIVE?
YES! GOD, YES--!
PLEASE, JUST--JUST TELL ME WHAT YOU WANT--!
TAKE IT.

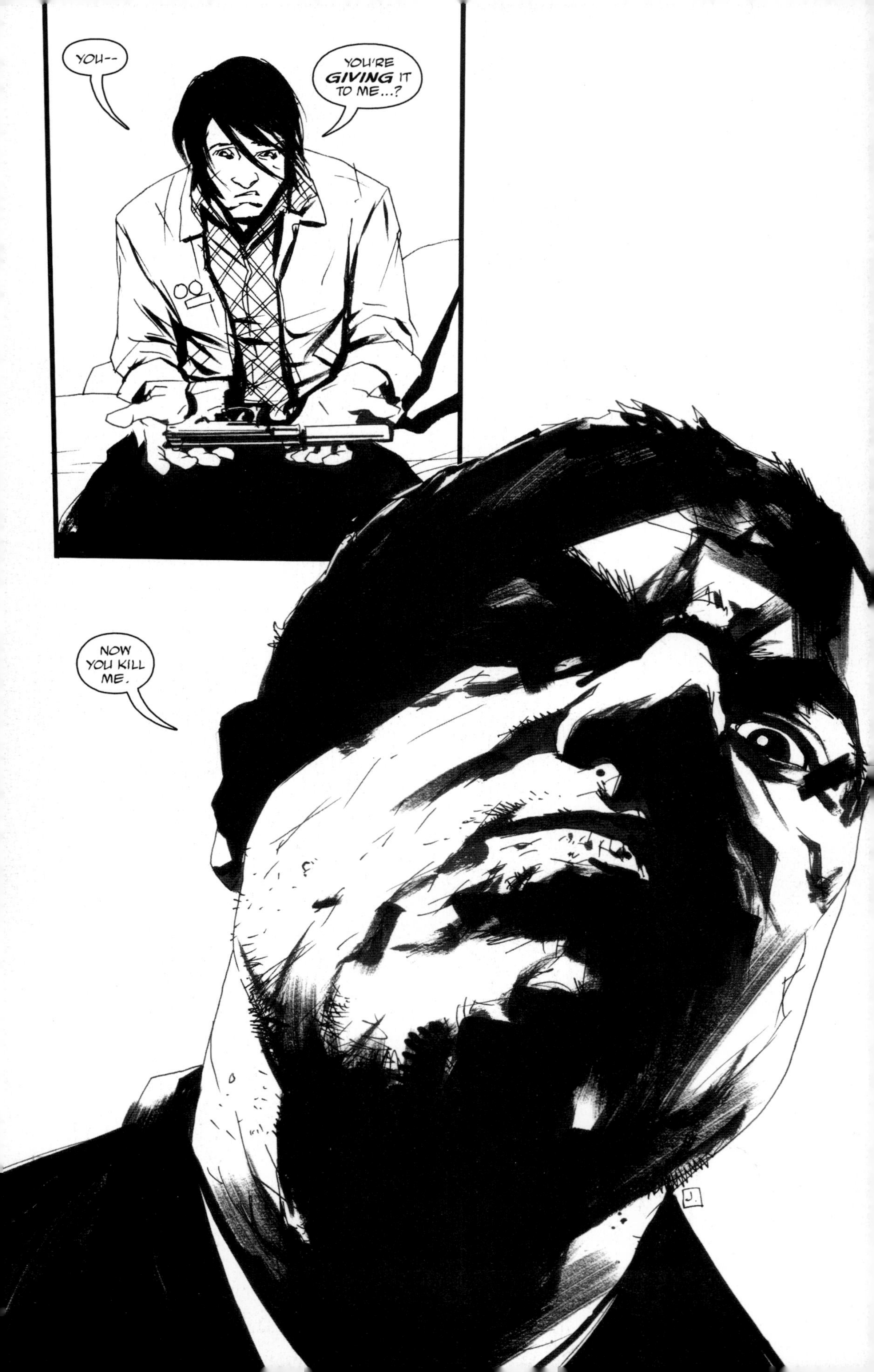
YOU--
YOU'RE GIVING IT TO ME...?
NOW YOU KILL ME.

CHAPTER TWO

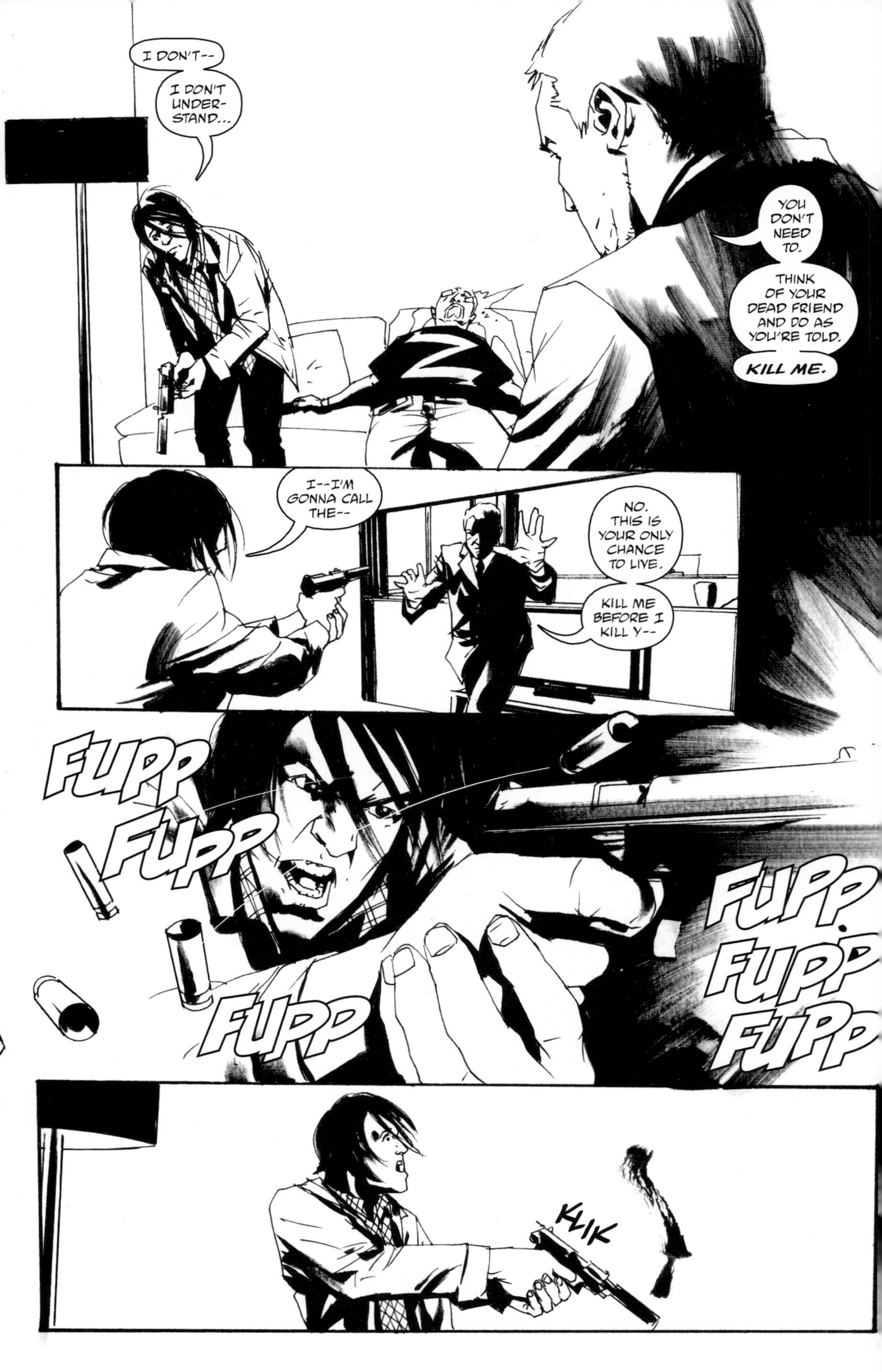
I DON'T--
I DON'T UNDER-STAND...
YOU DON'T NEED TO.
THINK OF YOUR DEAD FRIEND AND DO AS YOU'RE TOLD.
KILL ME.
I--I'M GONNA CALL THE--
NO. THIS IS YOUR ONLY CHANCE TO LIVE.
KILL ME BEFORE I KILL Y--
FUPP
FUPP
FUPP
FUPP.
FUPP
FUPP
KLIK

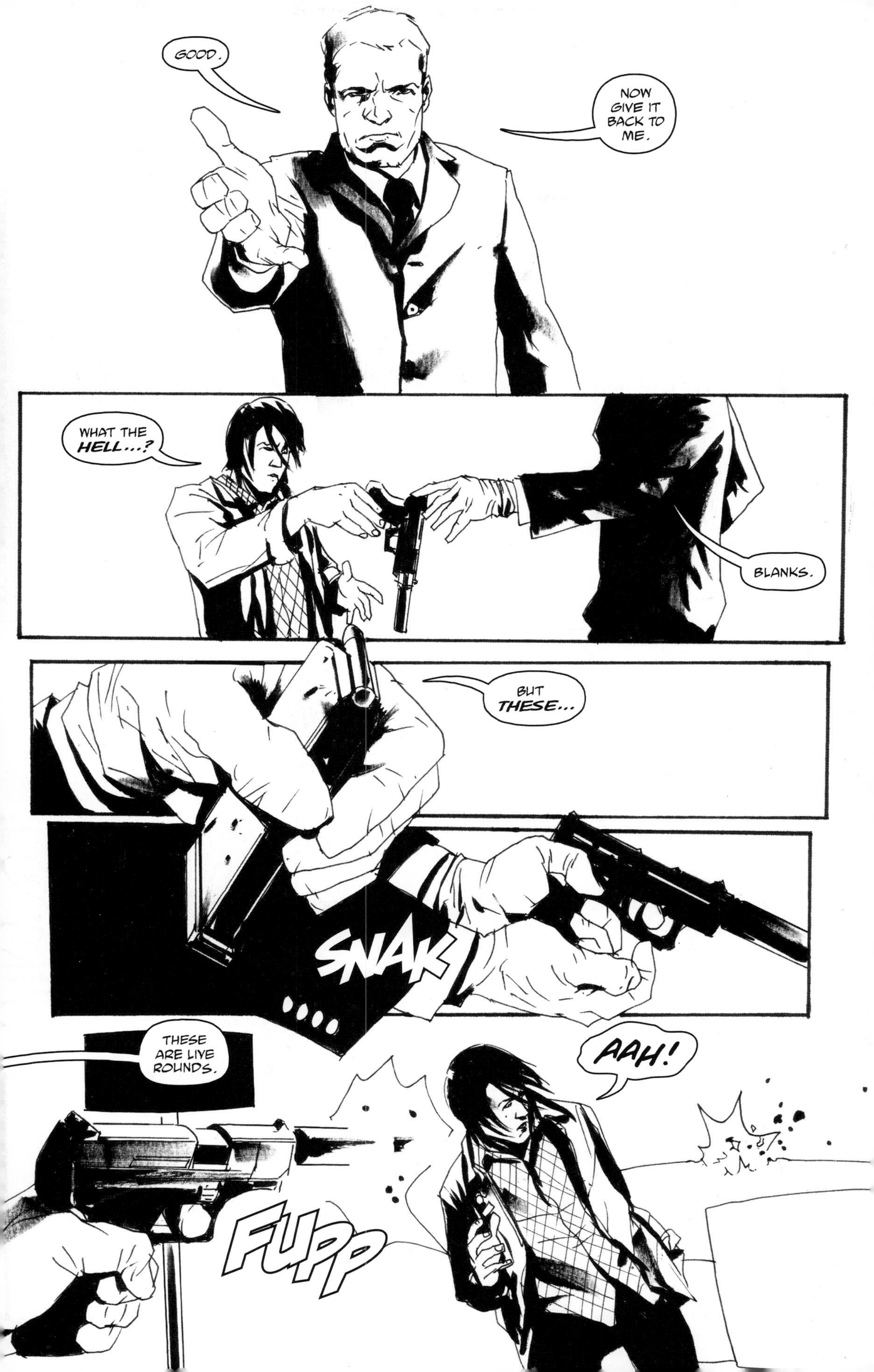
GOOD.
NOW GIVE IT BACK TO ME.
WHAT THE HELL...?
BLANKS.
BUT THESE...
SNAK
THESE ARE LIVE ROUNDS.
AAH!
FUPP

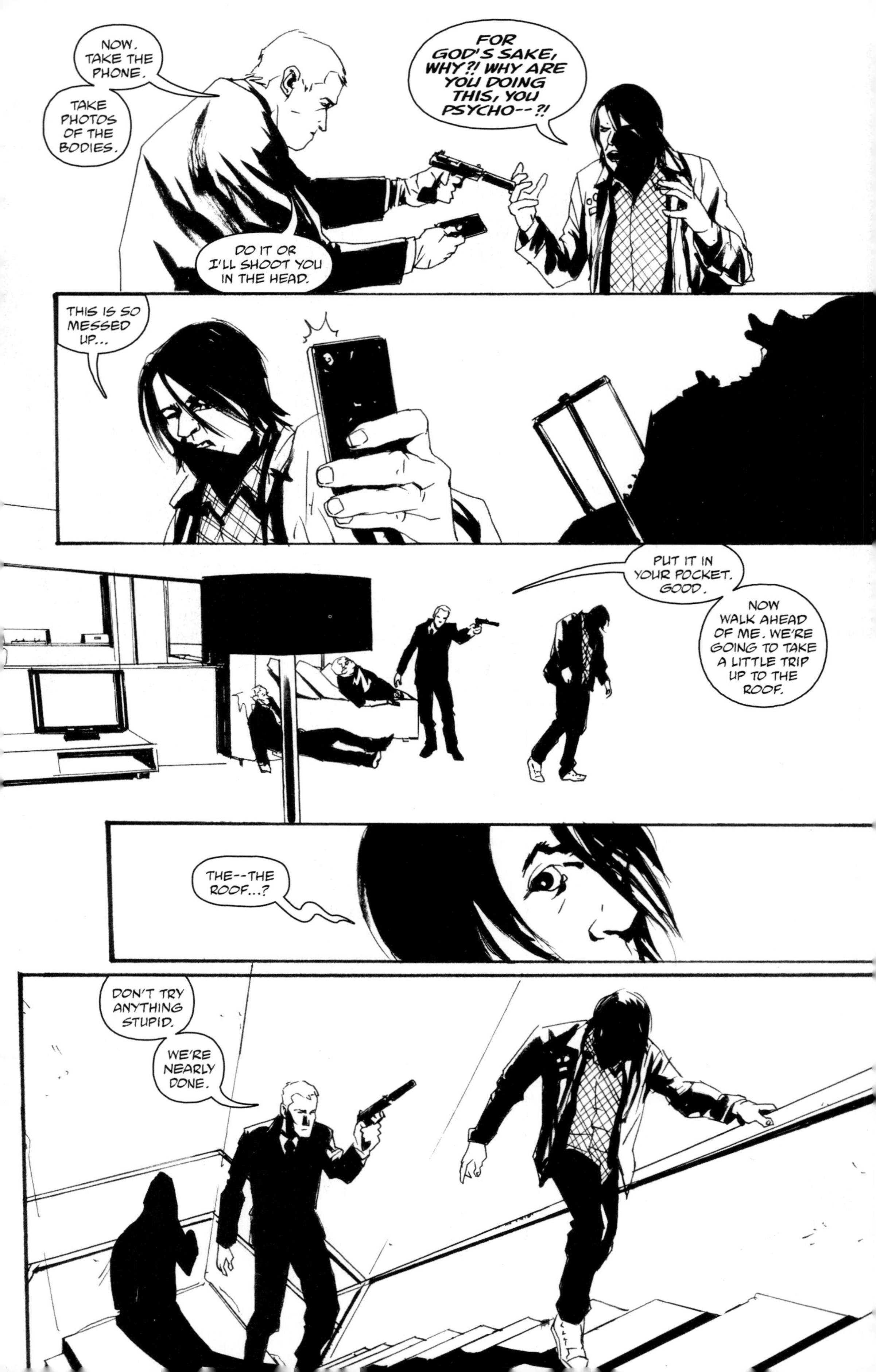

NOW. TAKE THE PHONE.
TAKE PHOTOS OF THE BODIES.
FOR GOD'S SAKE, WHY?! WHY ARE YOU DOING THIS, YOU PSYCHO--?!
DO IT OR I'LL SHOOT YOU IN THE HEAD.
THIS IS SO MESSED UP...
PUT IT IN YOUR POCKET. GOOD.
NOW WALK AHEAD OF ME. WE'RE GOING TO TAKE A LITTLE TRIP UP TO THE ROOF.
THE--THE ROOF...?
DON'T TRY ANYTHING STUPID.
WE'RE NEARLY DONE.

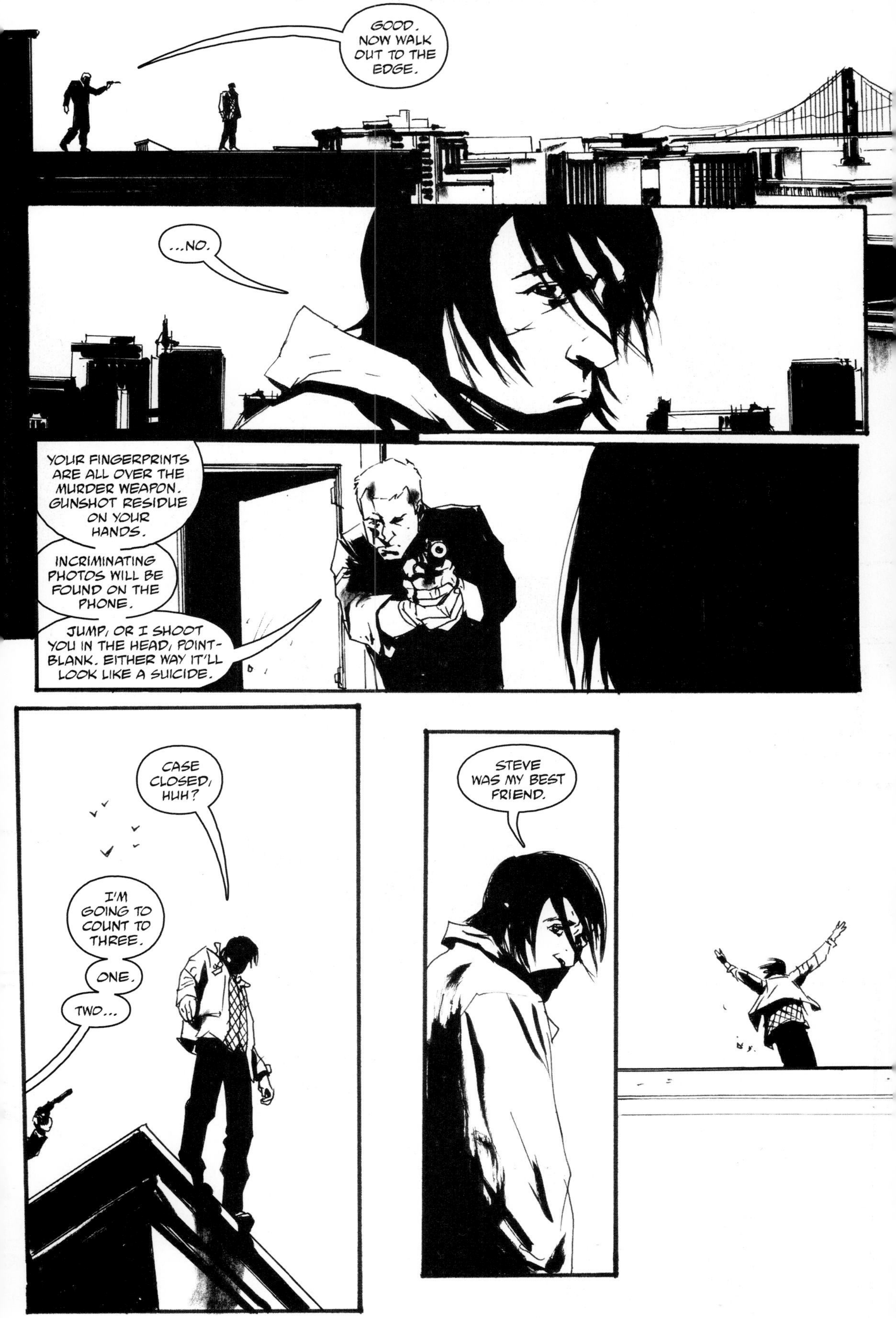
GOOD. NOW WALK OUT TO THE EDGE.
...NO.
YOUR FINGERPRINTS ARE ALL OVER THE MURDER WEAPON. GUNSHOT RESIDUE ON YOUR HANDS.
INCRIMINATING PHOTOS WILL BE FOUND ON THE PHONE.
JUMP, OR I SHOOT YOU IN THE HEAD, POINT-BLANK. EITHER WAY IT'LL LOOK LIKE A SUICIDE.
CASE CLOSED, HUH?
I'M GOING TO COUNT TO THREE.
ONE.
TWO...
STEVE WAS MY BEST FRIEND.

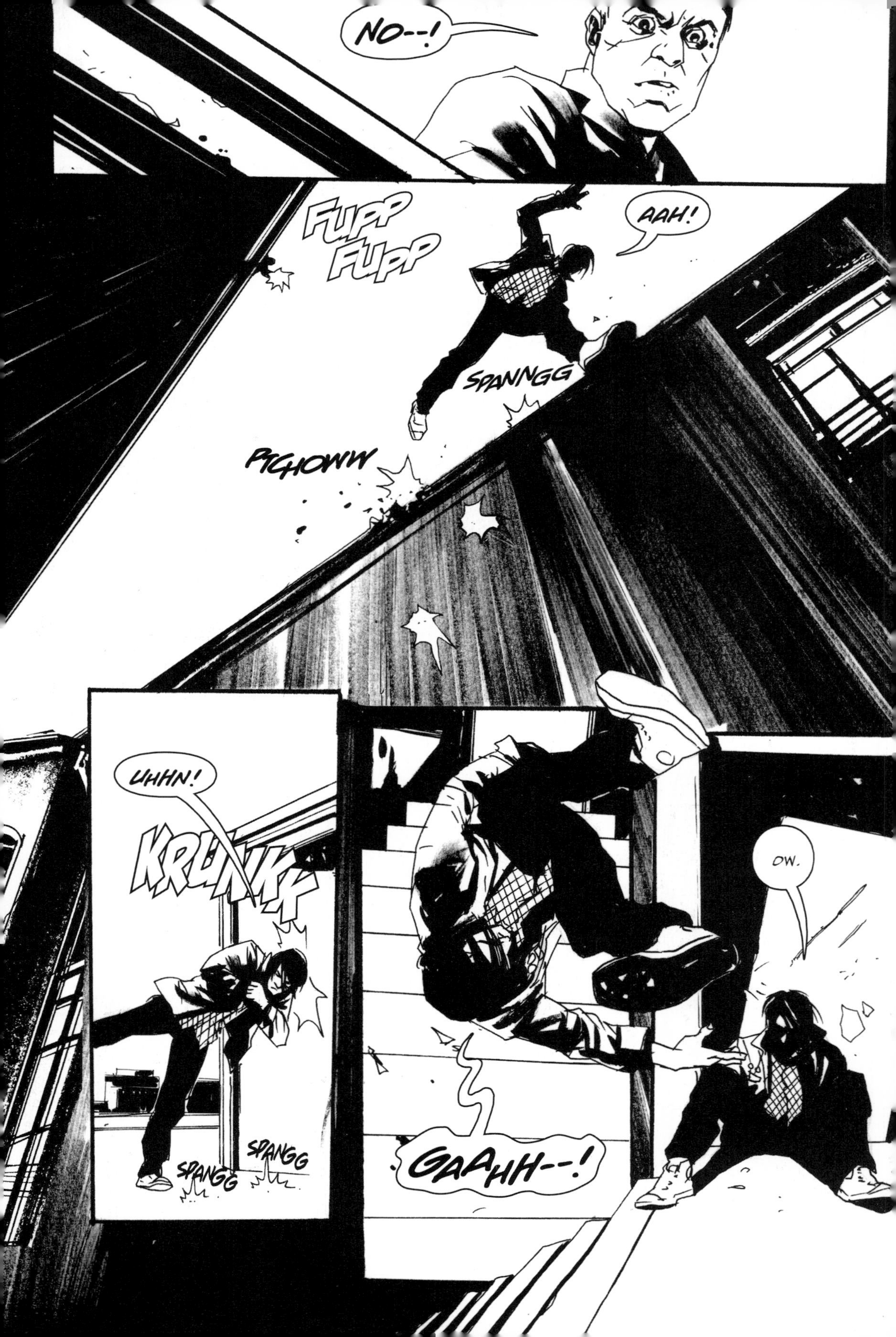
NO--!
FUPP FUPP
AAH!
SPANNGG
PIGHOWW
UHHN!
KRUNKK
SPANGG
SPANGG
OW.
GAAHH--!

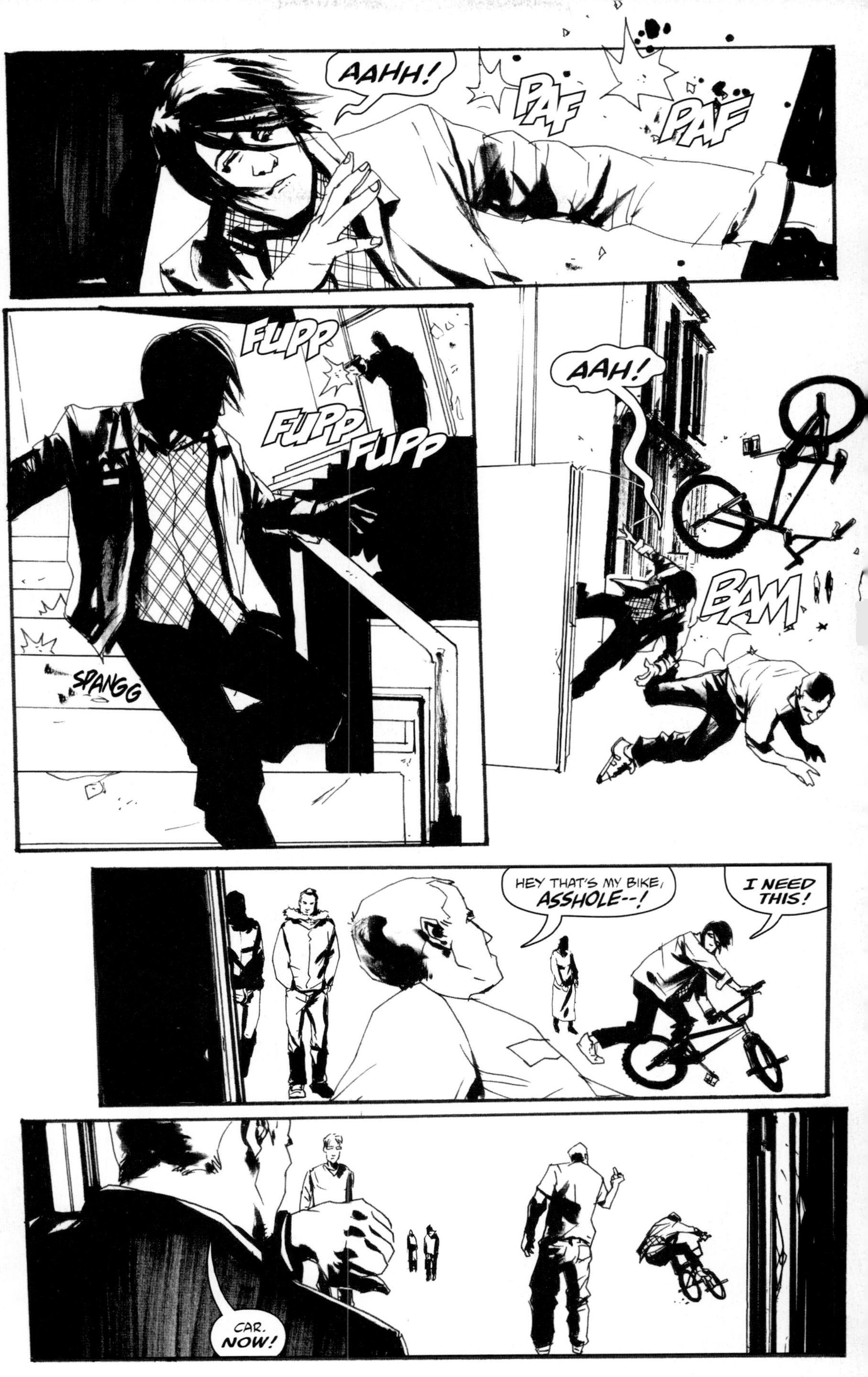
AAHH!
PAF
PAF
FUPP
FUPP
FUPP
SPANGG
AAH!
BAM
HEY THAT'S MY BIKE, ASSHOLE--!
I NEED THIS!
CAR. NOW!

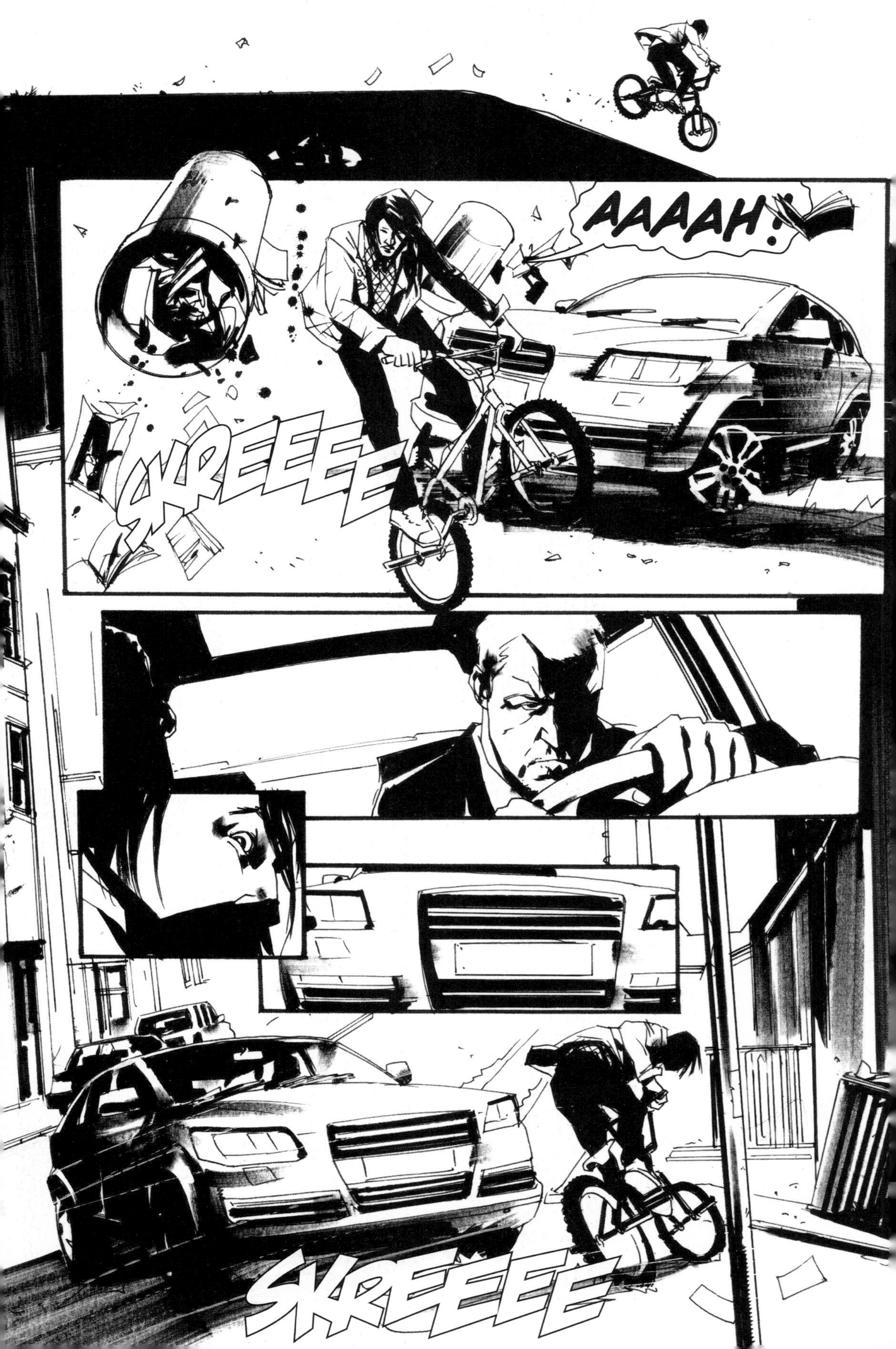
AAAAH!
SKREEEEE
SKREEEEE

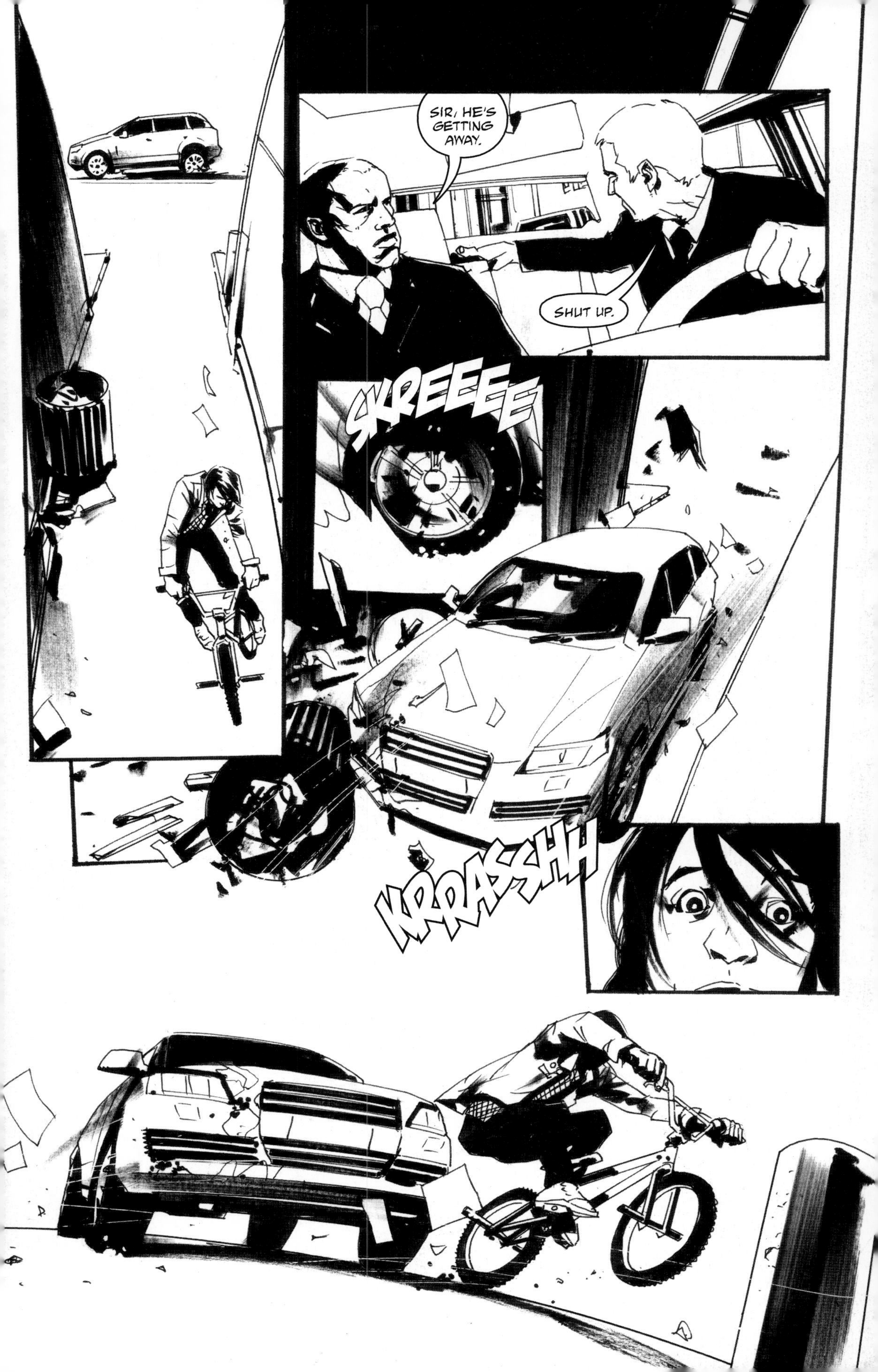
SIR, HE'S GETTING AWAY.
SHUT UP.
SKREEEEE
KRRASSHH

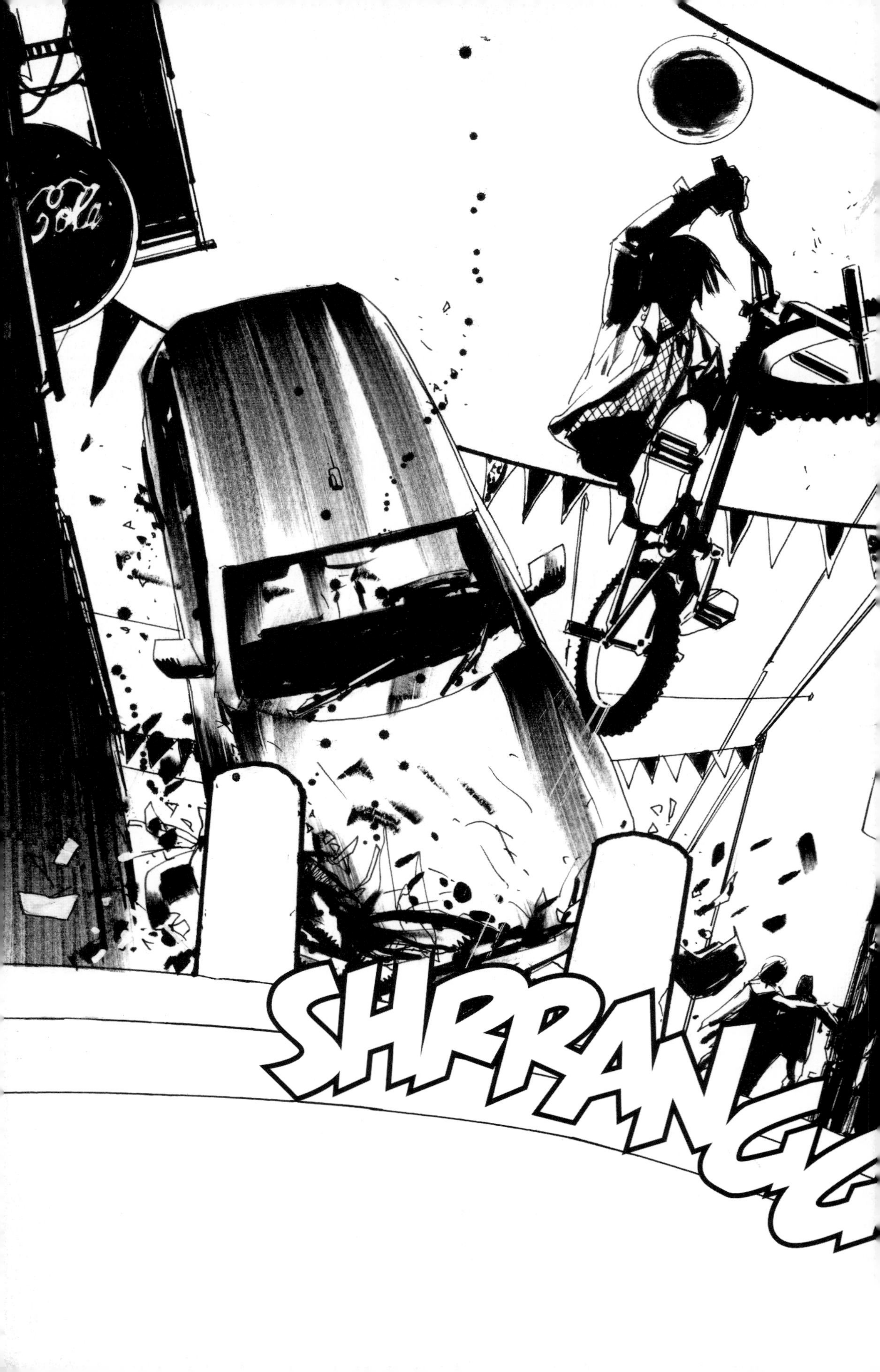
SHRRANGG

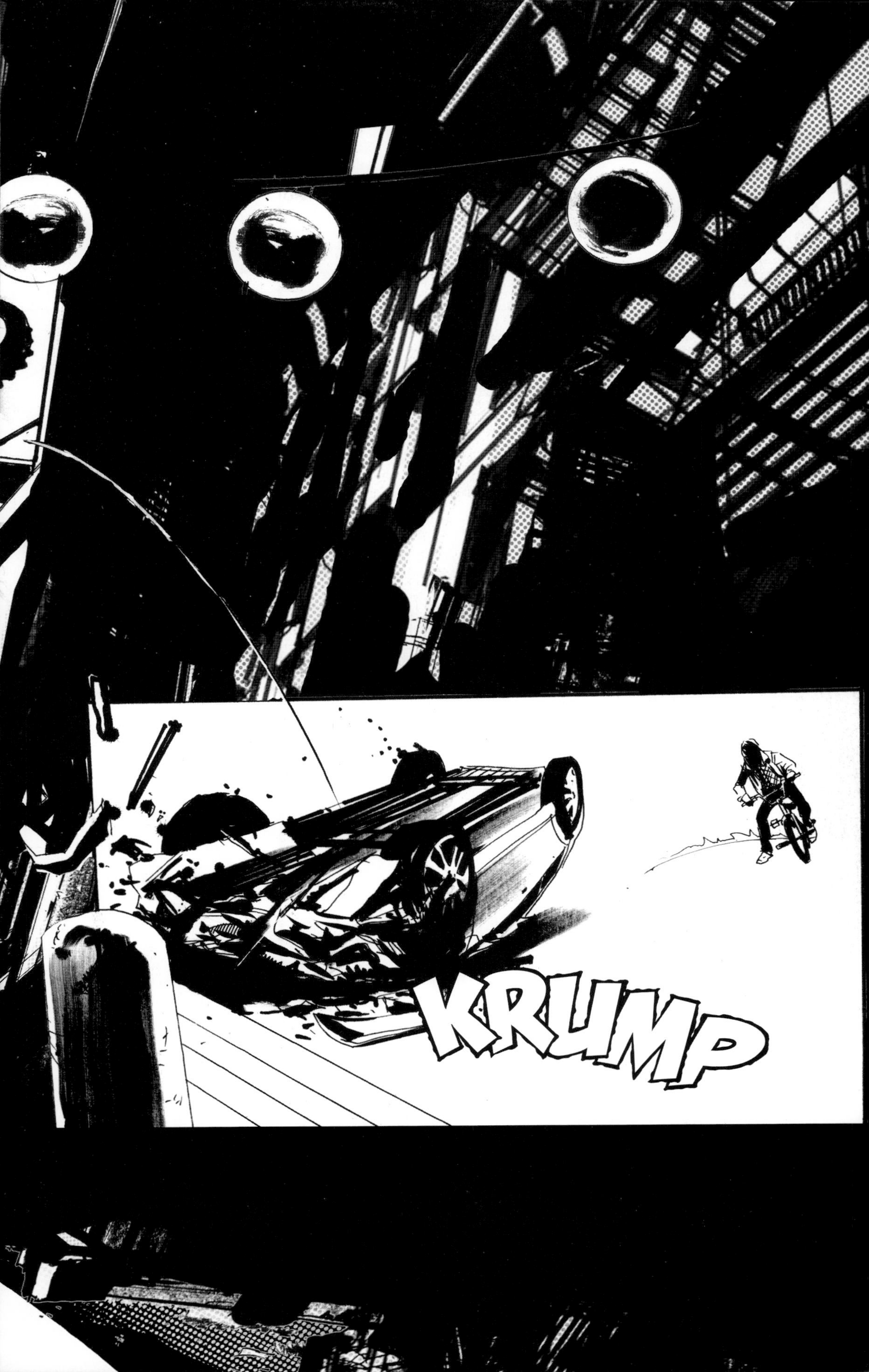
KRUMP

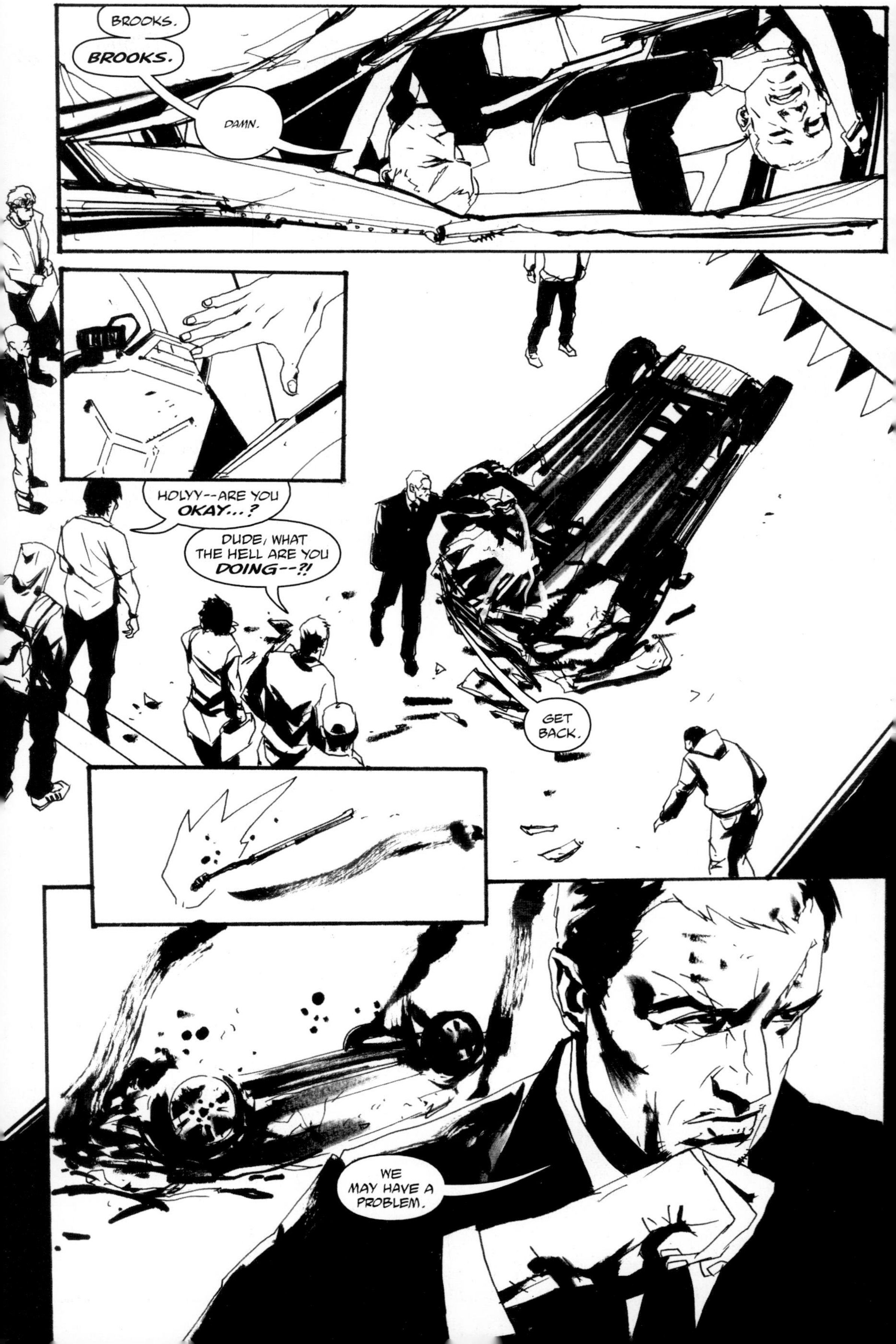
BROOKS.
BROOKS.
DAMN.
HOLYY--ARE YOU OKAY...?
DUDE, WHAT THE HELL ARE YOU DOING--?!
GET BACK.
WE MAY HAVE A PROBLEM.

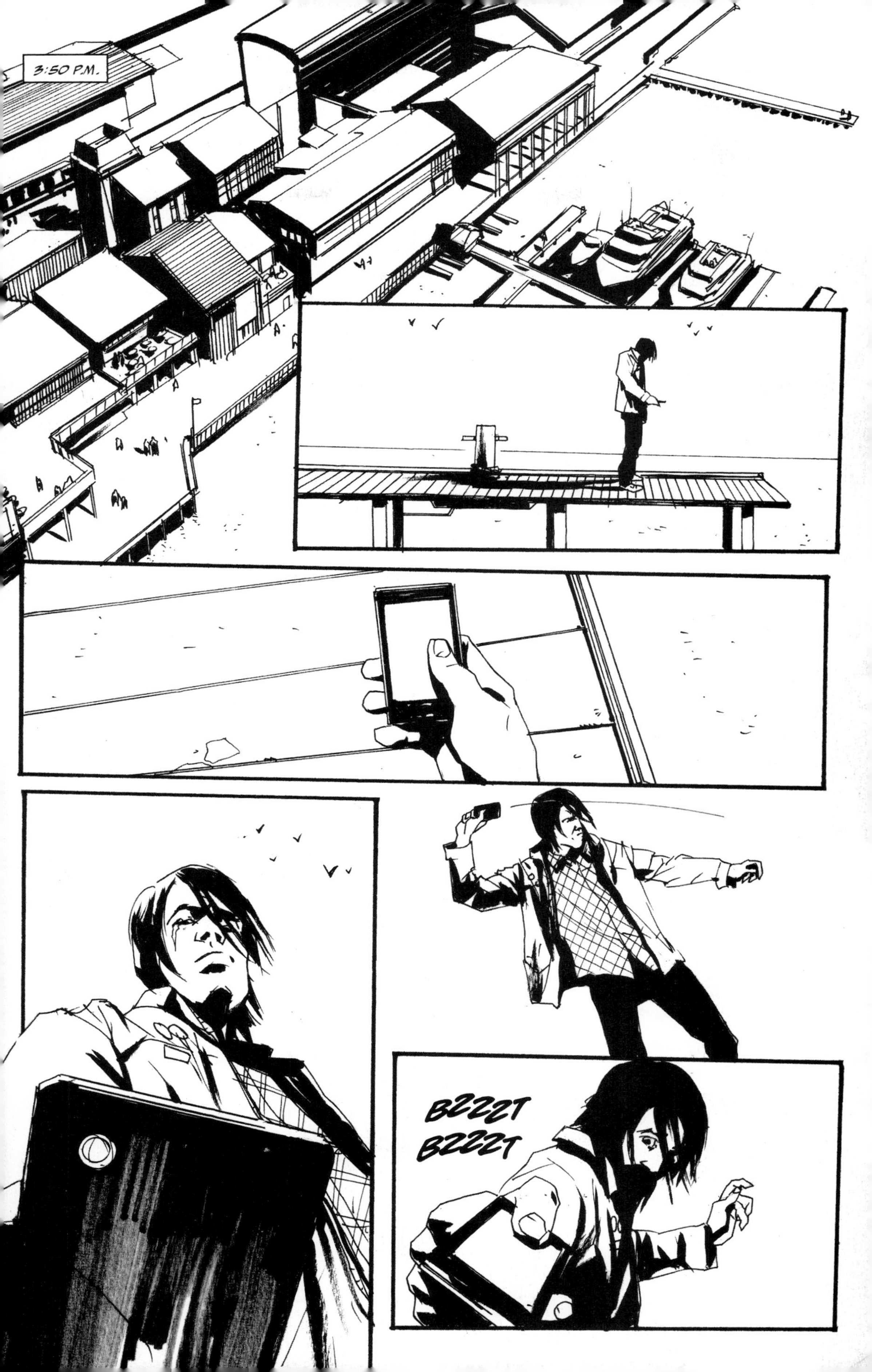
3:50 P.M.
BZZZT
BZZZT

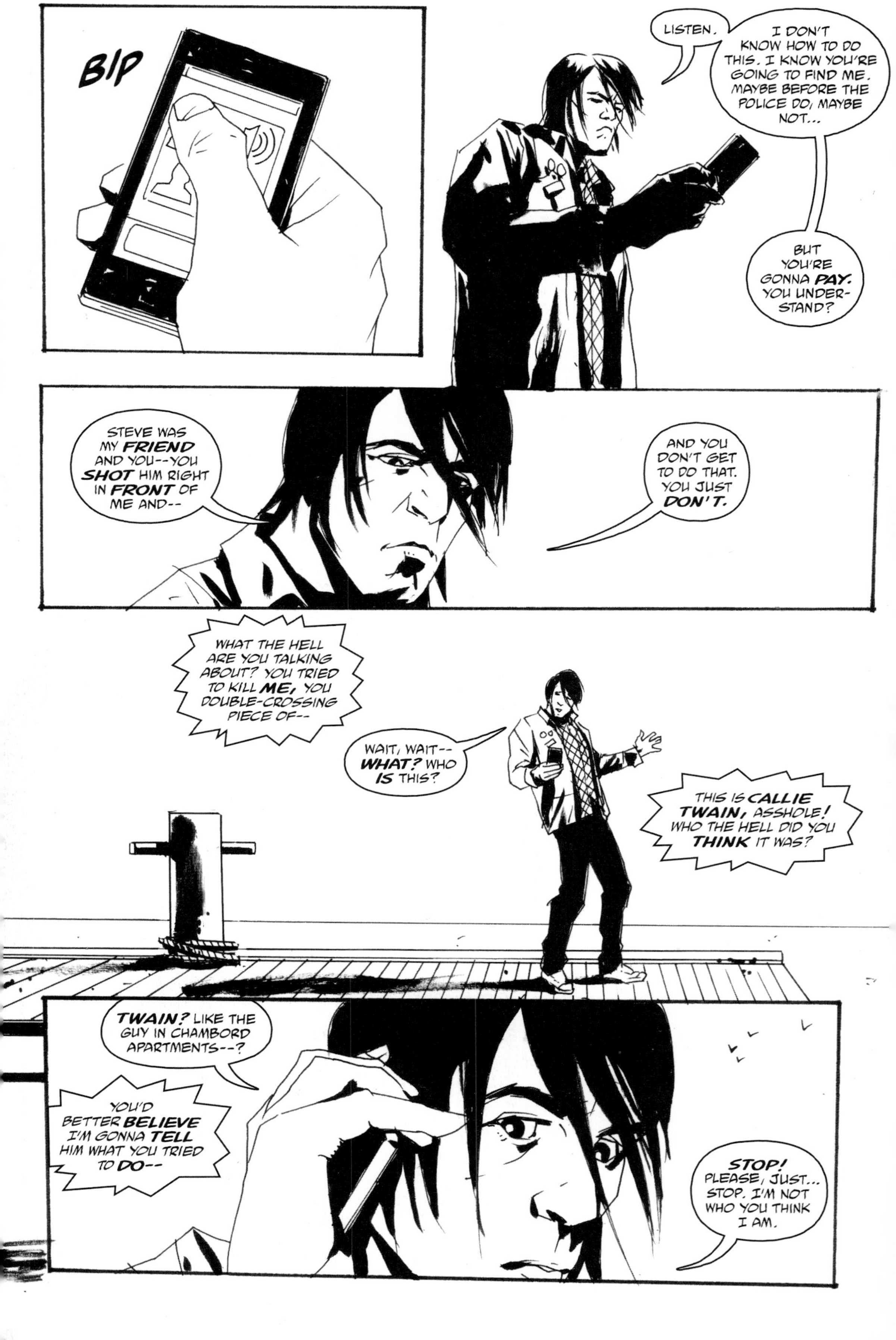
BIP
LISTEN.
I DON'T KNOW HOW TO DO THIS. I KNOW YOU'RE GOING TO FIND ME. MAYBE BEFORE THE POLICE DO, MAYBE NOT...
BUT YOU'RE GONNA PAY. YOU UNDER-STAND?
STEVE WAS MY FRIEND AND YOU--YOU SHOT HIM RIGHT IN FRONT OF ME AND--
AND YOU DON'T GET TO DO THAT. YOU JUST DON'T.
WHAT THE HELL ARE YOU TALKING ABOUT? YOU TRIED TO KILL ME, YOU DOUBLE-CROSSING PIECE OF--
WAIT, WAIT-- WHAT? WHO IS THIS?
THIS IS CALLIE TWAIN, ASSHOLE! WHO THE HELL DID YOU THINK IT WAS?
TWAIN? LIKE THE GUY IN CHAMBORD APARTMENTS--?
YOU'D BETTER BELIEVE I'M GONNA TELL HIM WHAT YOU TRIED TO DO--
STOP! PLEASE, JUST... STOP. I'M NOT WHO YOU THINK I AM.

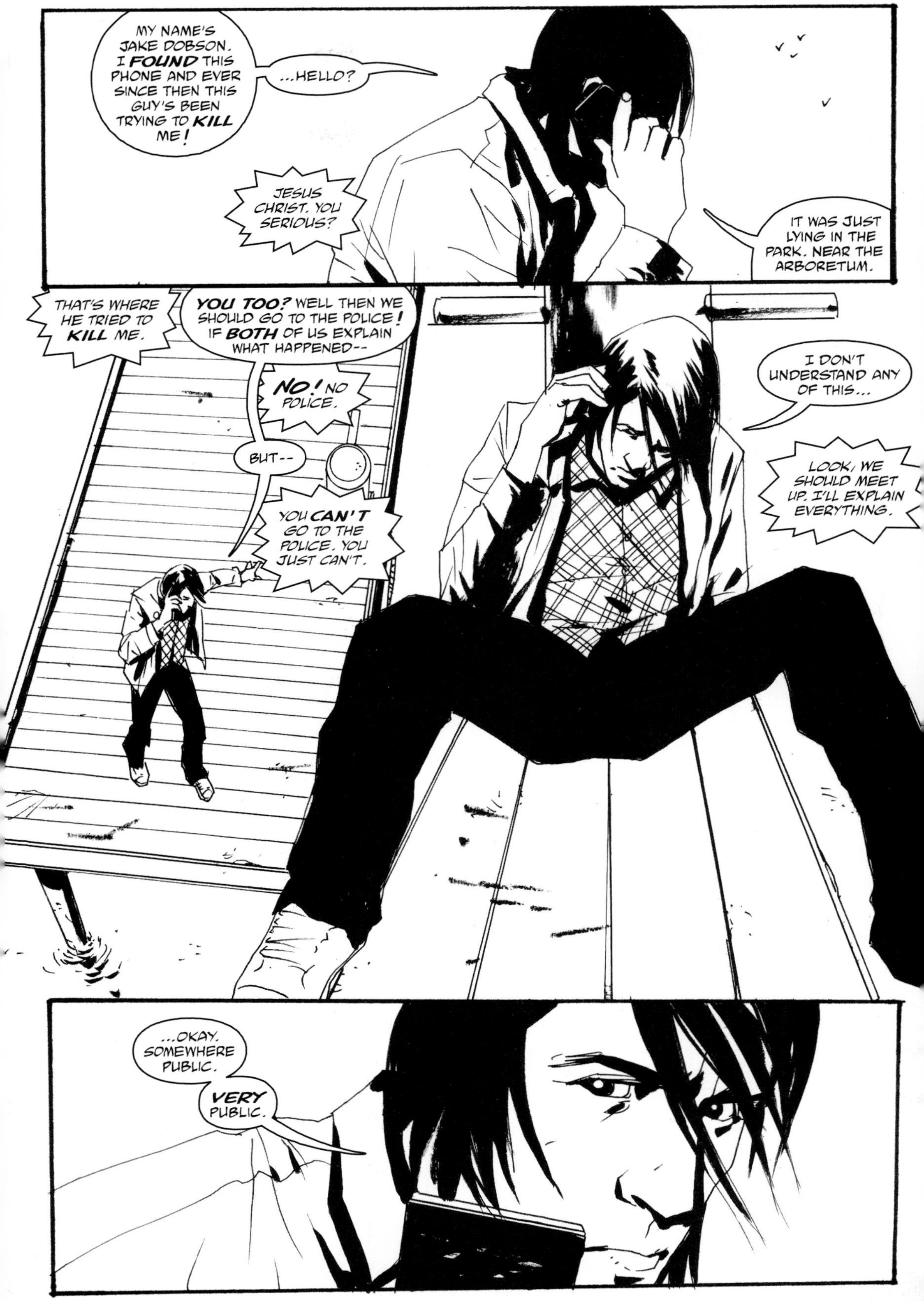
MY NAME'S JAKE DOBSON. I FOUND THIS PHONE AND EVER SINCE THEN THIS GUY'S BEEN TRYING TO KILL ME!
...HELLO?
JESUS CHRIST. YOU SERIOUS?
IT WAS JUST LYING IN THE PARK. NEAR THE ARBORETUM.
THAT'S WHERE HE TRIED TO KILL ME.
YOU TOO? WELL THEN WE SHOULD GO TO THE POLICE! IF BOTH OF US EXPLAIN WHAT HAPPENED--
NO! NO POLICE.
BUT--
YOU CAN'T GO TO THE POLICE. YOU JUST CAN'T.
I DON'T UNDERSTAND ANY OF THIS...
LOOK, WE SHOULD MEET UP. I'LL EXPLAIN EVERYTHING.
...OKAY. SOMEWHERE PUBLIC.
VERY PUBLIC.

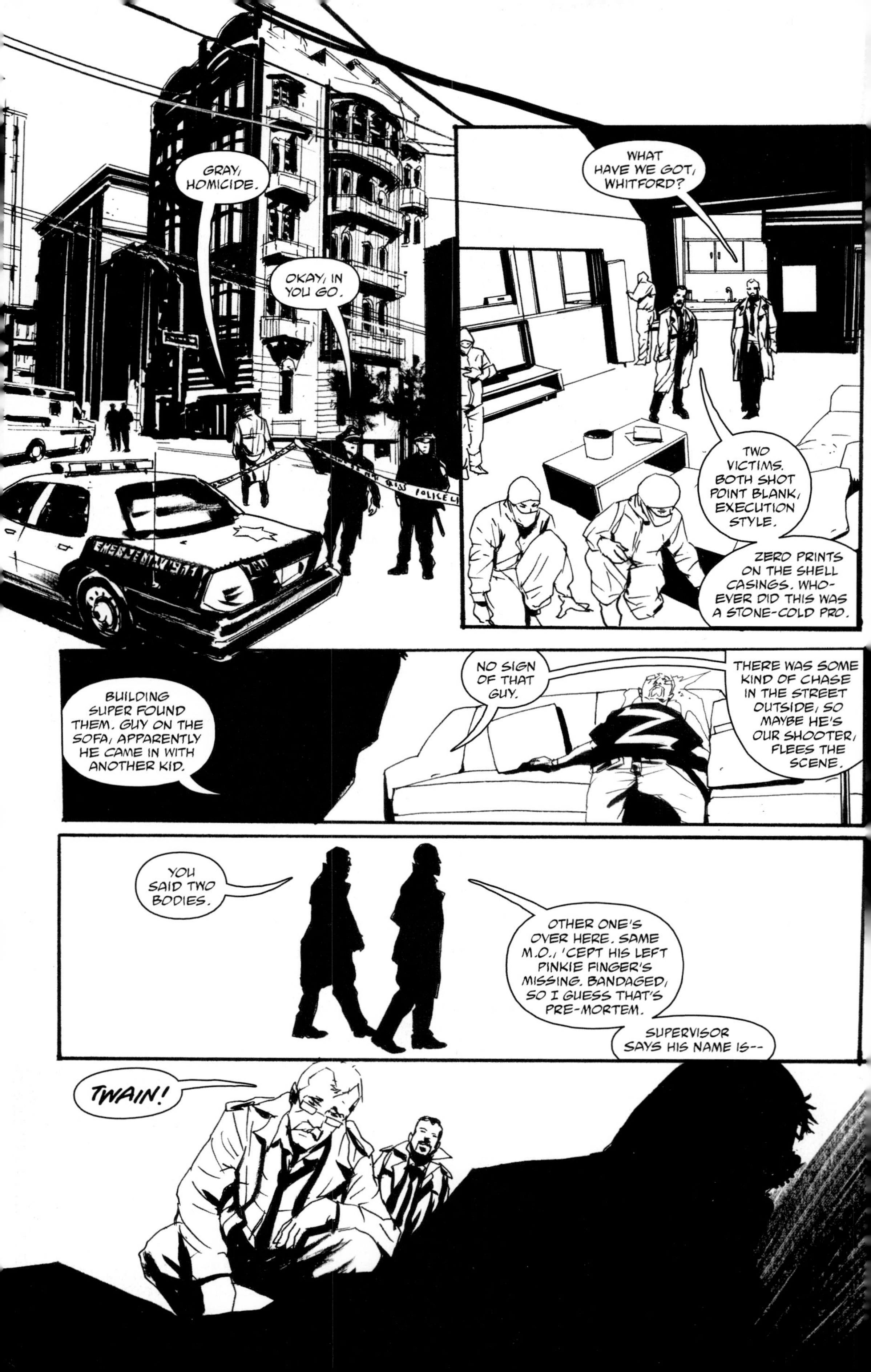
GRAY, HOMICIDE.
OKAY, IN YOU GO.
WHAT HAVE WE GOT, WHITFORD?
TWO VICTIMS. BOTH SHOT POINT BLANK, EXECUTION STYLE.
ZERO PRINTS ON THE SHELL CASINGS. WHOEVER DID THIS WAS A STONE-COLD PRO.
BUILDING SUPER FOUND THEM. GUY ON THE SOFA, APPARENTLY HE CAME IN WITH ANOTHER KID.
NO SIGN OF THAT GUY.
THERE WAS SOME KIND OF CHASE IN THE STREET OUTSIDE, SO MAYBE HE'S OUR SHOOTER, FLEES THE SCENE.
YOU SAID TWO BODIES.
OTHER ONE'S OVER HERE. SAME M.O., 'CEPT HIS LEFT PINKIE FINGER'S MISSING. BANDAGED, SO I GUESS THAT'S PRE-MORTEM.
SUPERVISOR SAYS HIS NAME IS--
TWAIN!

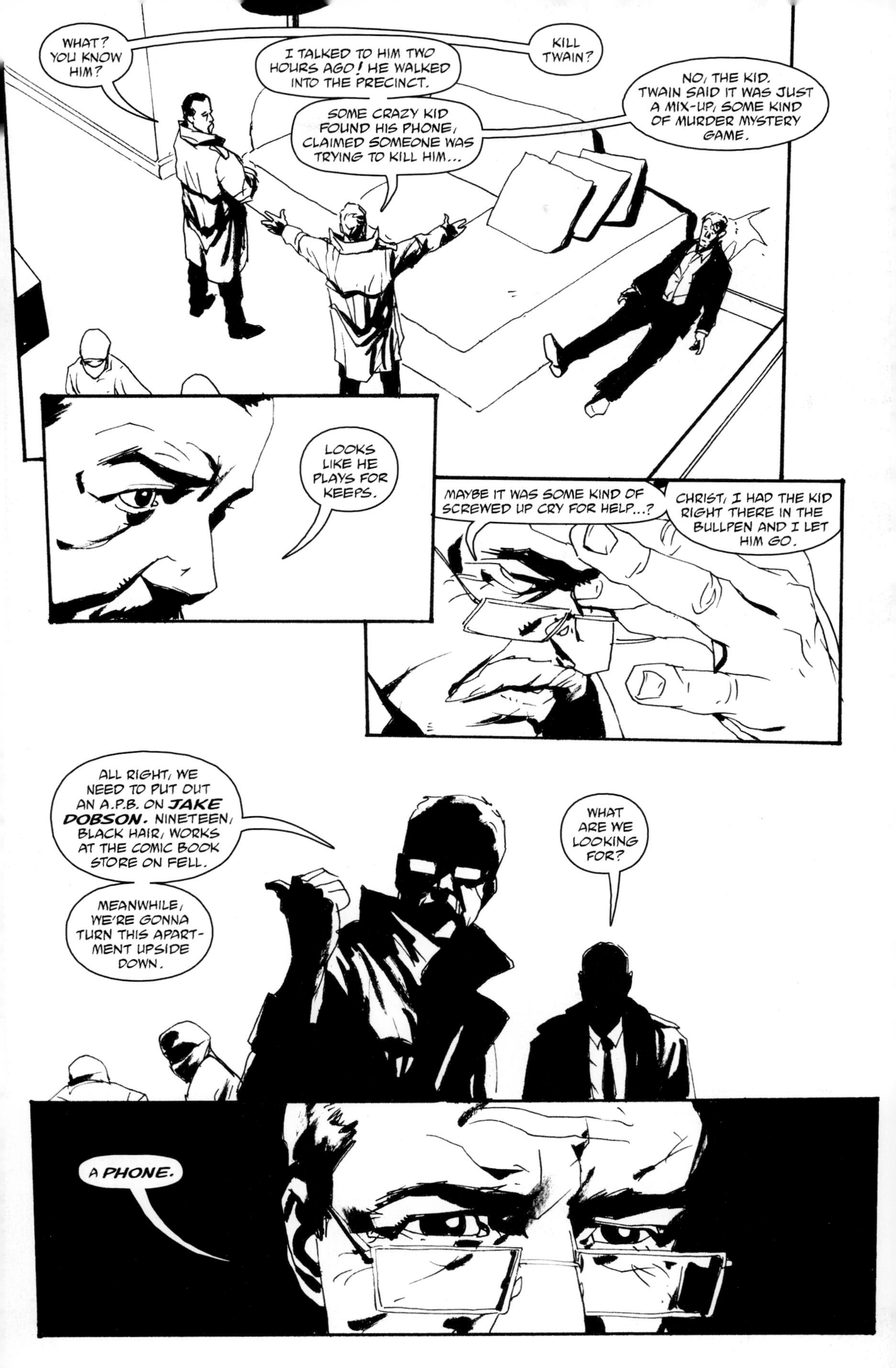
WHAT? YOU KNOW HIM?
KILL TWAIN?
I TALKED TO HIM TWO HOURS AGO! HE WALKED INTO THE PRECINCT.
SOME CRAZY KID FOUND HIS PHONE, CLAIMED SOMEONE WAS TRYING TO KILL HIM...
NO, THE KID. TWAIN SAID IT WAS JUST A MIX-UP, SOME KIND OF MURDER MYSTERY GAME.
LOOKS LIKE HE PLAYS FOR KEEPS.
MAYBE IT WAS SOME KIND OF SCREWED UP CRY FOR HELP...?
CHRIST, I HAD THE KID RIGHT THERE IN THE BULLPEN AND I LET HIM GO.
ALL RIGHT, WE NEED TO PUT OUT AN A.P.B. ON JAKE DOBSON. NINETEEN, BLACK HAIR, WORKS AT THE COMIC BOOK STORE ON FELL.
MEANWHILE, WE'RE GONNA TURN THIS APARTMENT UPSIDE DOWN.
WHAT ARE WE LOOKING FOR?
A PHONE.

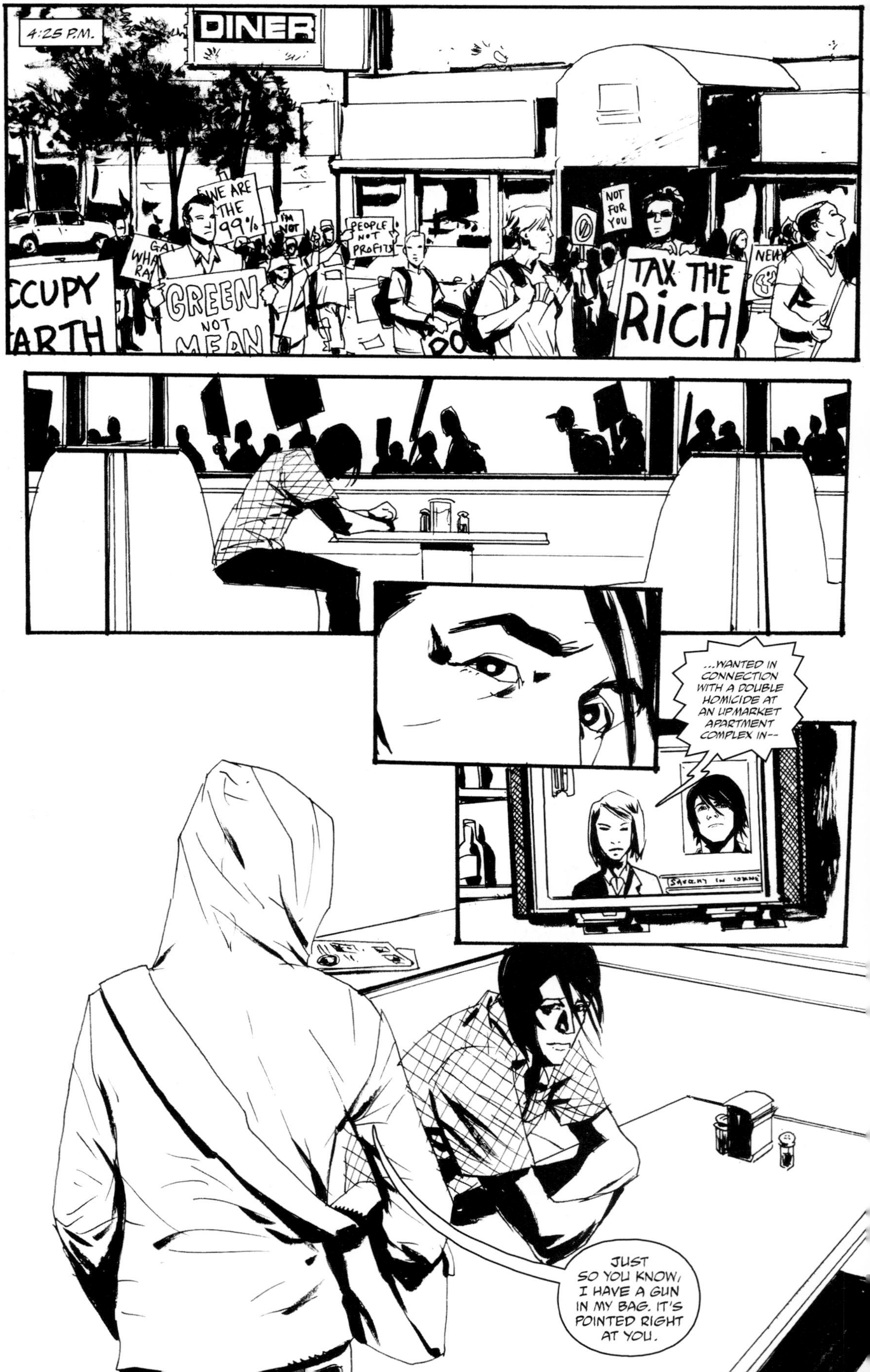
4:25 P.M.
DINER
WE ARE THE 99%
I'M NOT
PEOPLE NOT PROFITS
NOT FOR YOU
GREEN NOT
TAX THE RICH
...WANTED IN CONNECTION WITH A DOUBLE HOMICIDE AT AN UPMARKET APARTMENT COMPLEX IN--
JUST SO YOU KNOW, I HAVE A GUN IN MY BAG. IT'S POINTED RIGHT AT YOU.

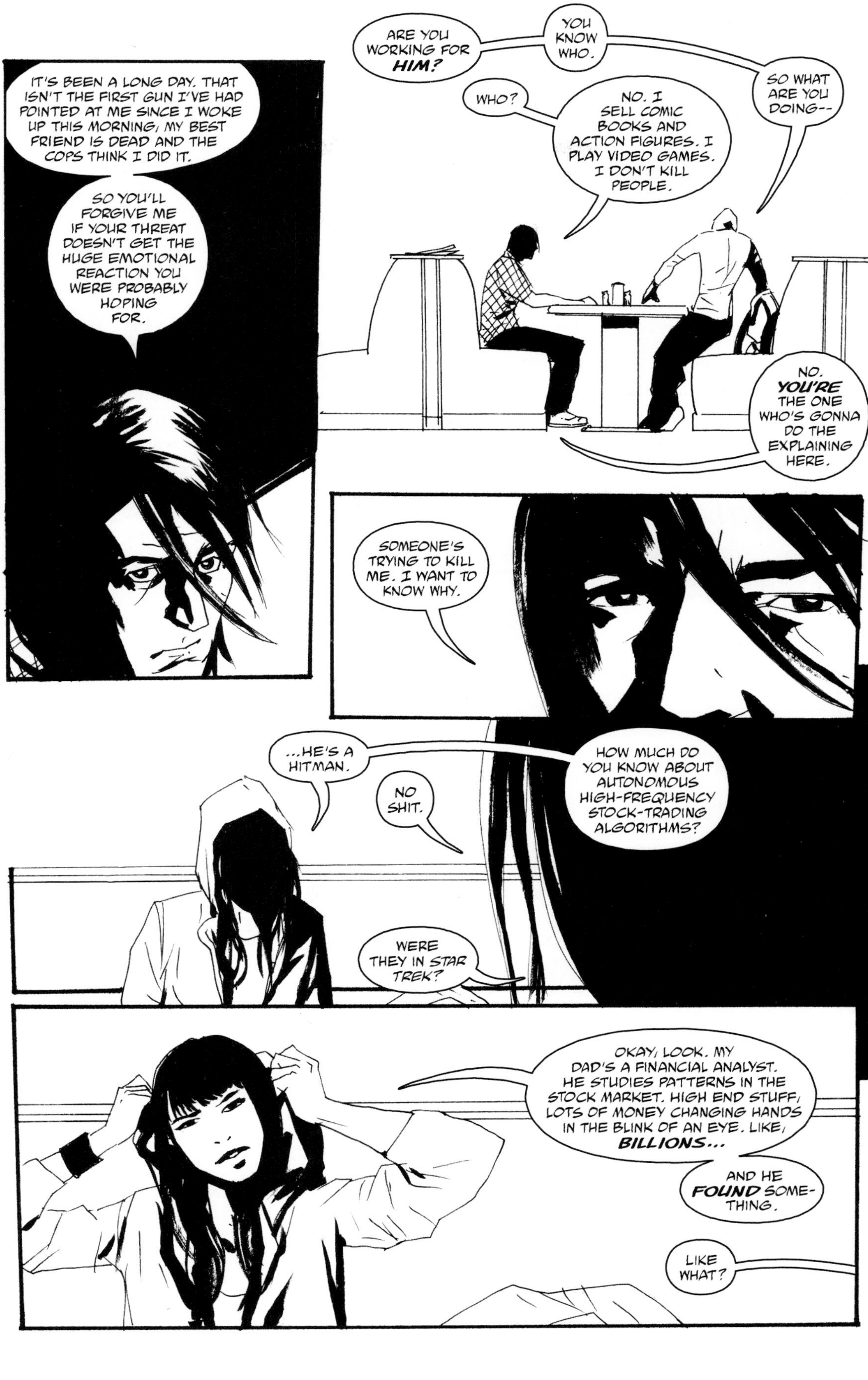

IT'S BEEN A LONG DAY. THAT ISN'T THE FIRST GUN I'VE HAD POINTED AT ME SINCE I WOKE UP THIS MORNING, MY BEST FRIEND IS DEAD AND THE COPS THINK I DID IT.
SO YOU'LL FORGIVE ME IF YOUR THREAT DOESN'T GET THE HUGE EMOTIONAL REACTION YOU WERE PROBABLY HOPING FOR.
ARE YOU WORKING FOR **HIM?**
WHO?
YOU KNOW WHO.
NO. I SELL COMIC BOOKS AND ACTION FIGURES. I PLAY VIDEO GAMES. I DON'T KILL PEOPLE.
SO WHAT ARE YOU DOING--
NO. ***YOU'RE*** THE ONE WHO'S GONNA DO THE EXPLAINING HERE.
SOMEONE'S TRYING TO KILL ME. I WANT TO KNOW WHY.
...HE'S A HITMAN.
NO SHIT.
HOW MUCH DO YOU KNOW ABOUT AUTONOMOUS HIGH-FREQUENCY STOCK-TRADING ALGORITHMS?
WERE THEY IN *STAR TREK?*
OKAY, LOOK. MY DAD'S A FINANCIAL ANALYST. HE STUDIES PATTERNS IN THE STOCK MARKET. HIGH END STUFF, LOTS OF MONEY CHANGING HANDS IN THE BLINK OF AN EYE. LIKE, ***BILLIONS...***
AND HE ***FOUND*** SOME-THING.
LIKE WHAT?

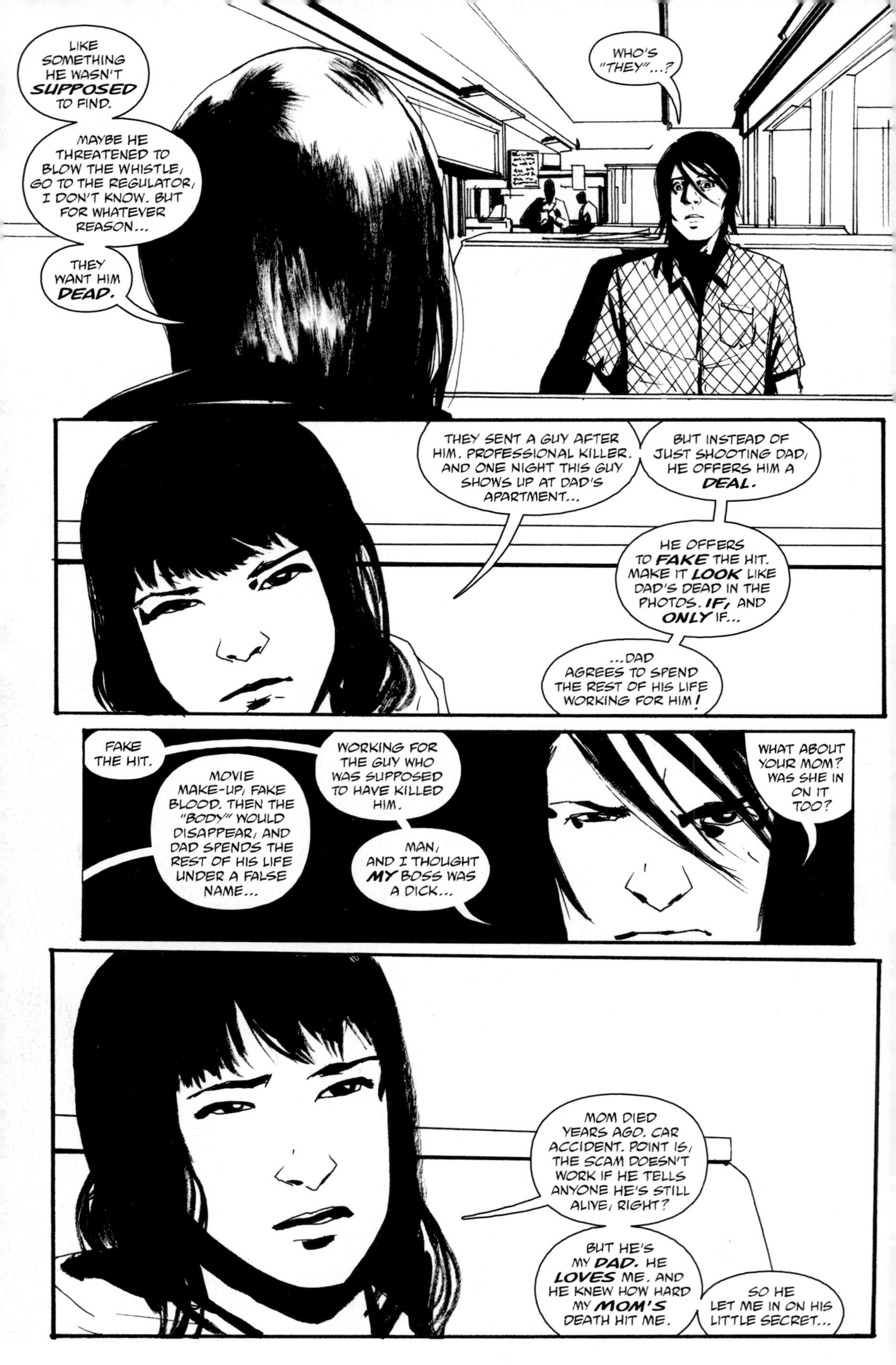
LIKE SOMETHING HE WASN'T SUPPOSED TO FIND.
MAYBE HE THREATENED TO BLOW THE WHISTLE, GO TO THE REGULATOR, I DON'T KNOW. BUT FOR WHATEVER REASON...
THEY WANT HIM DEAD.
WHO'S "THEY"...?
THEY SENT A GUY AFTER HIM. PROFESSIONAL KILLER. AND ONE NIGHT THIS GUY SHOWS UP AT DAD'S APARTMENT...
BUT INSTEAD OF JUST SHOOTING DAD, HE OFFERS HIM A DEAL.
HE OFFERS TO FAKE THE HIT. MAKE IT LOOK LIKE DAD'S DEAD IN THE PHOTOS. IF, AND ONLY IF...
...DAD AGREES TO SPEND THE REST OF HIS LIFE WORKING FOR HIM!
FAKE THE HIT.
MOVIE MAKE-UP, FAKE BLOOD. THEN THE "BODY" WOULD DISAPPEAR, AND DAD SPENDS THE REST OF HIS LIFE UNDER A FALSE NAME...
WORKING FOR THE GUY WHO WAS SUPPOSED TO HAVE KILLED HIM.
MAN, AND I THOUGHT MY BOSS WAS A DICK...
WHAT ABOUT YOUR MOM? WAS SHE IN ON IT TOO?
MOM DIED YEARS AGO. CAR ACCIDENT. POINT IS, THE SCAM DOESN'T WORK IF HE TELLS ANYONE HE'S STILL ALIVE, RIGHT?
BUT HE'S MY DAD. HE LOVES ME. AND HE KNEW HOW HARD MY MOM'S DEATH HIT ME.
SO HE LET ME IN ON HIS LITTLE SECRET...

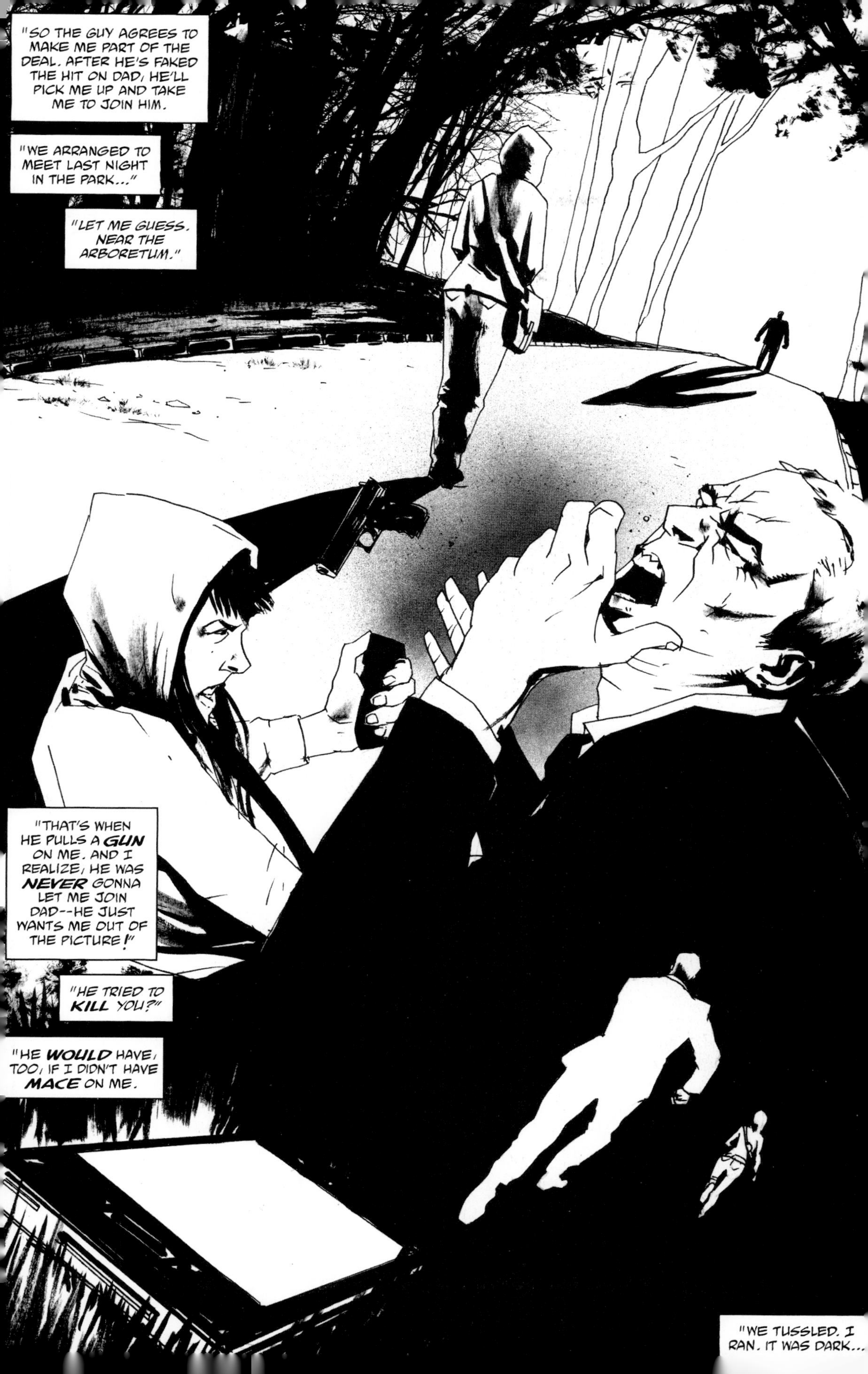
"SO THE GUY AGREES TO MAKE ME PART OF THE DEAL. AFTER HE'S FAKED THE HIT ON DAD, HE'LL PICK ME UP AND TAKE ME TO JOIN HIM.
"WE ARRANGED TO MEET LAST NIGHT IN THE PARK..."
"LET ME GUESS. NEAR THE ARBORETUM."
"THAT'S WHEN HE PULLS A **GUN** ON ME. AND I REALIZE, HE WAS **NEVER** GONNA LET ME JOIN DAD--HE JUST WANTS ME OUT OF THE PICTURE!"
"HE TRIED TO **KILL** YOU?"
"HE **WOULD** HAVE, TOO, IF I DIDN'T HAVE **MACE** ON ME.
"WE TUSSLED. I RAN. IT WAS DARK...

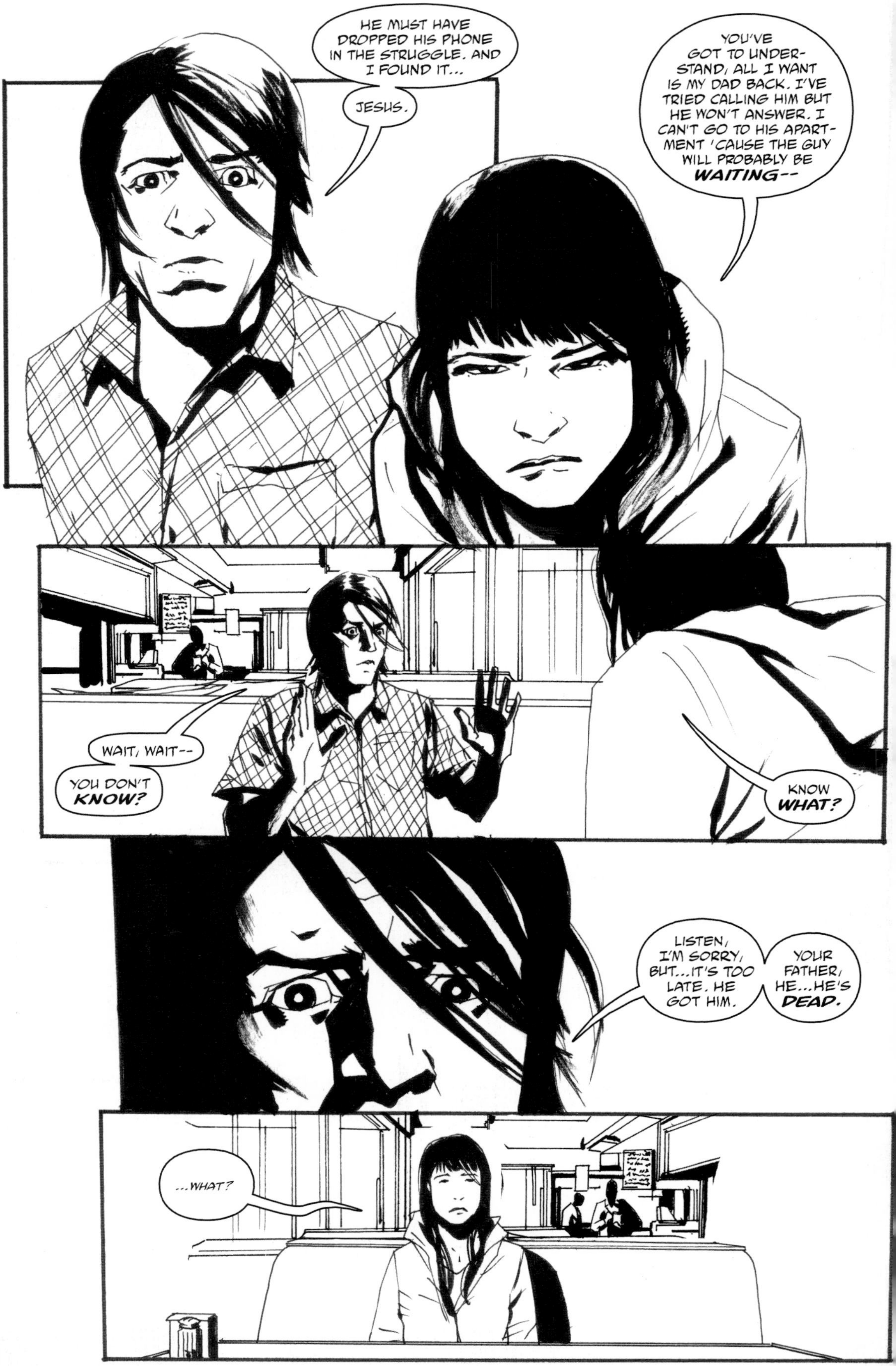
HE MUST HAVE DROPPED HIS PHONE IN THE STRUGGLE. AND I FOUND IT...
JESUS.
YOU'VE GOT TO UNDER-STAND, ALL I WANT IS MY DAD BACK. I'VE TRIED CALLING HIM BUT HE WON'T ANSWER. I CAN'T GO TO HIS APART-MENT 'CAUSE THE GUY WILL PROBABLY BE **WAITING**--
WAIT, WAIT--
YOU DON'T **KNOW?**
KNOW **WHAT?**
LISTEN, I'M SORRY, BUT...IT'S TOO LATE. HE GOT HIM.
YOUR FATHER, HE...HE'S **DEAD.**
...WHAT?

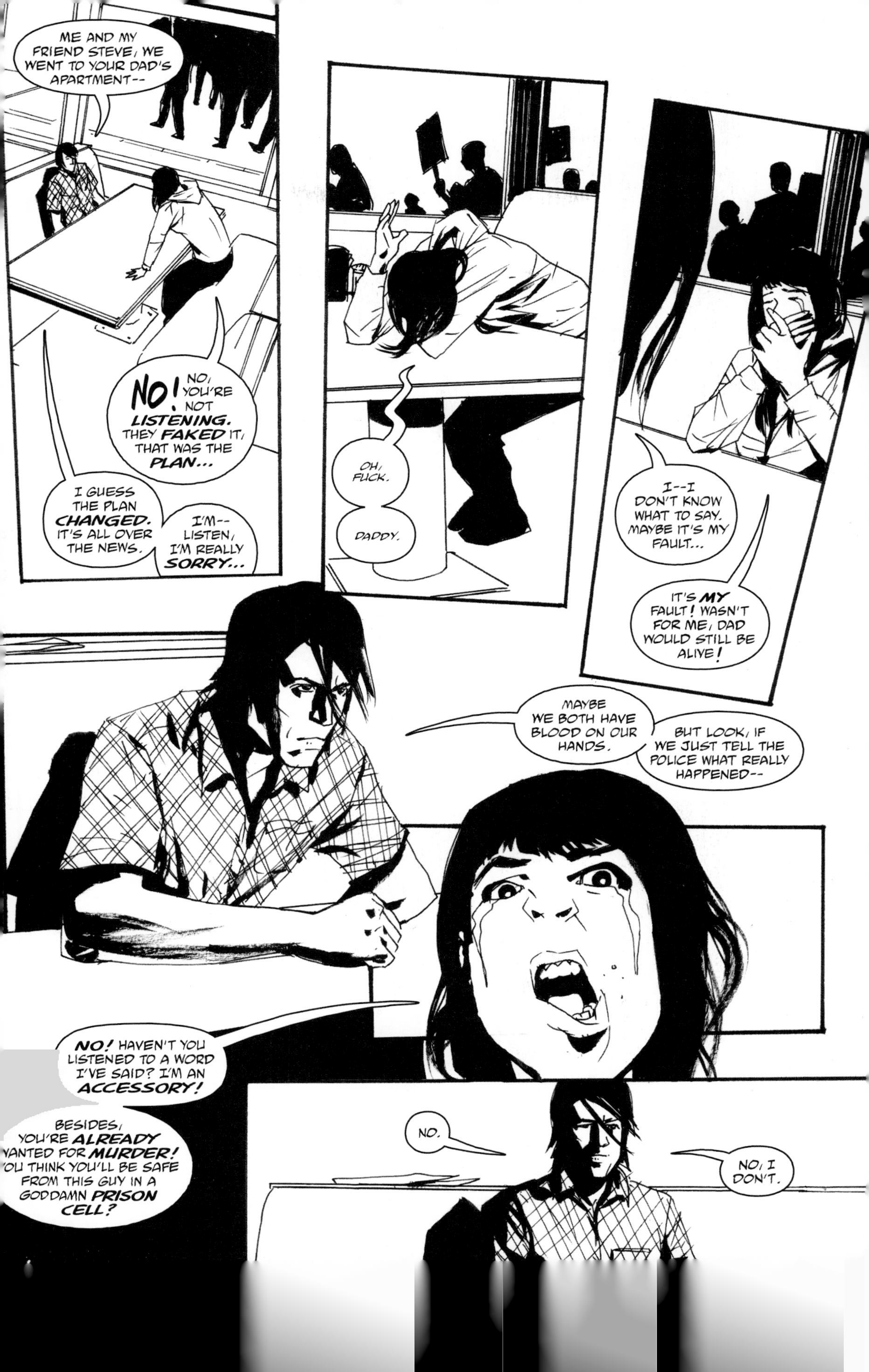
ME AND MY FRIEND STEVE, WE WENT TO YOUR DAD'S APARTMENT--
NO! NO, YOU'RE NOT LISTENING. THEY FAKED IT, THAT WAS THE PLAN...
I GUESS THE PLAN CHANGED. IT'S ALL OVER THE NEWS.
I'M-- LISTEN, I'M REALLY SORRY...
OH, FUCK.
DADDY.
I--I DON'T KNOW WHAT TO SAY. MAYBE IT'S MY FAULT...
IT'S MY FAULT! WASN'T FOR ME, DAD WOULD STILL BE ALIVE!
MAYBE WE BOTH HAVE BLOOD ON OUR HANDS.
BUT LOOK, IF WE JUST TELL THE POLICE WHAT REALLY HAPPENED--
NO! HAVEN'T YOU LISTENED TO A WORD I'VE SAID? I'M AN ACCESSORY!
BESIDES, YOU'RE ALREADY WANTED FOR MURDER! YOU THINK YOU'LL BE SAFE FROM THIS GUY IN A GODDAMN PRISON CELL?
NO.
NO, I DON'T.

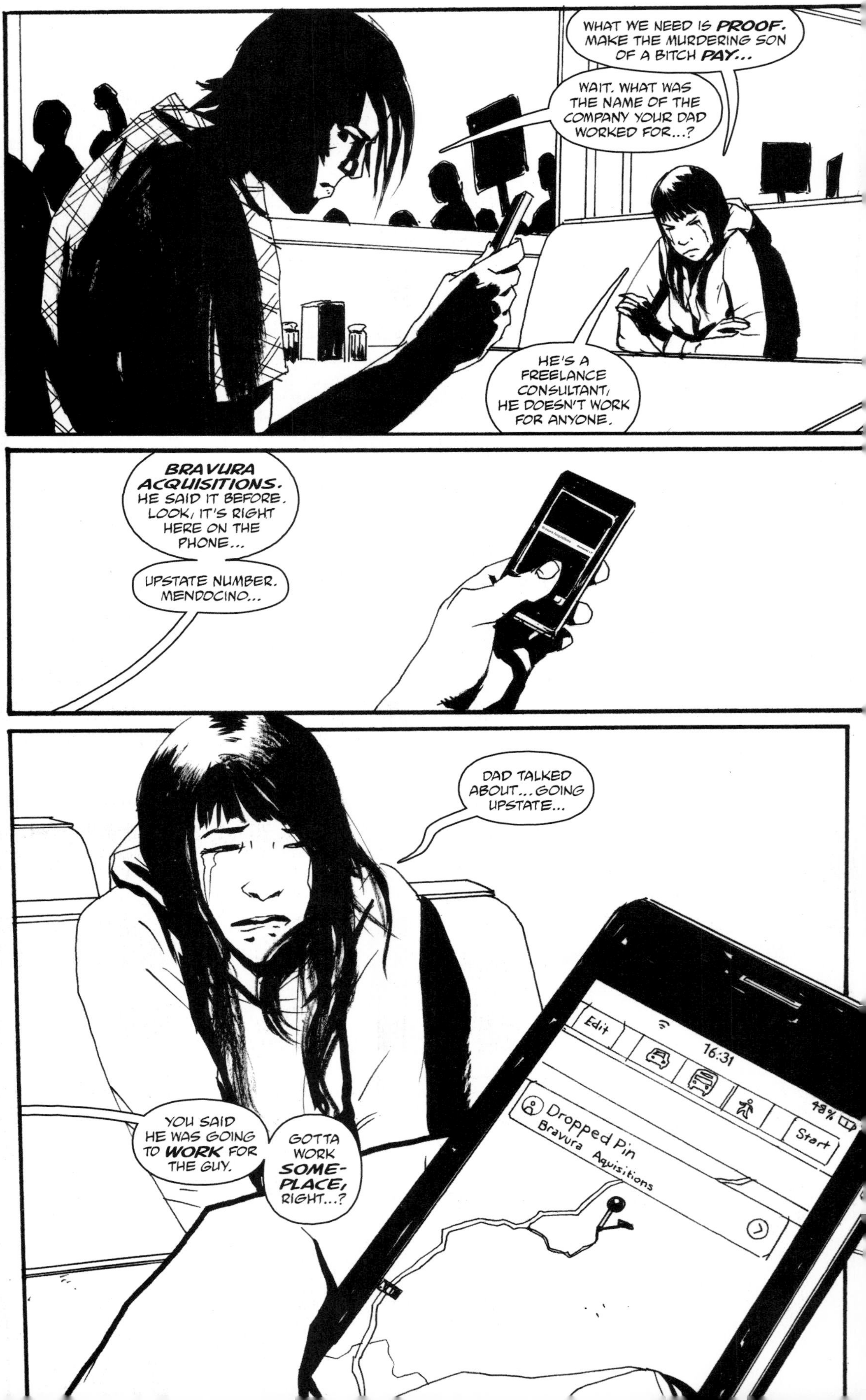
WHAT WE NEED IS PROOF. MAKE THE MURDERING SON OF A BITCH PAY...
WAIT. WHAT WAS THE NAME OF THE COMPANY YOUR DAD WORKED FOR...?
HE'S A FREELANCE CONSULTANT, HE DOESN'T WORK FOR ANYONE.
BRAVURA ACQUISITIONS. HE SAID IT BEFORE. LOOK, IT'S RIGHT HERE ON THE PHONE...
UPSTATE NUMBER. MENDOCINO...
DAD TALKED ABOUT... GOING UPSTATE...
Edit
16:31
48%
Dropped Pin
Bravura Aquisitions
Start
YOU SAID HE WAS GOING TO WORK FOR THE GUY.
GOTTA WORK SOME-PLACE, RIGHT...?

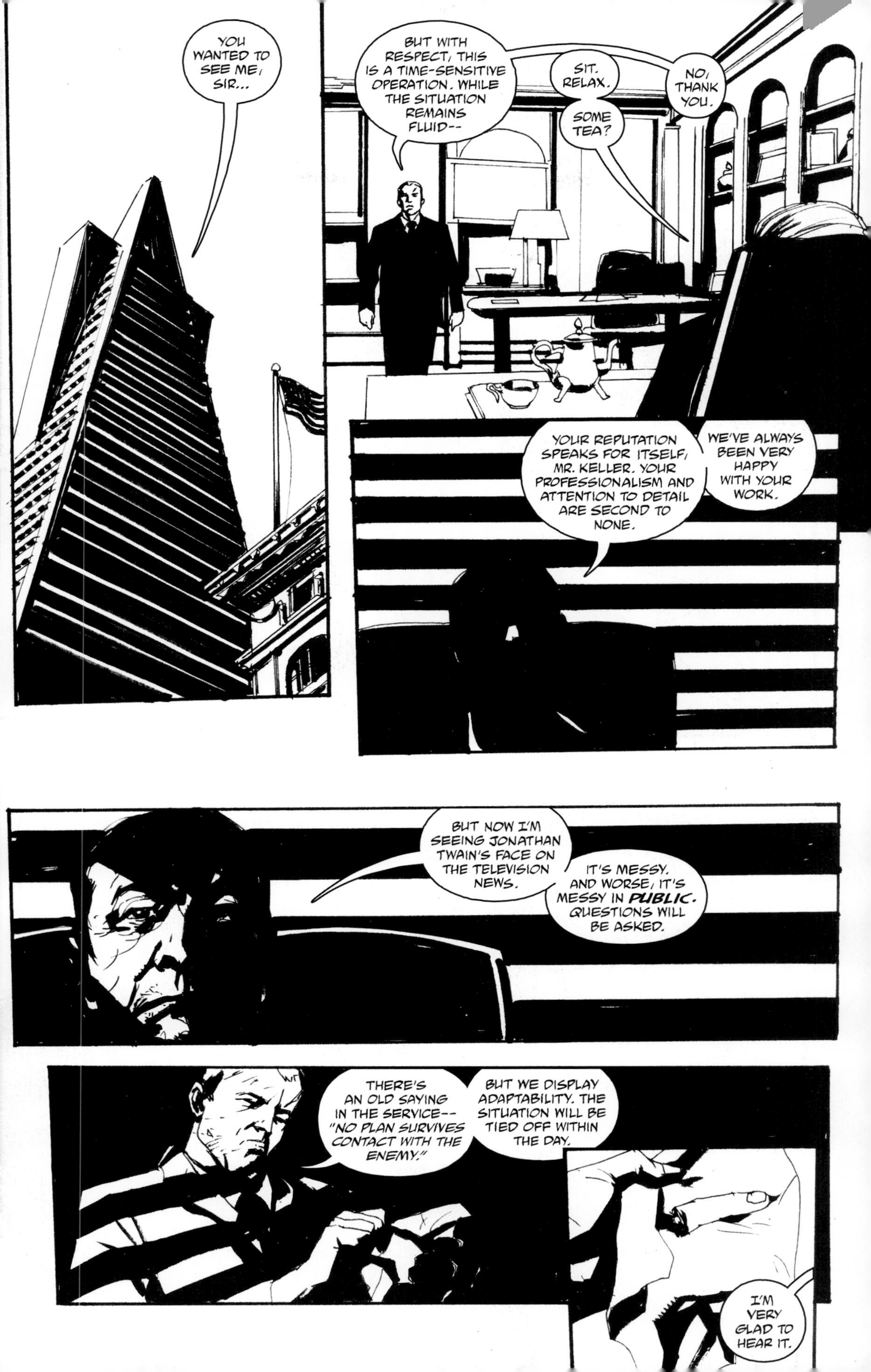
YOU WANTED TO SEE ME, SIR...
BUT WITH RESPECT, THIS IS A TIME-SENSITIVE OPERATION. WHILE THE SITUATION REMAINS FLUID--
SIT. RELAX.
SOME TEA?
NO, THANK YOU.
YOUR REPUTATION SPEAKS FOR ITSELF, MR. KELLER. YOUR PROFESSIONALISM AND ATTENTION TO DETAIL ARE SECOND TO NONE.
WE'VE ALWAYS BEEN VERY HAPPY WITH YOUR WORK.
BUT NOW I'M SEEING JONATHAN TWAIN'S FACE ON THE TELEVISION NEWS.
IT'S MESSY. AND WORSE, IT'S MESSY IN PUBLIC. QUESTIONS WILL BE ASKED.
THERE'S AN OLD SAYING IN THE SERVICE-- "NO PLAN SURVIVES CONTACT WITH THE ENEMY."
BUT WE DISPLAY ADAPTABILITY. THE SITUATION WILL BE TIED OFF WITHIN THE DAY.
I'M VERY GLAD TO HEAR IT.

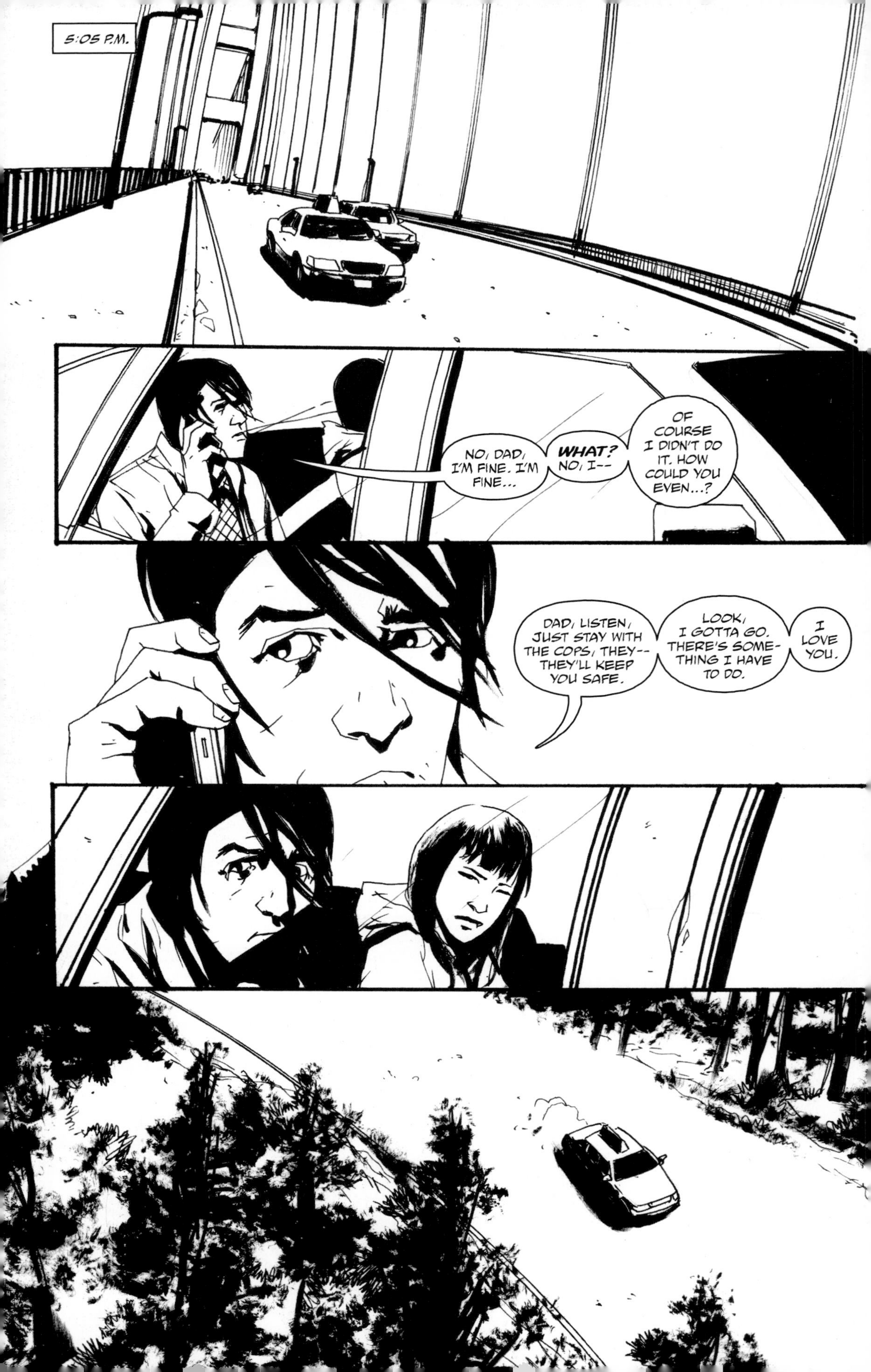
5:05 P.M.
NO, DAD, I'M FINE. I'M FINE...
WHAT? NO, I--
OF COURSE I DIDN'T DO IT. HOW COULD YOU EVEN...?
DAD, LISTEN, JUST STAY WITH THE COPS, THEY--THEY'LL KEEP YOU SAFE.
LOOK, I GOTTA GO. THERE'S SOME-THING I HAVE TO DO.
I LOVE YOU.

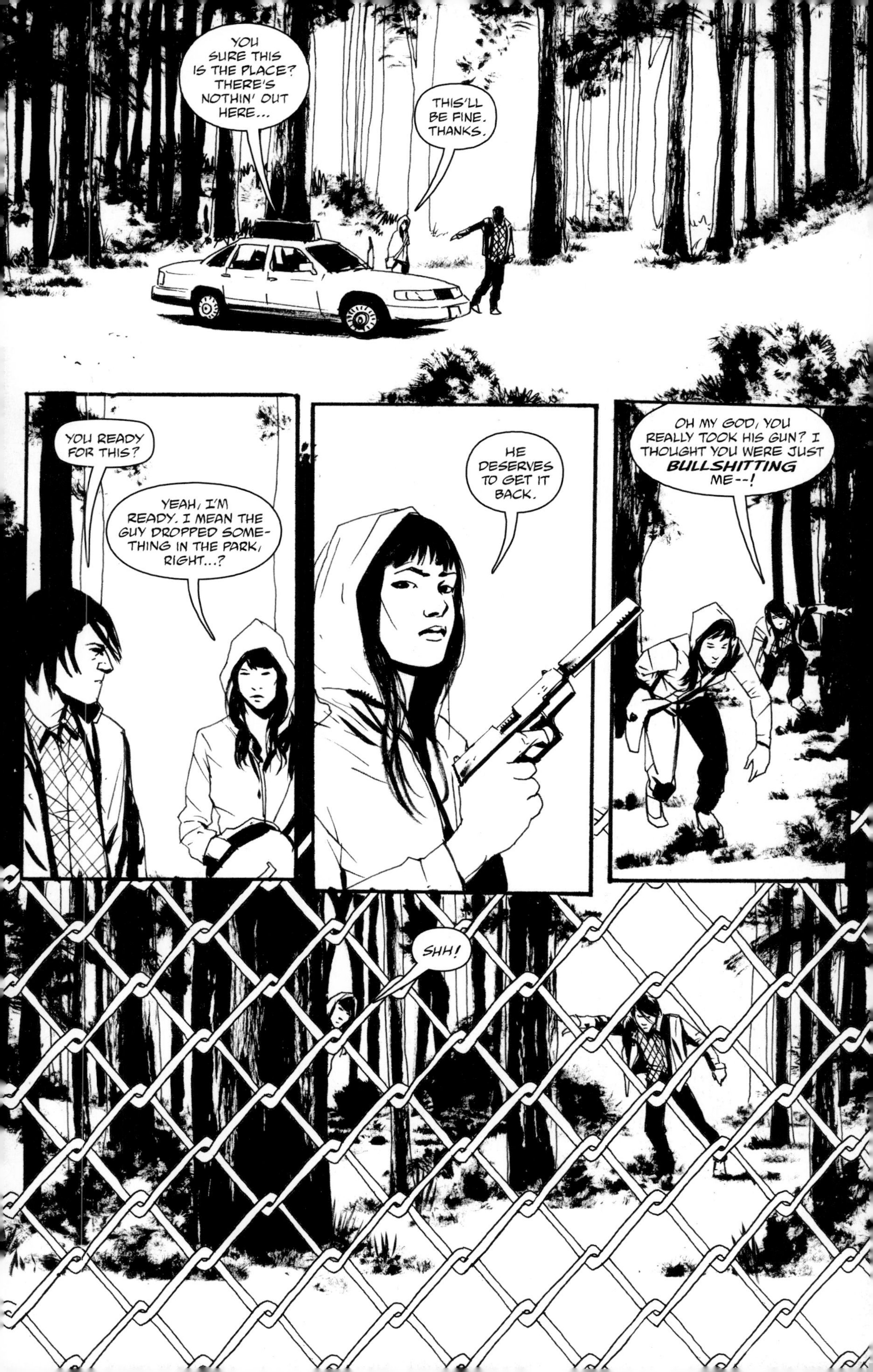
YOU SURE THIS IS THE PLACE? THERE'S NOTHIN' OUT HERE...
THIS'LL BE FINE. THANKS.
YOU READY FOR THIS?
YEAH, I'M READY. I MEAN THE GUY DROPPED SOMETHING IN THE PARK, RIGHT...?
HE DESERVES TO GET IT BACK.
OH MY GOD, YOU REALLY TOOK HIS GUN? I THOUGHT YOU WERE JUST **BULLSHITTING** ME--!
SHH!

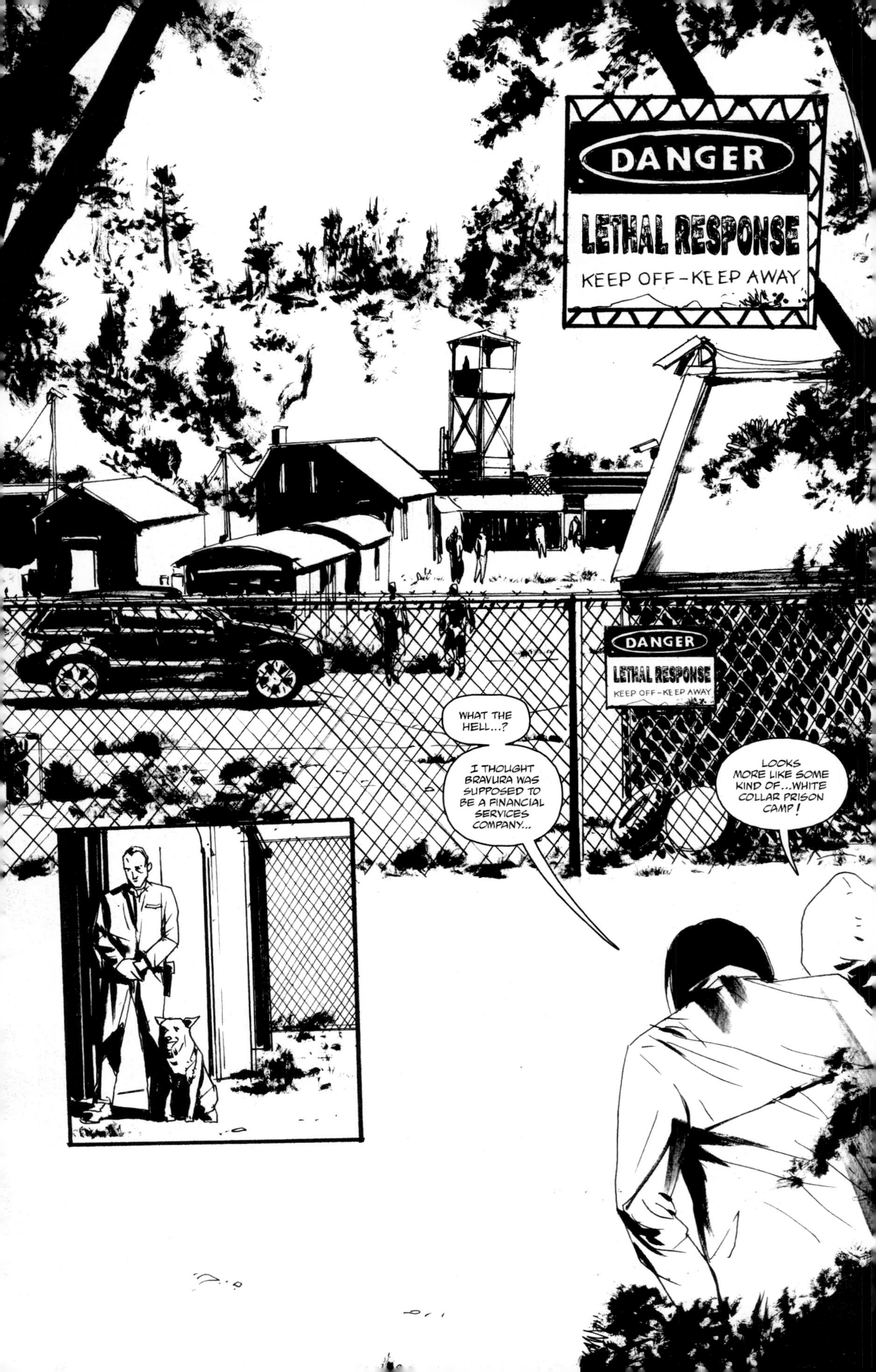
DANGER
LETHAL RESPONSE
KEEP OFF - KEEP AWAY
DANGER
LETHAL RESPONSE
KEEP OFF - KEEP AWAY
WHAT THE HELL...?
I THOUGHT BRAVURA WAS SUPPOSED TO BE A FINANCIAL SERVICES COMPANY...
LOOKS MORE LIKE SOME KIND OF...WHITE COLLAR PRISON CAMP!

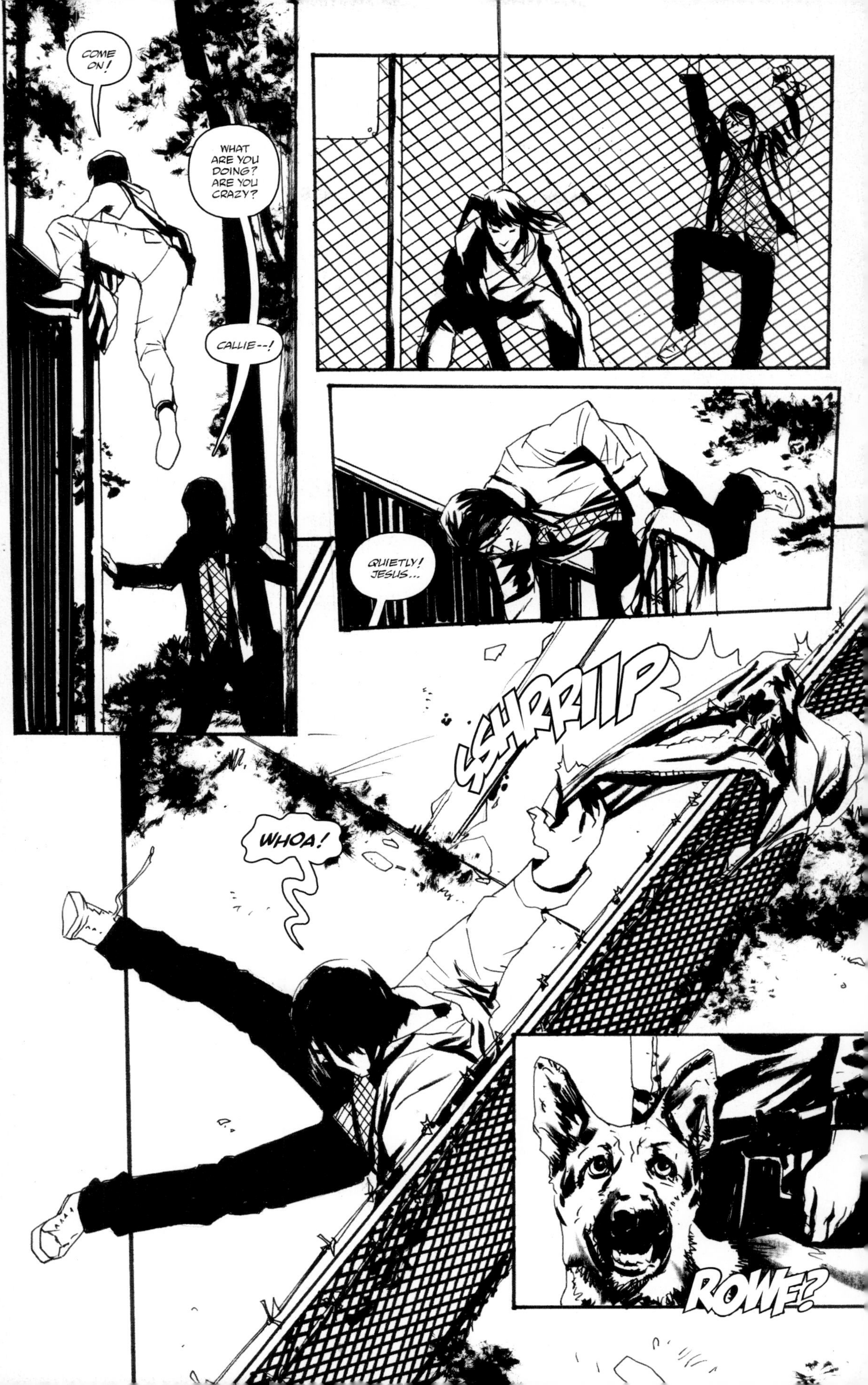
COME ON!
WHAT ARE YOU DOING? ARE YOU CRAZY?
CALLIE--!
QUIETLY! JESUS...
SHRRIIP
WHOA!
ROWF?

CHAPTER THREE

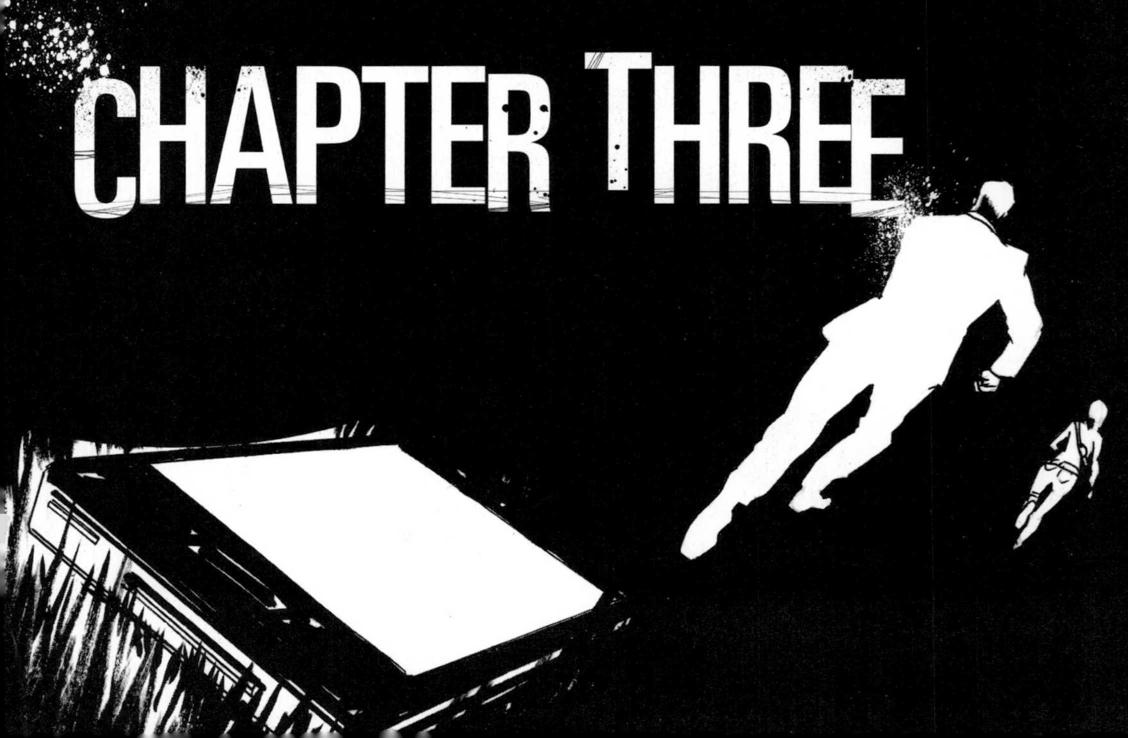

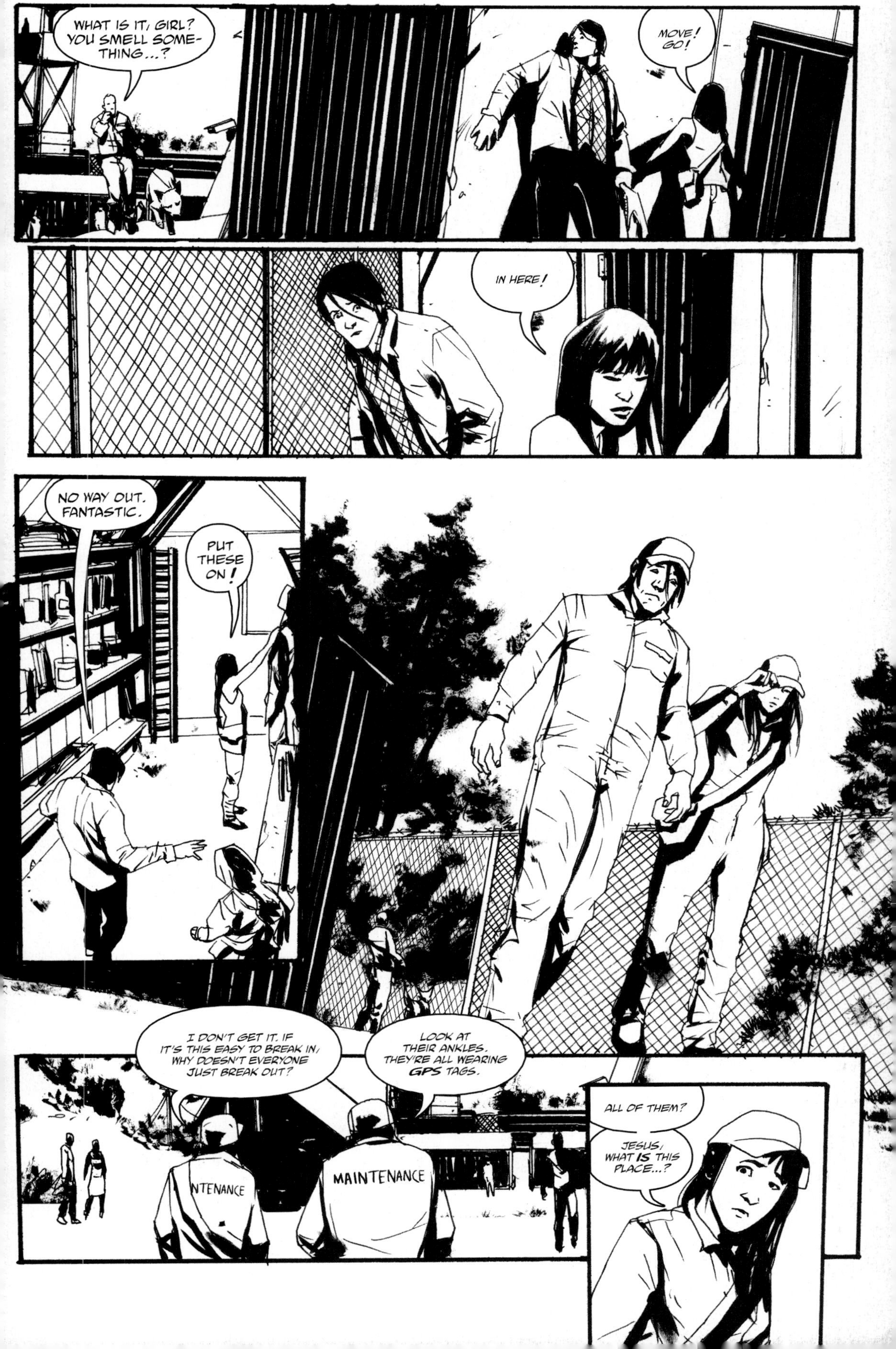
WHAT IS IT, GIRL? YOU SMELL SOME-THING...?
MOVE! GO!
IN HERE!
NO WAY OUT. FANTASTIC.
PUT THESE ON!
I DON'T GET IT. IF IT'S THIS EASY TO BREAK IN, WHY DOESN'T EVERYONE JUST BREAK OUT?
LOOK AT THEIR ANKLES. THEY'RE ALL WEARING GPS TAGS.
NTENANCE
MAINTENANCE
ALL OF THEM?
JESUS, WHAT IS THIS PLACE...?

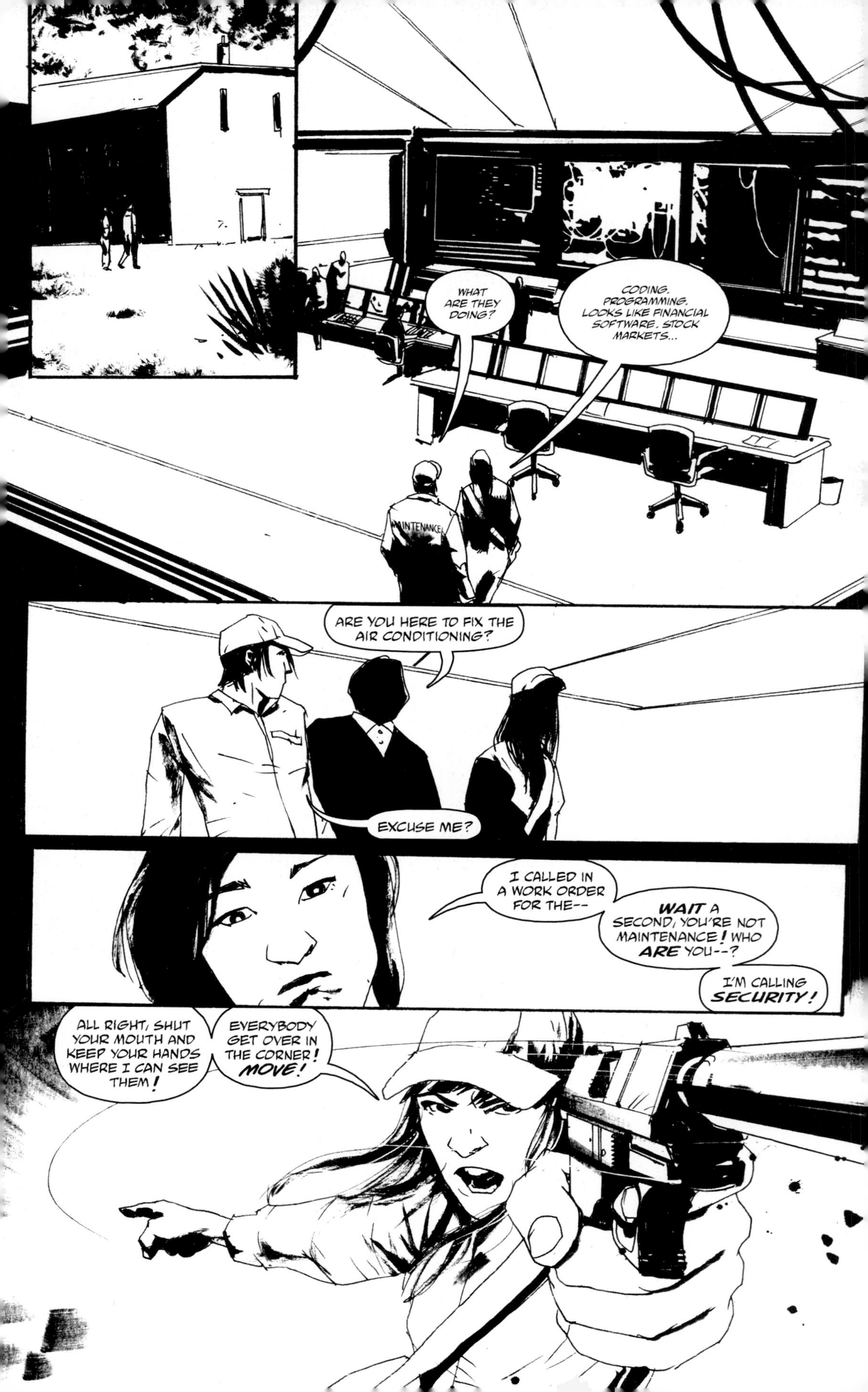
WHAT ARE THEY DOING?
CODING. PROGRAMMING. LOOKS LIKE FINANCIAL SOFTWARE. STOCK MARKETS...
MAINTENANCE
ARE YOU HERE TO FIX THE AIR CONDITIONING?
EXCUSE ME?
I CALLED IN A WORK ORDER FOR THE--
WAIT A SECOND, YOU'RE NOT MAINTENANCE! WHO ARE YOU--?
I'M CALLING SECURITY!
ALL RIGHT, SHUT YOUR MOUTH AND KEEP YOUR HANDS WHERE I CAN SEE THEM!
EVERYBODY GET OVER IN THE CORNER! MOVE!

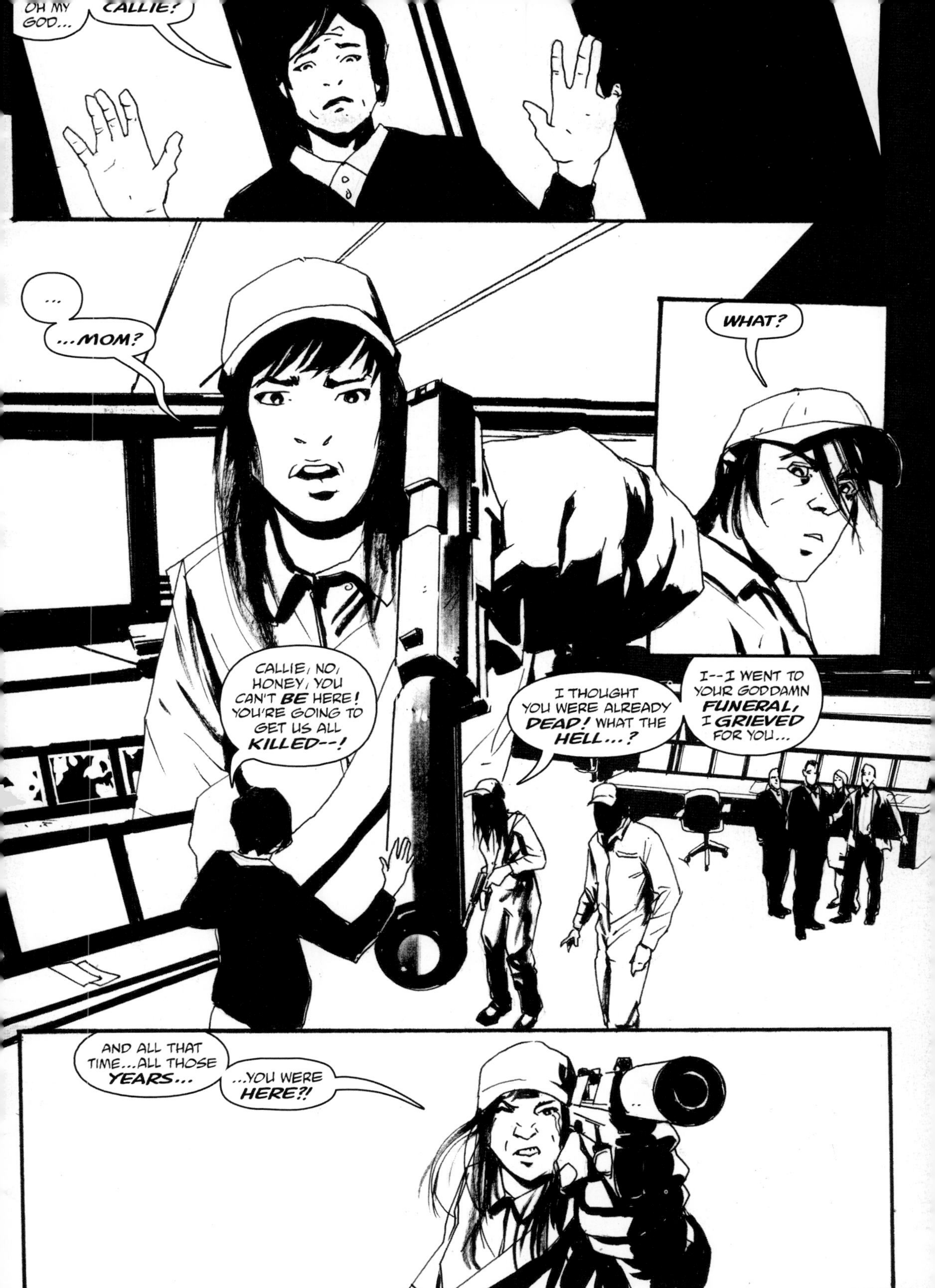
OH MY GOD...
CALLIE?
...
...MOM?
WHAT?
CALLIE, NO, HONEY, YOU CAN'T BE HERE! YOU'RE GOING TO GET US ALL KILLED--!
I THOUGHT YOU WERE ALREADY DEAD! WHAT THE HELL...?
I--I WENT TO YOUR GODDAMN FUNERAL, I GRIEVED FOR YOU...
AND ALL THAT TIME...ALL THOSE YEARS...
...YOU WERE HERE?!

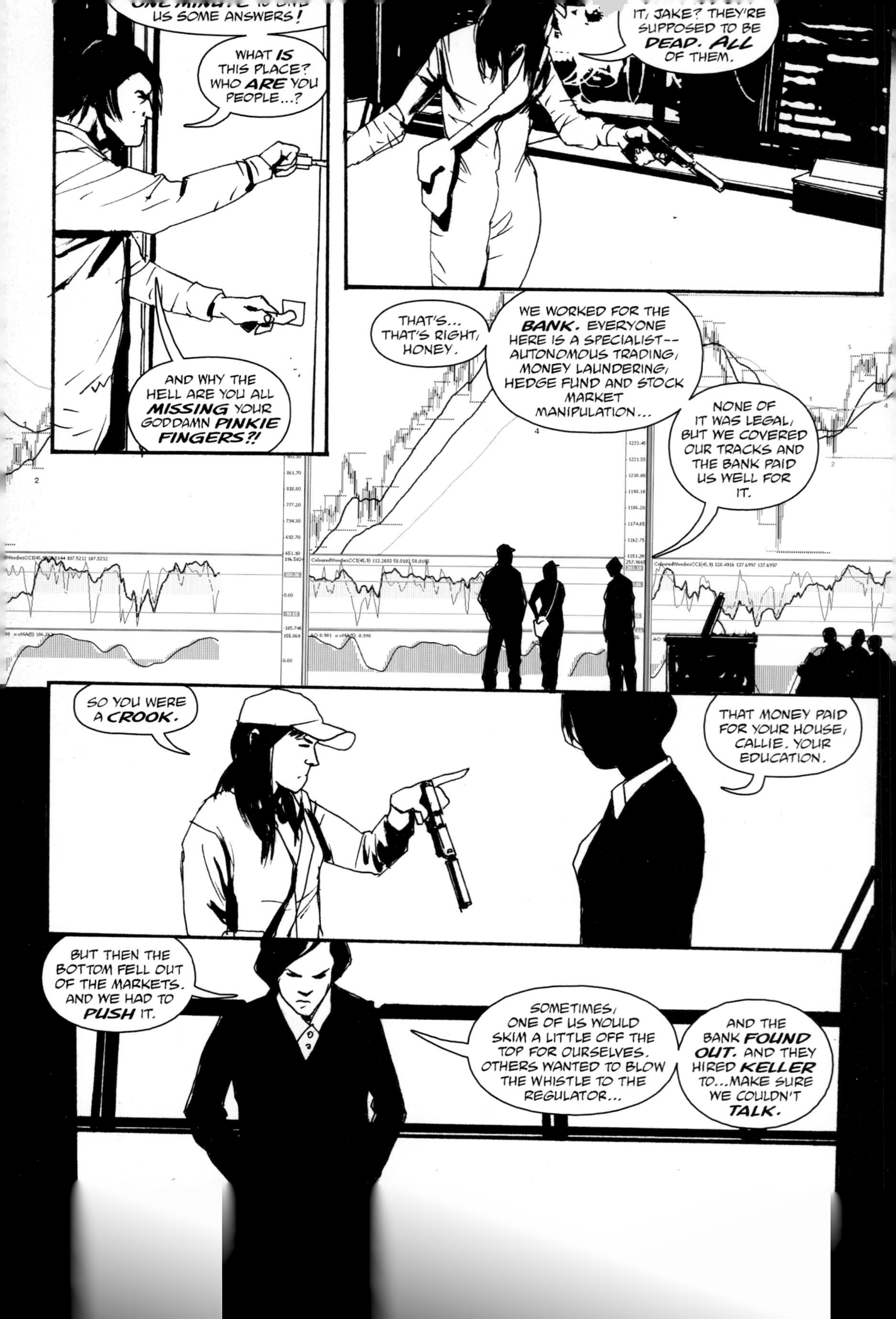
US SOME ANSWERS!
WHAT IS THIS PLACE? WHO ARE YOU PEOPLE...?
AND WHY THE HELL ARE YOU ALL MISSING YOUR GODDAMN PINKIE FINGERS?!
IT, JAKE? THEY'RE SUPPOSED TO BE DEAD. ALL OF THEM.
THAT'S... THAT'S RIGHT, HONEY.
WE WORKED FOR THE BANK. EVERYONE HERE IS A SPECIALIST-- AUTONOMOUS TRADING, MONEY LAUNDERING, HEDGE FUND AND STOCK MARKET MANIPULATION...
NONE OF IT WAS LEGAL, BUT WE COVERED OUR TRACKS AND THE BANK PAID US WELL FOR IT.
SO YOU WERE A CROOK.
THAT MONEY PAID FOR YOUR HOUSE, CALLIE. YOUR EDUCATION.
BUT THEN THE BOTTOM FELL OUT OF THE MARKETS. AND WE HAD TO PUSH IT.
SOMETIMES, ONE OF US WOULD SKIM A LITTLE OFF THE TOP FOR OURSELVES. OTHERS WANTED TO BLOW THE WHISTLE TO THE REGULATOR...
AND THE BANK FOUND OUT. AND THEY HIRED KELLER TO...MAKE SURE WE COULDN'T TALK.

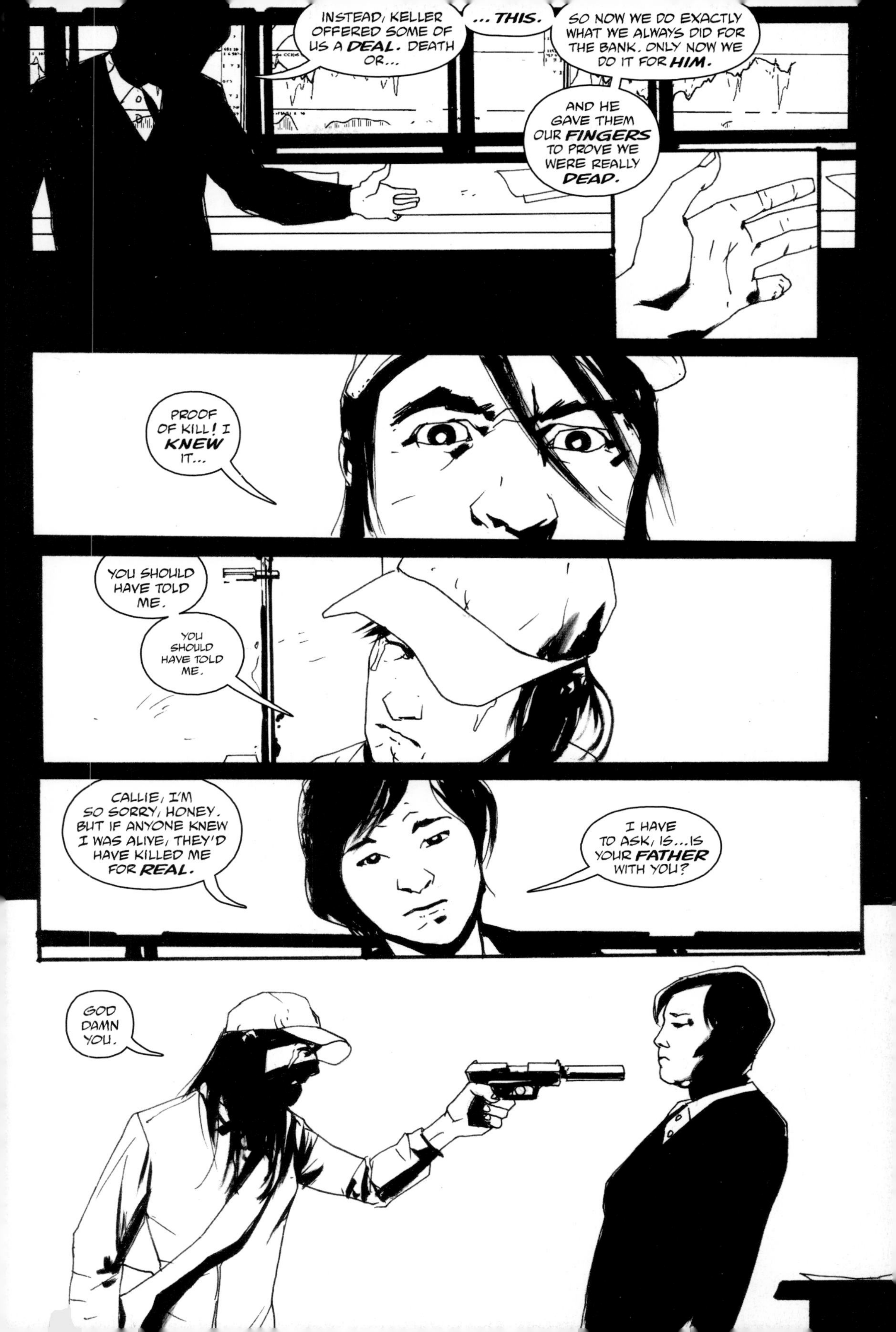
INSTEAD, KELLER OFFERED SOME OF US A DEAL. DEATH OR...
...THIS.
SO NOW WE DO EXACTLY WHAT WE ALWAYS DID FOR THE BANK. ONLY NOW WE DO IT FOR HIM.
AND HE GAVE THEM OUR FINGERS TO PROVE WE WERE REALLY DEAD.
PROOF OF KILL! I KNEW IT...
YOU SHOULD HAVE TOLD ME.
YOU SHOULD HAVE TOLD ME.
CALLIE, I'M SO SORRY, HONEY. BUT IF ANYONE KNEW I WAS ALIVE, THEY'D HAVE KILLED ME FOR REAL.
I HAVE TO ASK, IS...IS YOUR FATHER WITH YOU?
GOD DAMN YOU.

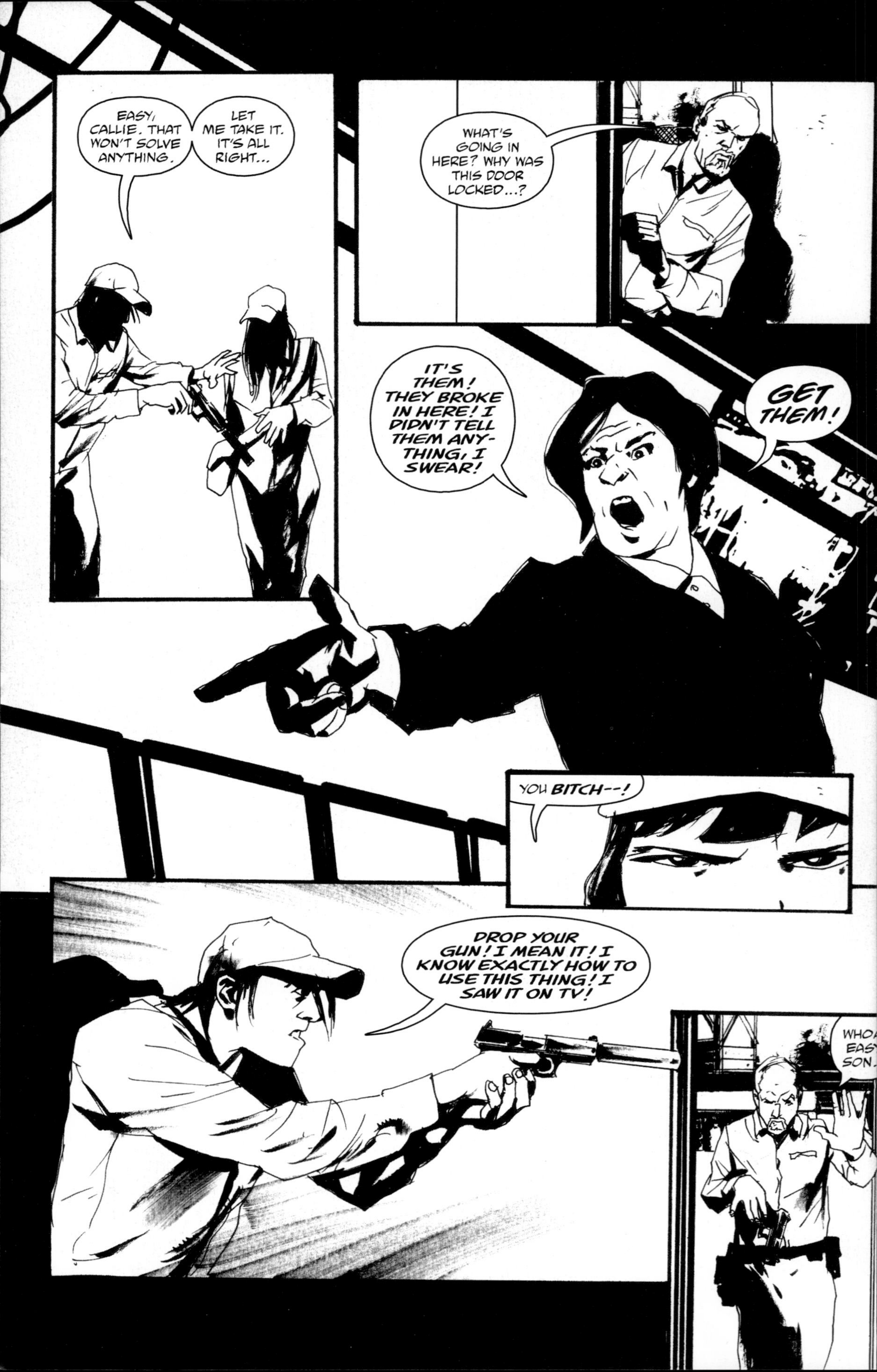
EASY, CALLIE. THAT WON'T SOLVE ANYTHING.
LET ME TAKE IT. IT'S ALL RIGHT...
WHAT'S GOING IN HERE? WHY WAS THIS DOOR LOCKED...?
IT'S THEM! THEY BROKE IN HERE! I DIDN'T TELL THEM ANYTHING, I SWEAR!
GET THEM!
YOU BITCH--!
DROP YOUR GUN! I MEAN IT! I KNOW EXACTLY HOW TO USE THIS THING! I SAW IT ON TV!

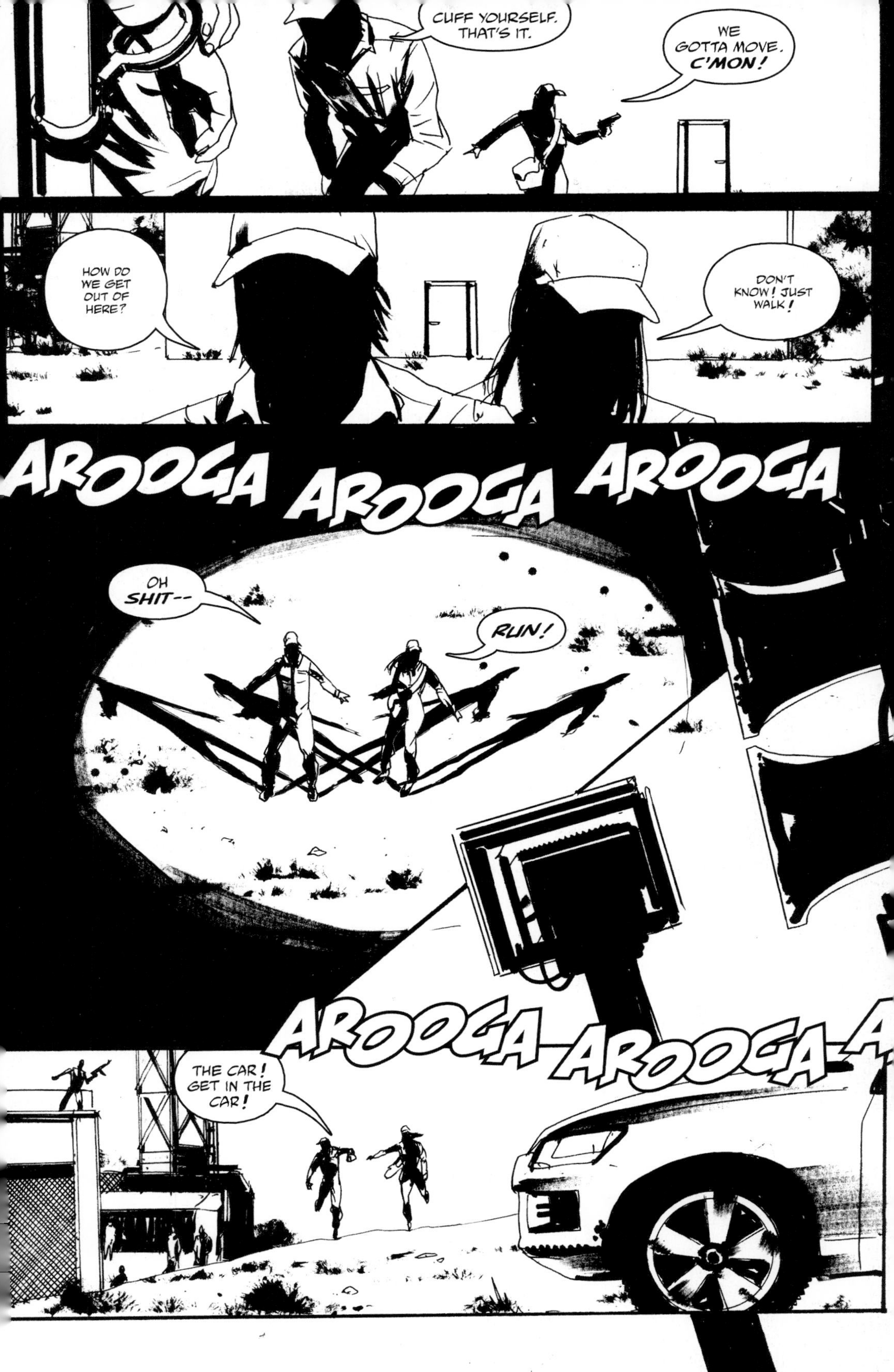
CUFF YOURSELF. THAT'S IT.
WE GOTTA MOVE. C'MON!
HOW DO WE GET OUT OF HERE?
DON'T KNOW! JUST WALK!
AROOGA AROOGA AROOGA
OH SHIT--
RUN!
AROOGA AROOGA A
THE CAR! GET IN THE CAR!

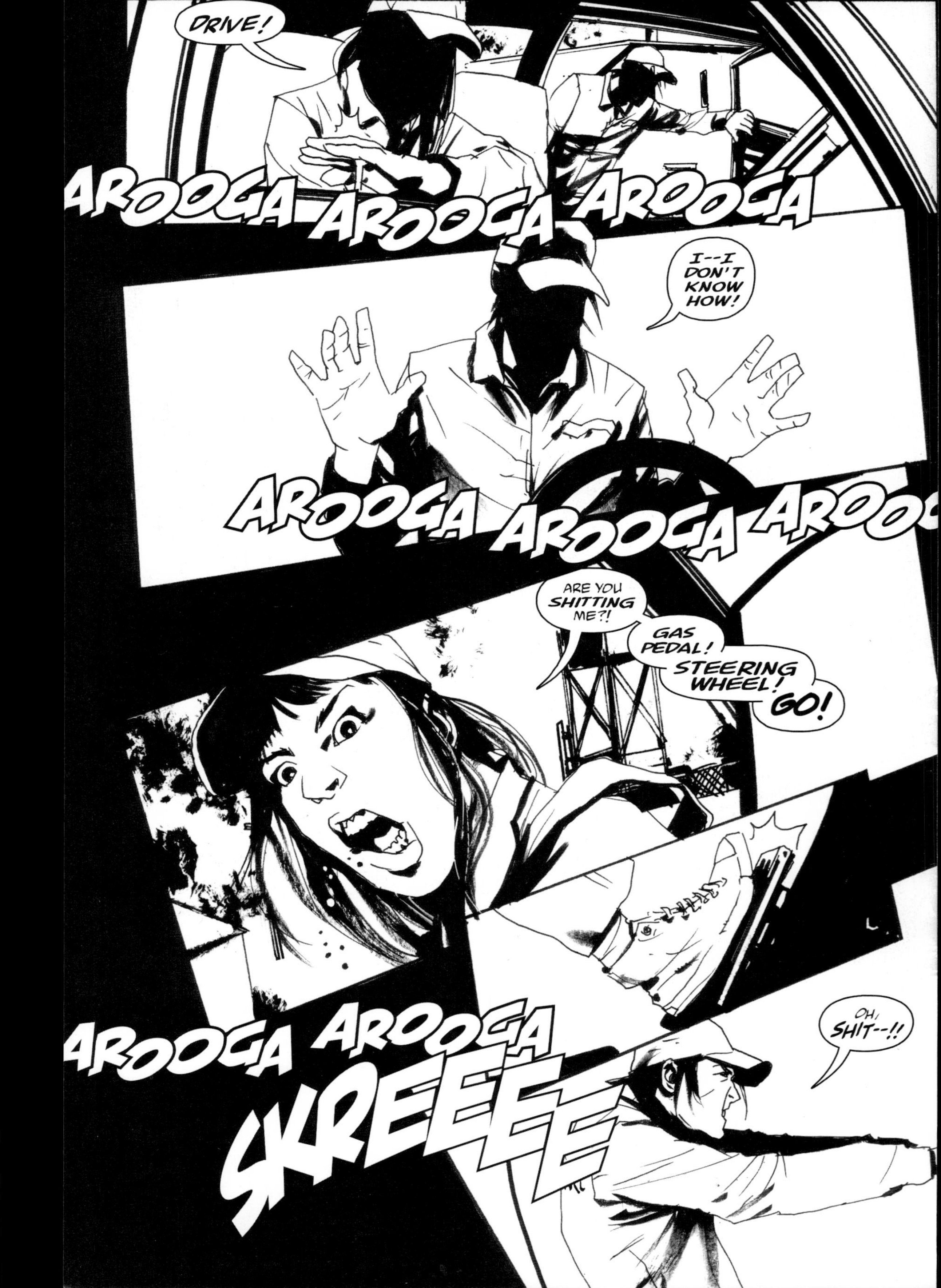
DRIVE!
AROOGA AROOGA AROOGA
I--I DON'T KNOW HOW!
AROOGA AROOGA AROO
ARE YOU SHITTING ME?!
GAS PEDAL! STEERING WHEEL! GO!
AROOGA AROOGA
SKREEEEE
OH, SHIT--!!

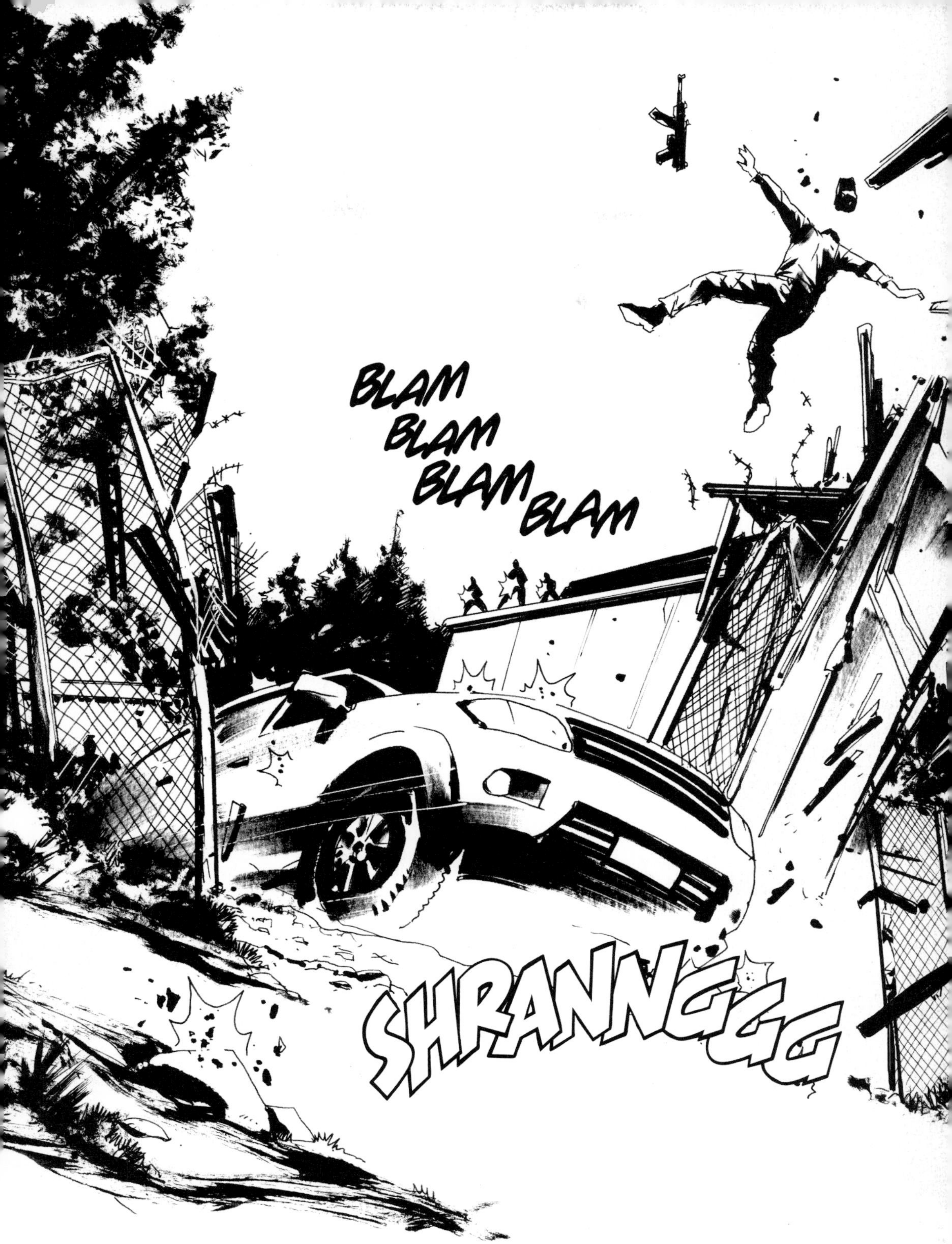
BLAM
BLAM
BLAM
BLAM
SHRANNGGG

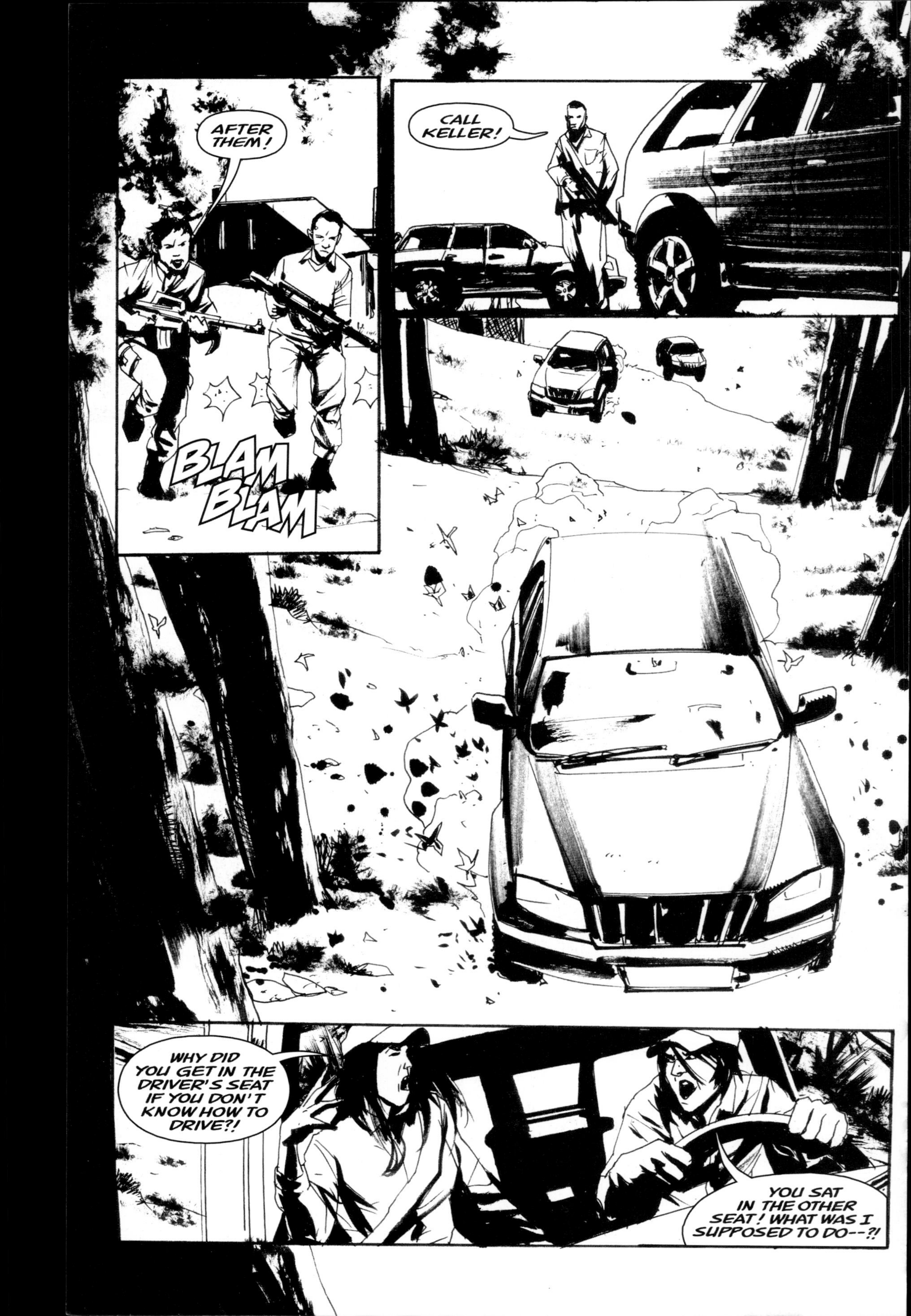

AFTER THEM!
BLAM BLAM
CALL KELLER!
WHY DID YOU GET IN THE DRIVER'S SEAT IF YOU DON'T KNOW HOW TO DRIVE?!
YOU SAT IN THE OTHER SEAT! WHAT WAS I SUPPOSED TO DO--?!

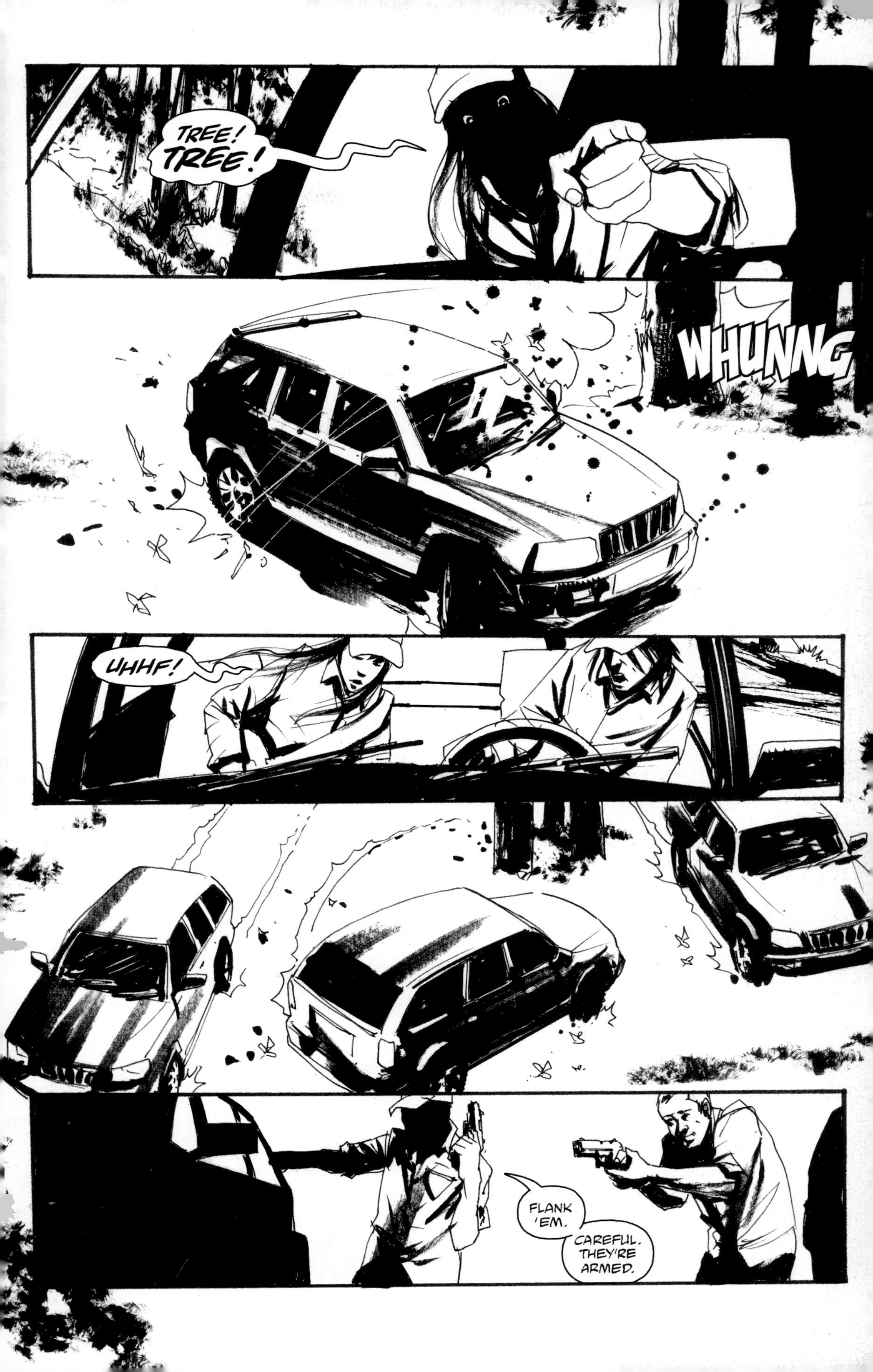
TREE! TREE!
WHUNNG
UHHF!
FLANK 'EM.
CAREFUL. THEY'RE ARMED.

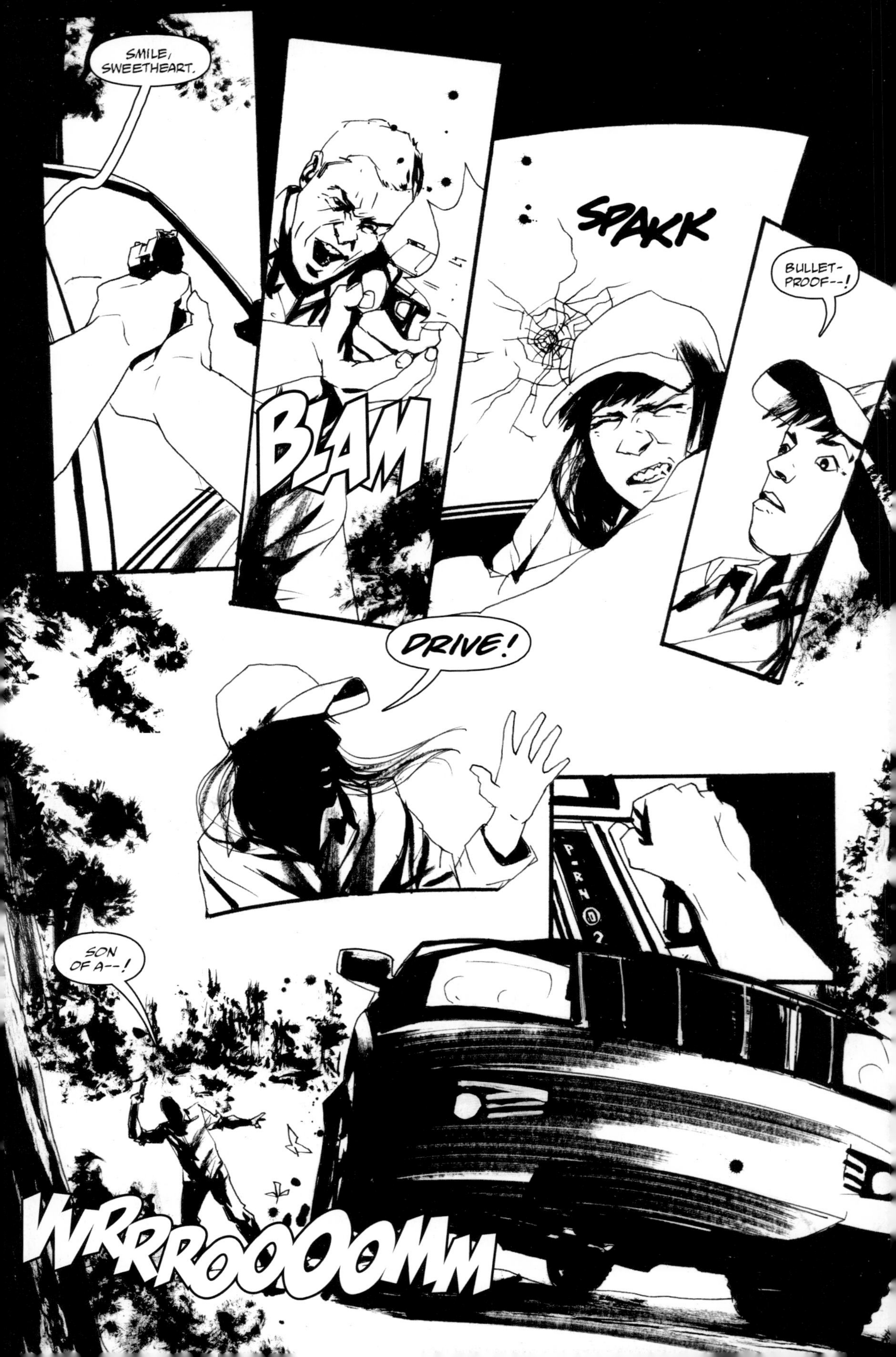
SMILE, SWEETHEART.
BLAM
SPAKK
BULLET-PROOF--!
DRIVE!
SON OF A--!
WRRROOOOOMM

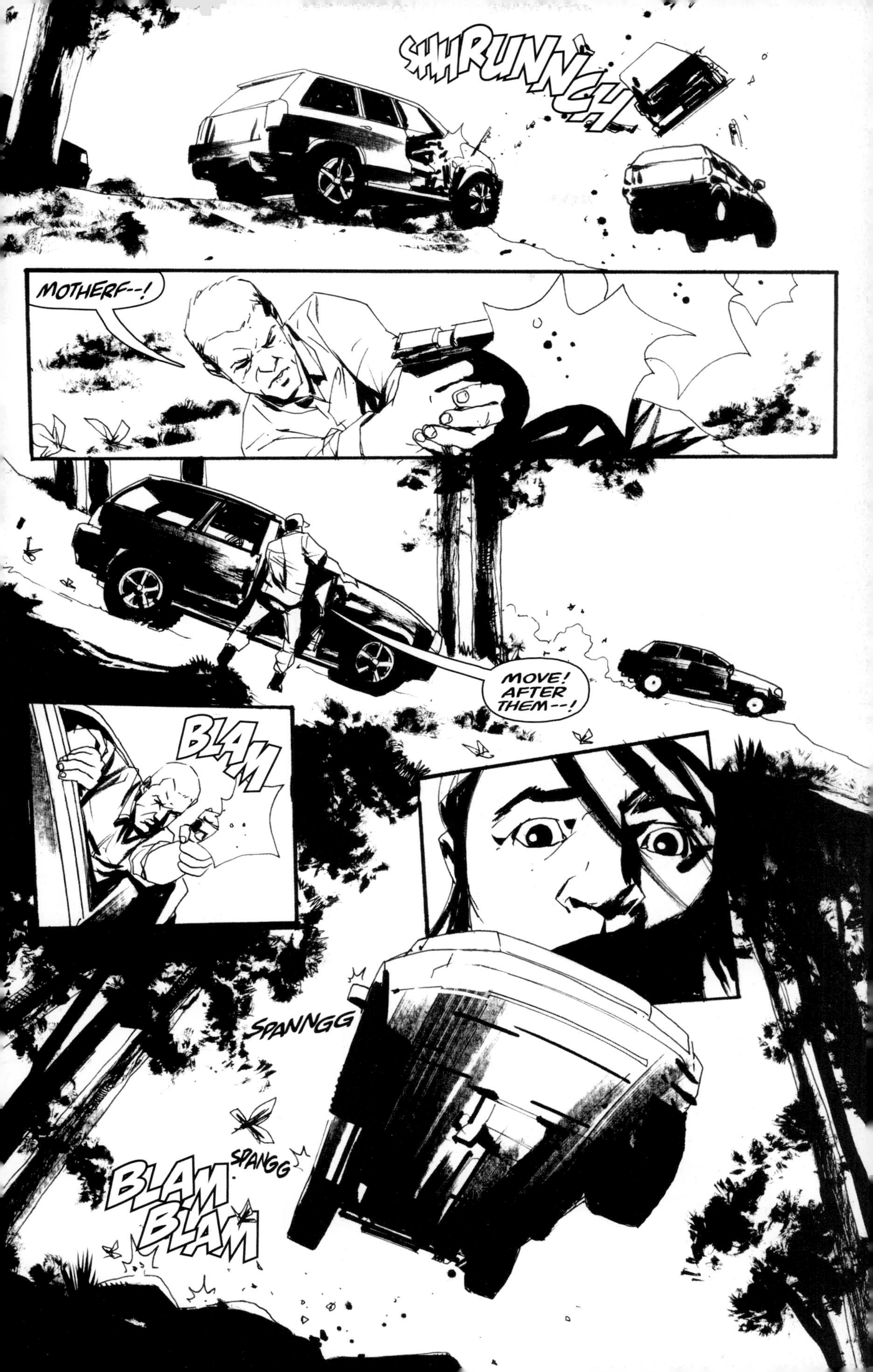
SHHRUNNCH
MOTHERF--!
MOVE! AFTER THEM--!
BLAM
SPANNGG
SPANGG
BLAM BLAM

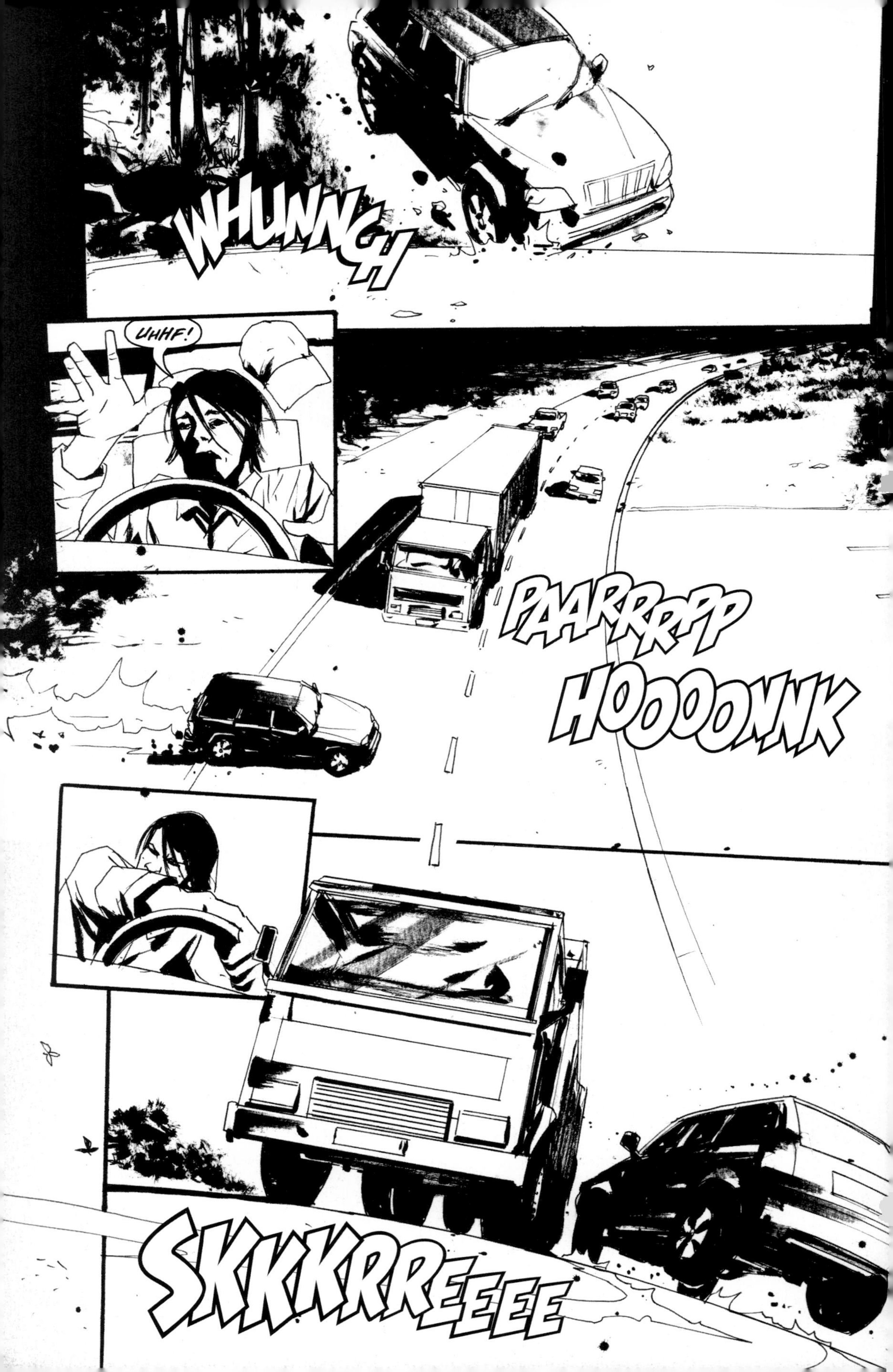
WHUNNCH
UHHF!
PAARRRPP
HOOOONNK
SKKKRREEEE

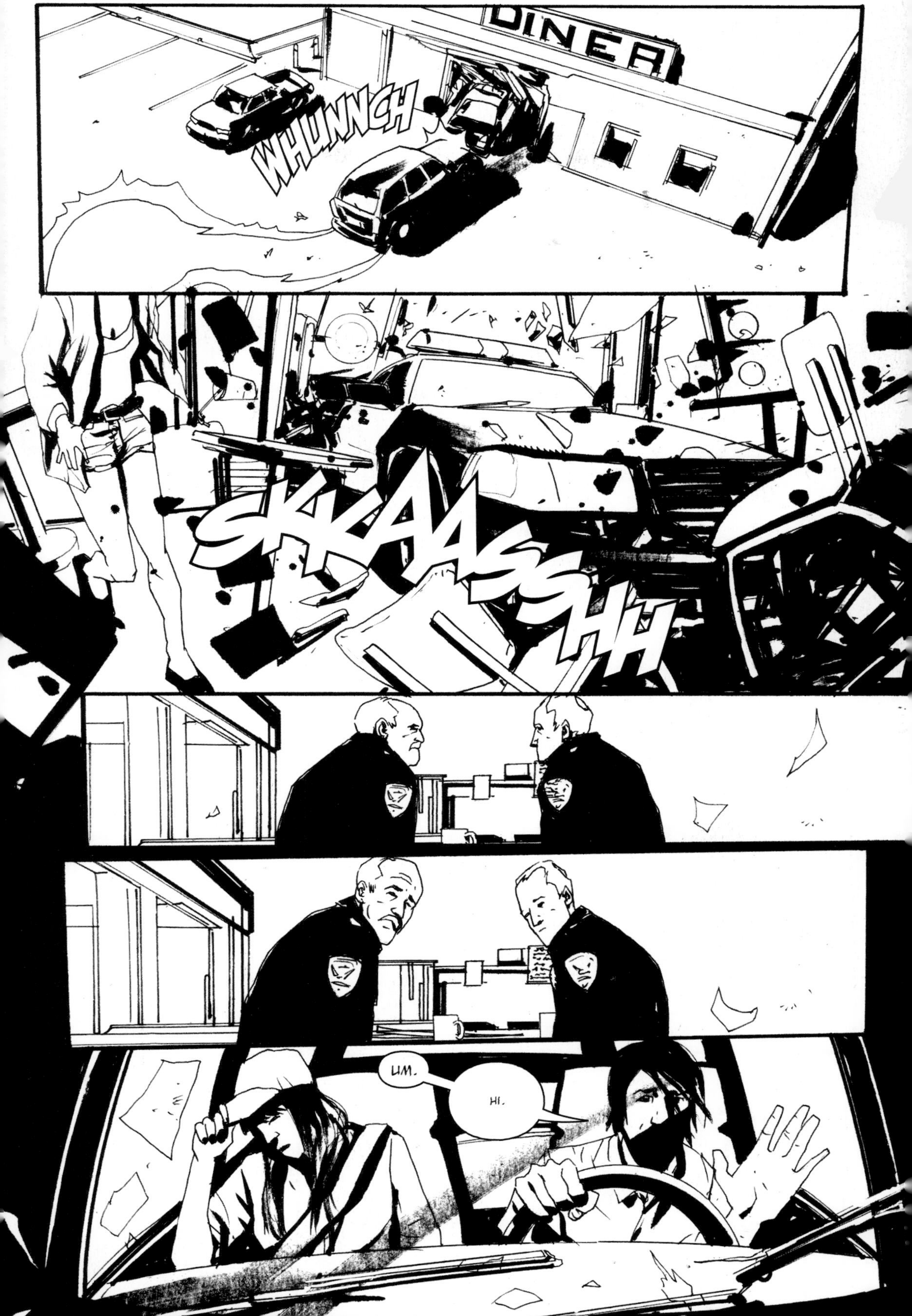
DINER
WHUNNCH
SKAASSHH
UM.
HI.

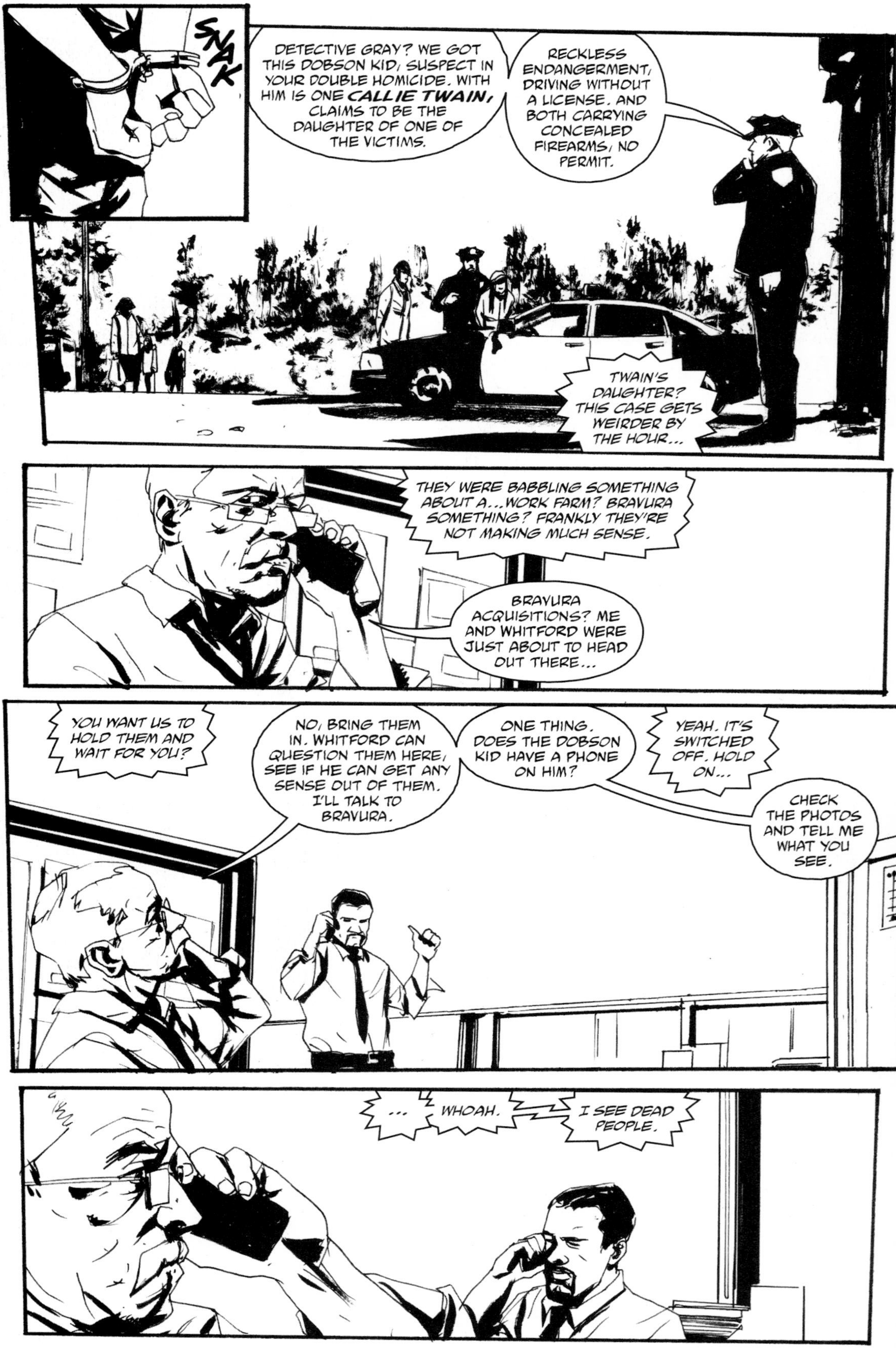
SNAK
DETECTIVE GRAY? WE GOT THIS DOBSON KID, SUSPECT IN YOUR DOUBLE HOMICIDE. WITH HIM IS ONE CALLIE TWAIN, CLAIMS TO BE THE DAUGHTER OF ONE OF THE VICTIMS.
RECKLESS ENDANGERMENT, DRIVING WITHOUT A LICENSE. AND BOTH CARRYING CONCEALED FIREARMS, NO PERMIT.
TWAIN'S DAUGHTER? THIS CASE GETS WEIRDER BY THE HOUR...
THEY WERE BABBLING SOMETHING ABOUT A...WORK FARM? BRAVURA SOMETHING? FRANKLY THEY'RE NOT MAKING MUCH SENSE.
BRAVURA ACQUISITIONS? ME AND WHITFORD WERE JUST ABOUT TO HEAD OUT THERE...
YOU WANT US TO HOLD THEM AND WAIT FOR YOU?
NO, BRING THEM IN. WHITFORD CAN QUESTION THEM HERE, SEE IF HE CAN GET ANY SENSE OUT OF THEM. I'LL TALK TO BRAVURA.
ONE THING. DOES THE DOBSON KID HAVE A PHONE ON HIM?
YEAH. IT'S SWITCHED OFF. HOLD ON...
CHECK THE PHOTOS AND TELL ME WHAT YOU SEE.
...
WHOAH.
I SEE DEAD PEOPLE.

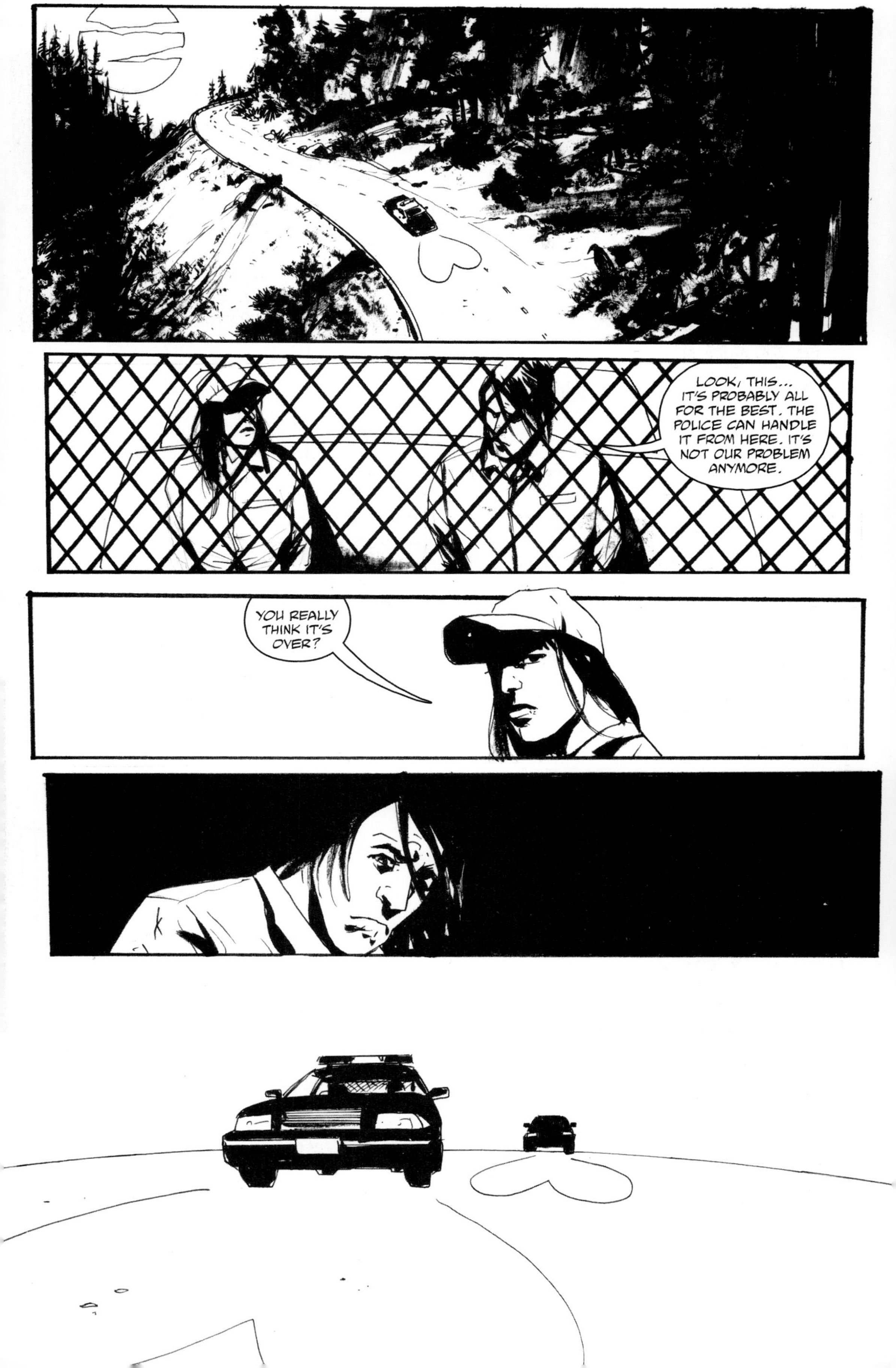
LOOK, THIS... IT'S PROBABLY ALL FOR THE BEST. THE POLICE CAN HANDLE IT FROM HERE. IT'S NOT OUR PROBLEM ANYMORE.
YOU REALLY THINK IT'S OVER?

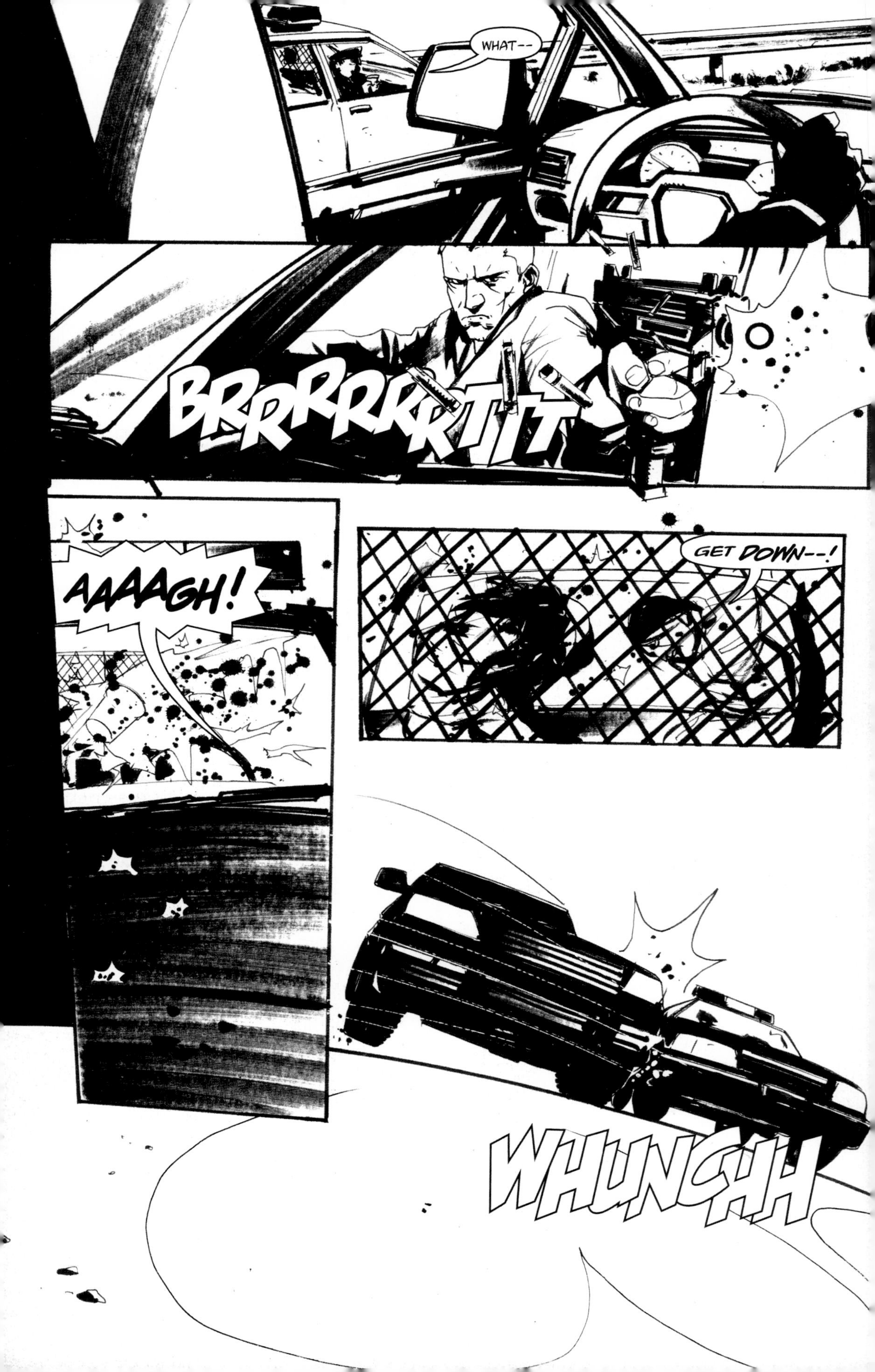
WHAT--
BRRRRRRRTTT
AAAAGH!
GET DOWN--!
WHUNCHH

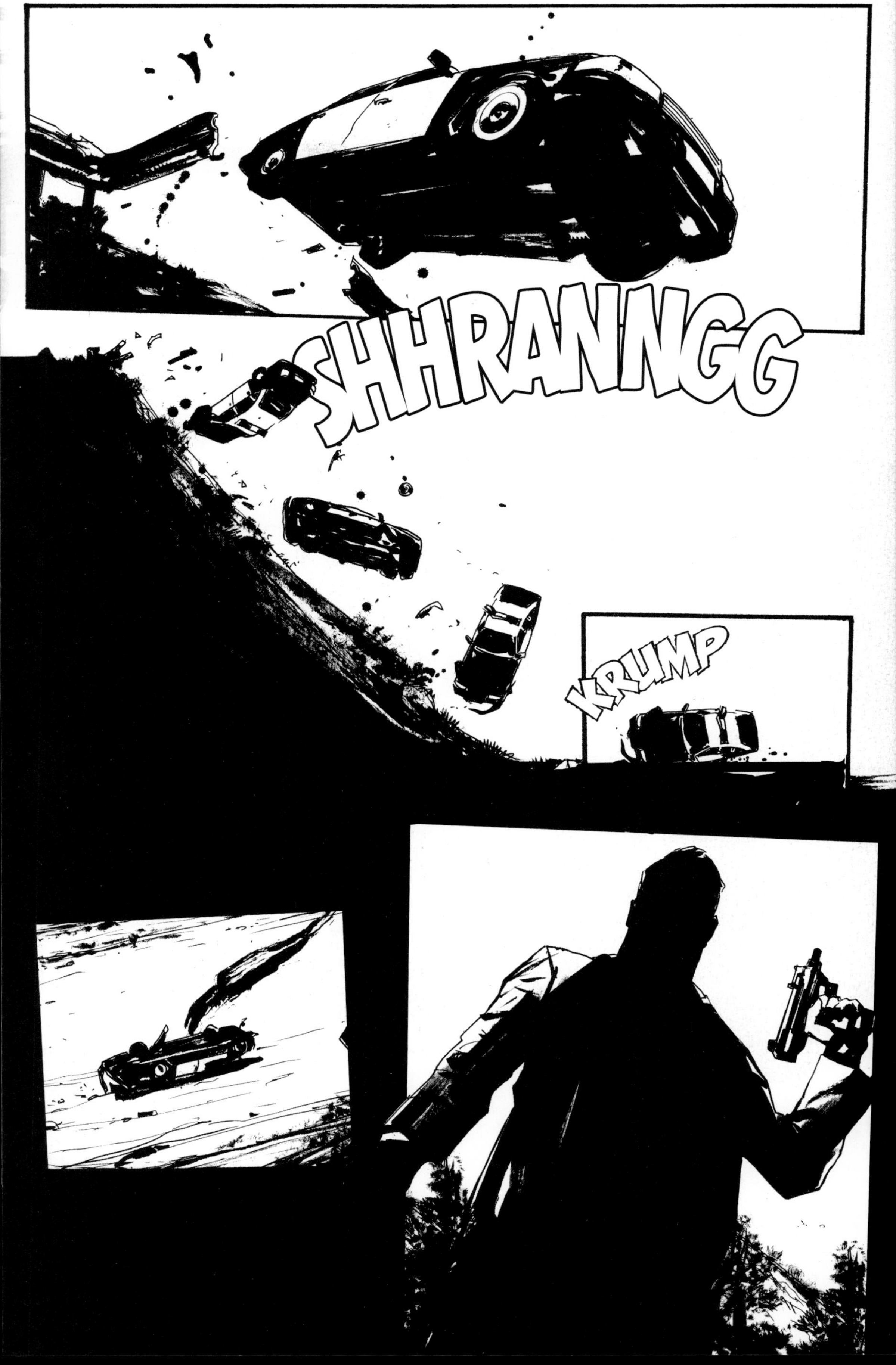
SHHRANNGG
KRUMP

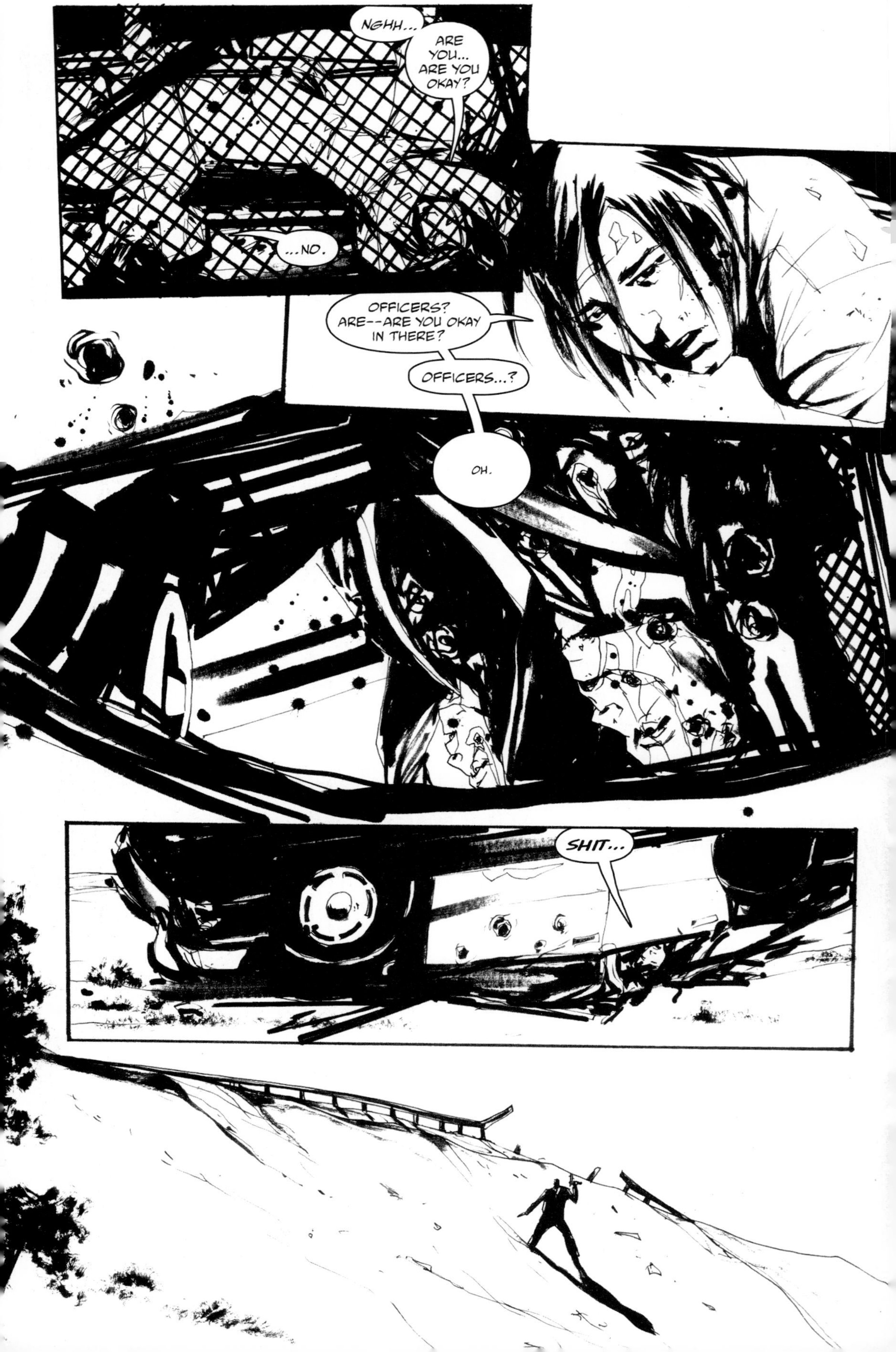
NGHH...
ARE YOU... ARE YOU OKAY?
...NO.
OFFICERS? ARE--ARE YOU OKAY IN THERE?
OFFICERS...?
OH.
SHIT...

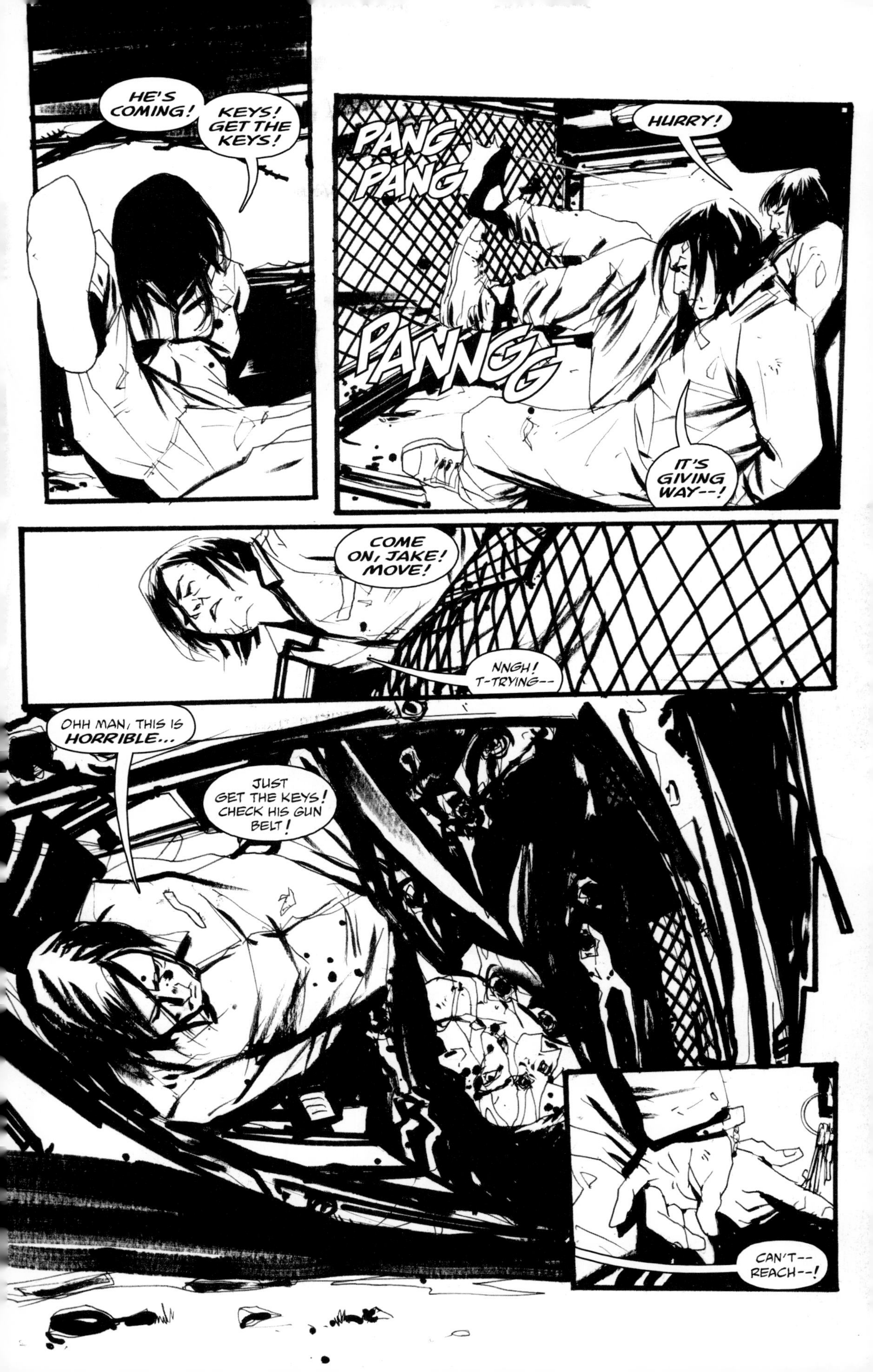
HE'S COMING!
KEYS! GET THE KEYS!
PANG PANG
HURRY!
PANNGG
IT'S GIVING WAY--!
COME ON, JAKE! MOVE!
NNGH! T-TRYING--
OHH MAN, THIS IS HORRIBLE...
JUST GET THE KEYS! CHECK HIS GUN BELT!
CAN'T-- REACH--!

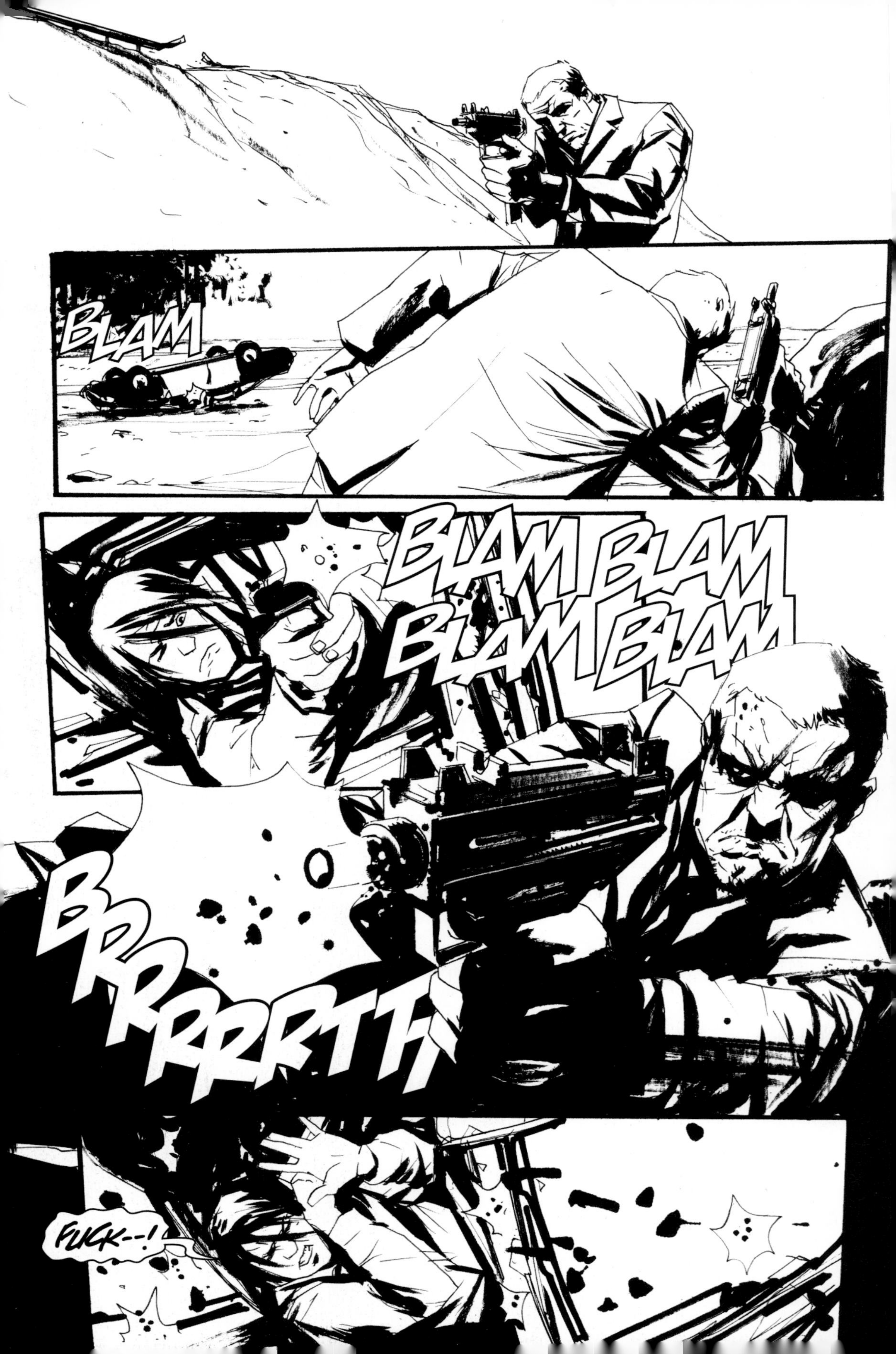
BLAM
BLAM BLAM
BLAM BLAM
BRRRRRTTT
FUCK--!

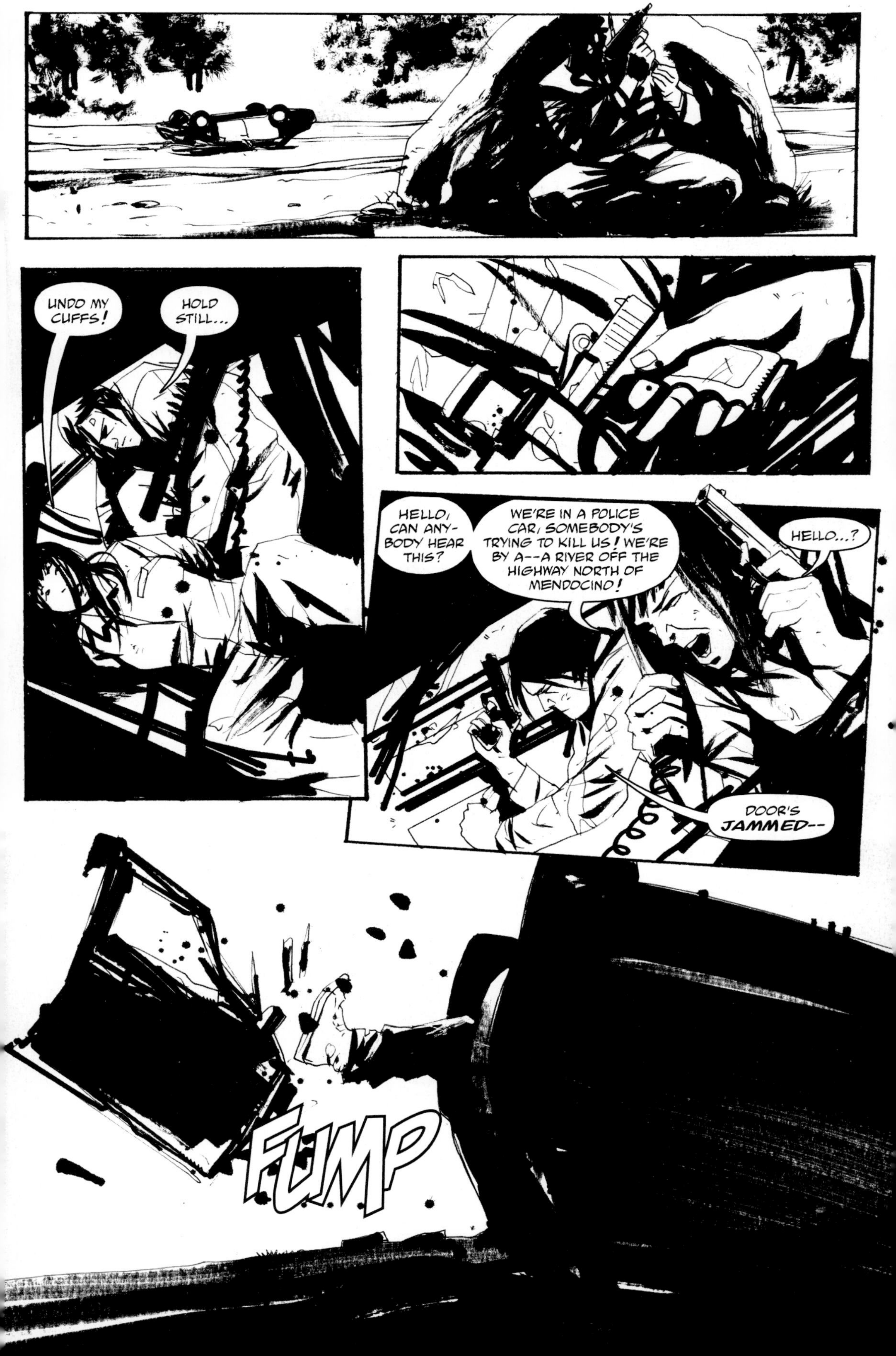
UNDO MY CUFFS!
HOLD STILL...
HELLO, CAN ANY-BODY HEAR THIS?
WE'RE IN A POLICE CAR, SOMEBODY'S TRYING TO KILL US! WE'RE BY A--A RIVER OFF THE HIGHWAY NORTH OF MENDOCINO!
HELLO...?
DOOR'S JAMMED--
FUMP

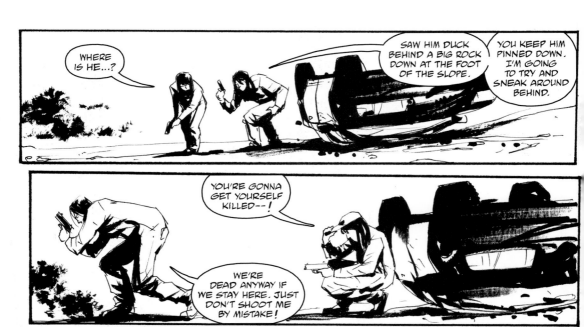

WHERE IS HE...?

SAW HIM DUCK BEHIND A BIG ROCK DOWN AT THE FOOT OF THE SLOPE.

YOU KEEP HIM PINNED DOWN. I'M GOING TO TRY AND SNEAK AROUND BEHIND.

YOU'RE GONNA GET YOURSELF KILLED--!

WE'RE DEAD ANYWAY IF WE STAY HERE. JUST DON'T SHOOT ME BY MISTAKE!

BLAM

BLAM

BLAM BLAM

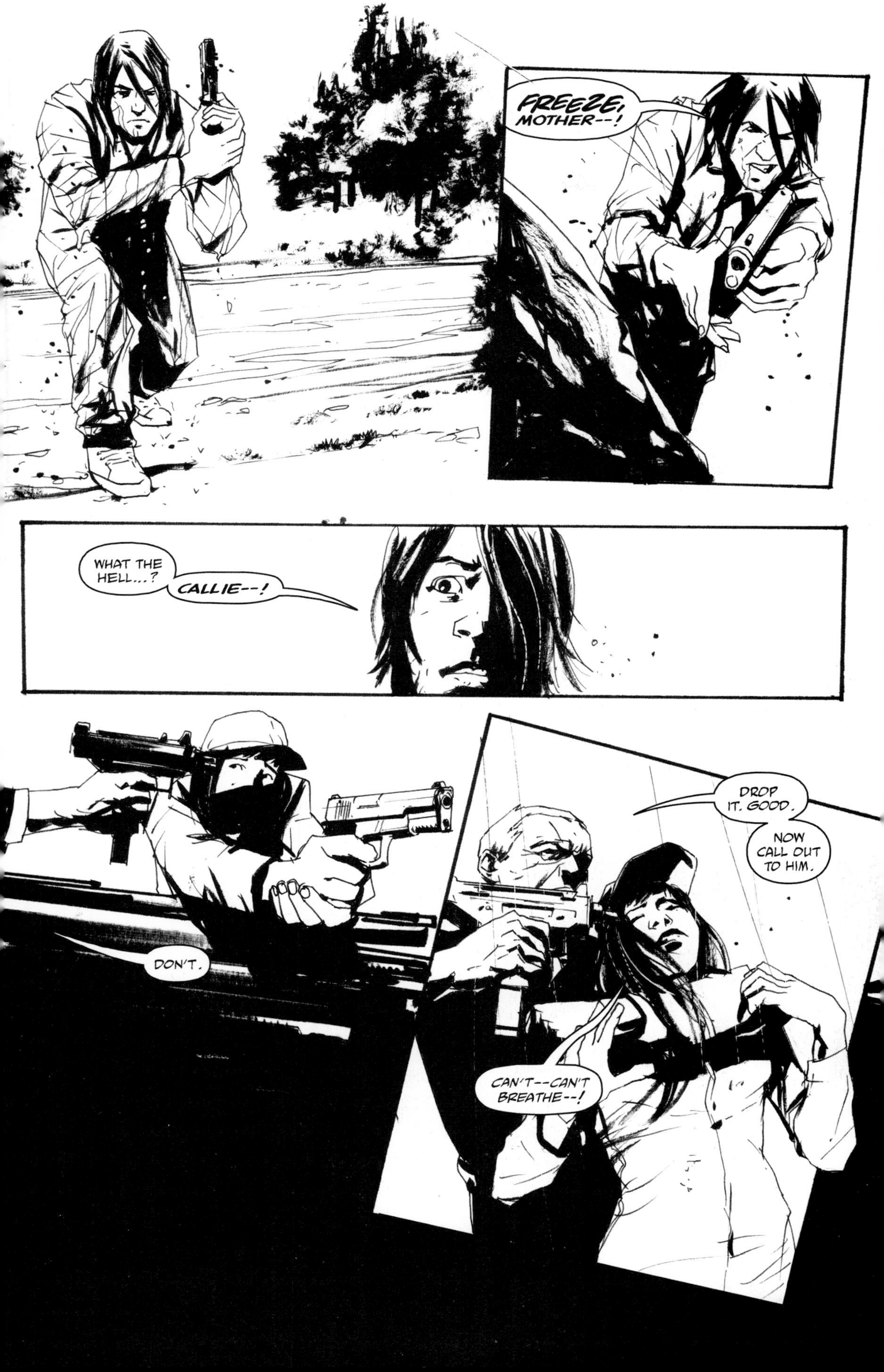
FREEZE, MOTHER--!
WHAT THE HELL...?
CALLIE--!
DON'T.
DROP IT. GOOD.
NOW CALL OUT TO HIM.
CAN'T--CAN'T BREATHE--!

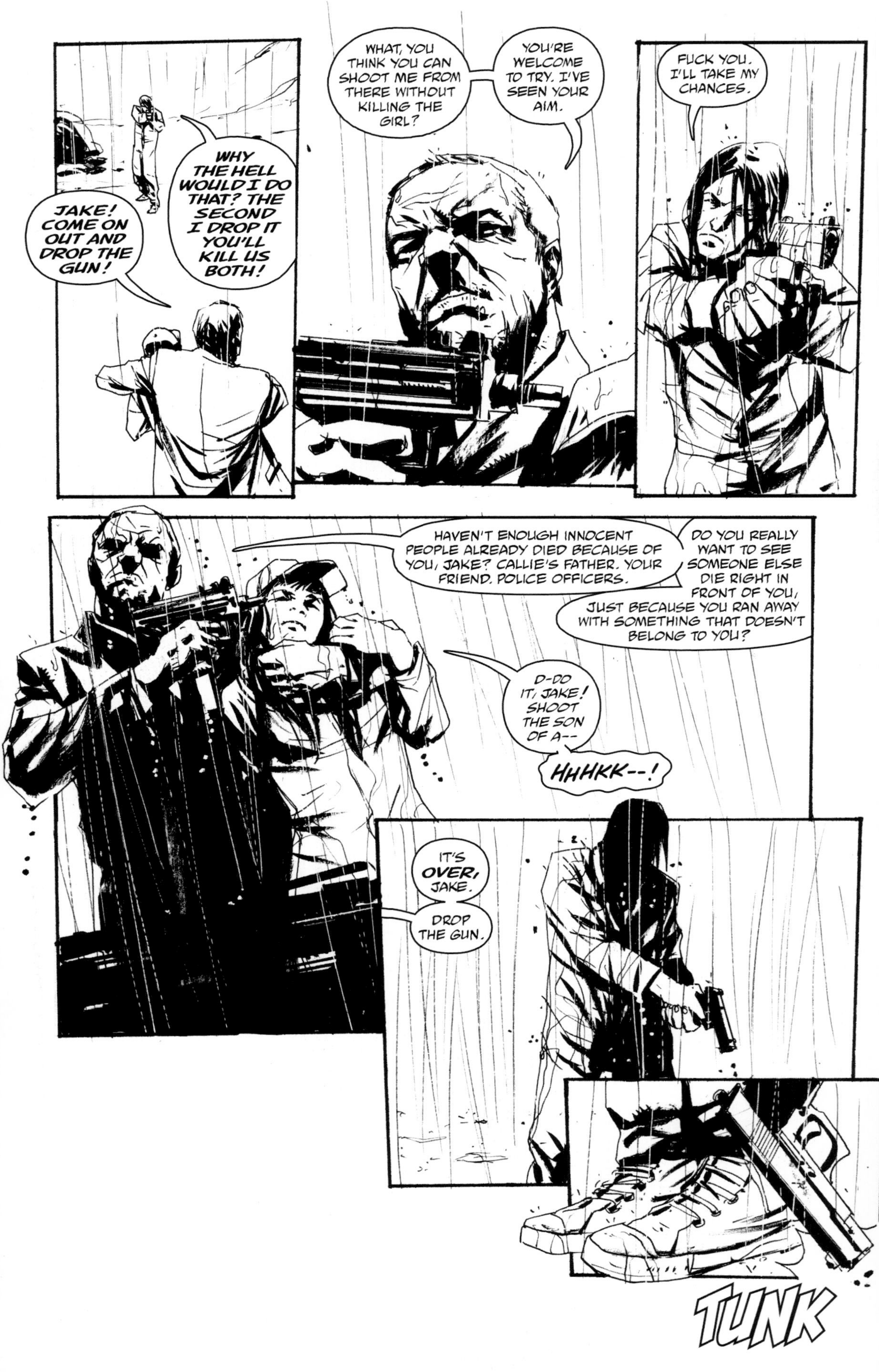

JAKE! COME ON OUT AND DROP THE GUN!
WHY THE HELL WOULD I DO THAT? THE SECOND I DROP IT YOU'LL KILL US BOTH!
WHAT, YOU THINK YOU CAN SHOOT ME FROM THERE WITHOUT KILLING THE GIRL?
YOU'RE WELCOME TO TRY. I'VE SEEN YOUR AIM.
FUCK YOU. I'LL TAKE MY CHANCES.
HAVEN'T ENOUGH INNOCENT PEOPLE ALREADY DIED BECAUSE OF YOU, JAKE? CALLIE'S FATHER. YOUR FRIEND. POLICE OFFICERS.
DO YOU REALLY WANT TO SEE SOMEONE ELSE DIE RIGHT IN FRONT OF YOU, JUST BECAUSE YOU RAN AWAY WITH SOMETHING THAT DOESN'T BELONG TO YOU?
D-DO IT, JAKE! SHOOT THE SON OF A--
HHHKK--!
IT'S OVER, JAKE.
DROP THE GUN.
TUNK

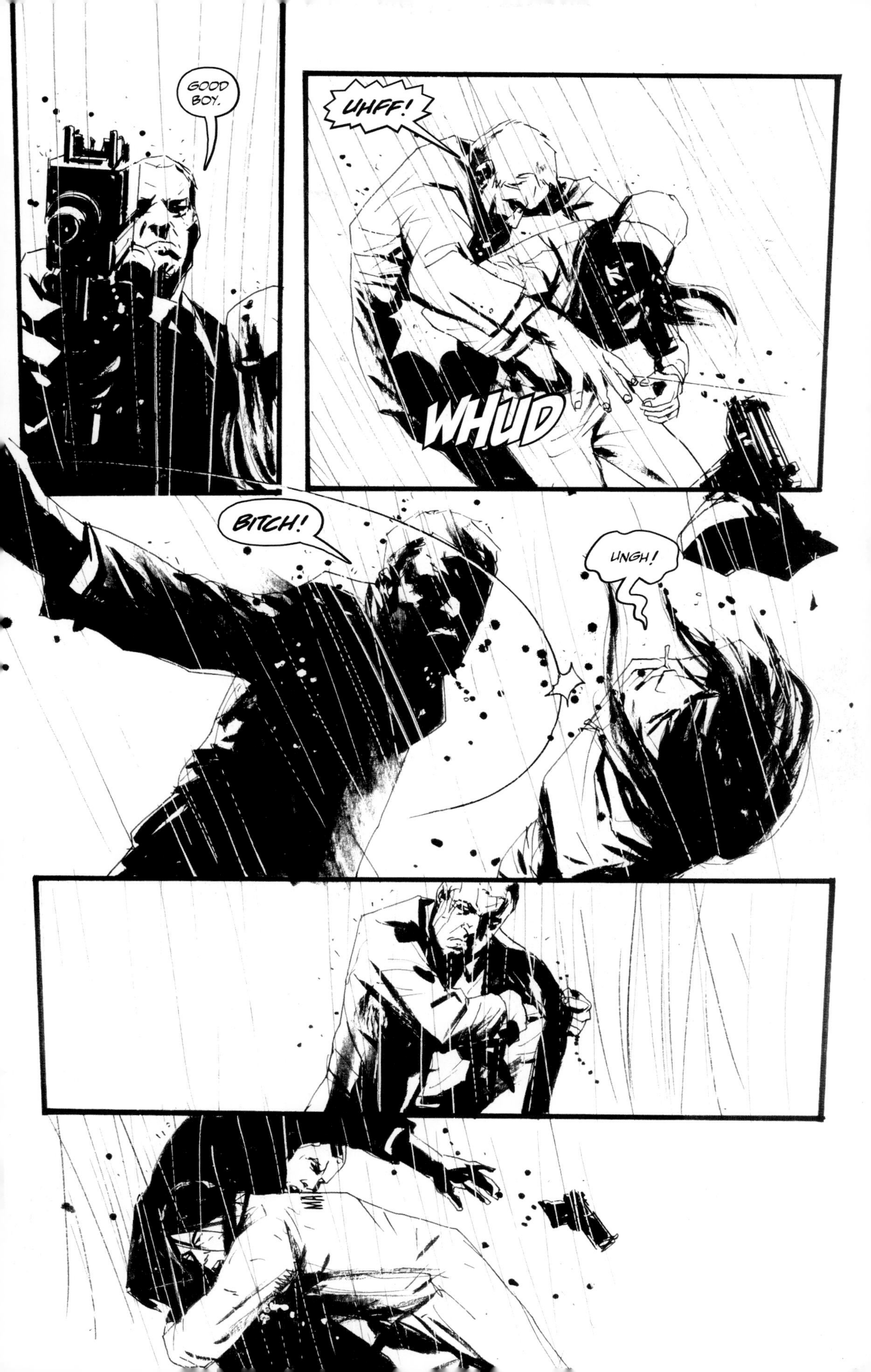
GOOD BOY.
UHFF!
WHUD
BITCH!
UNGH!

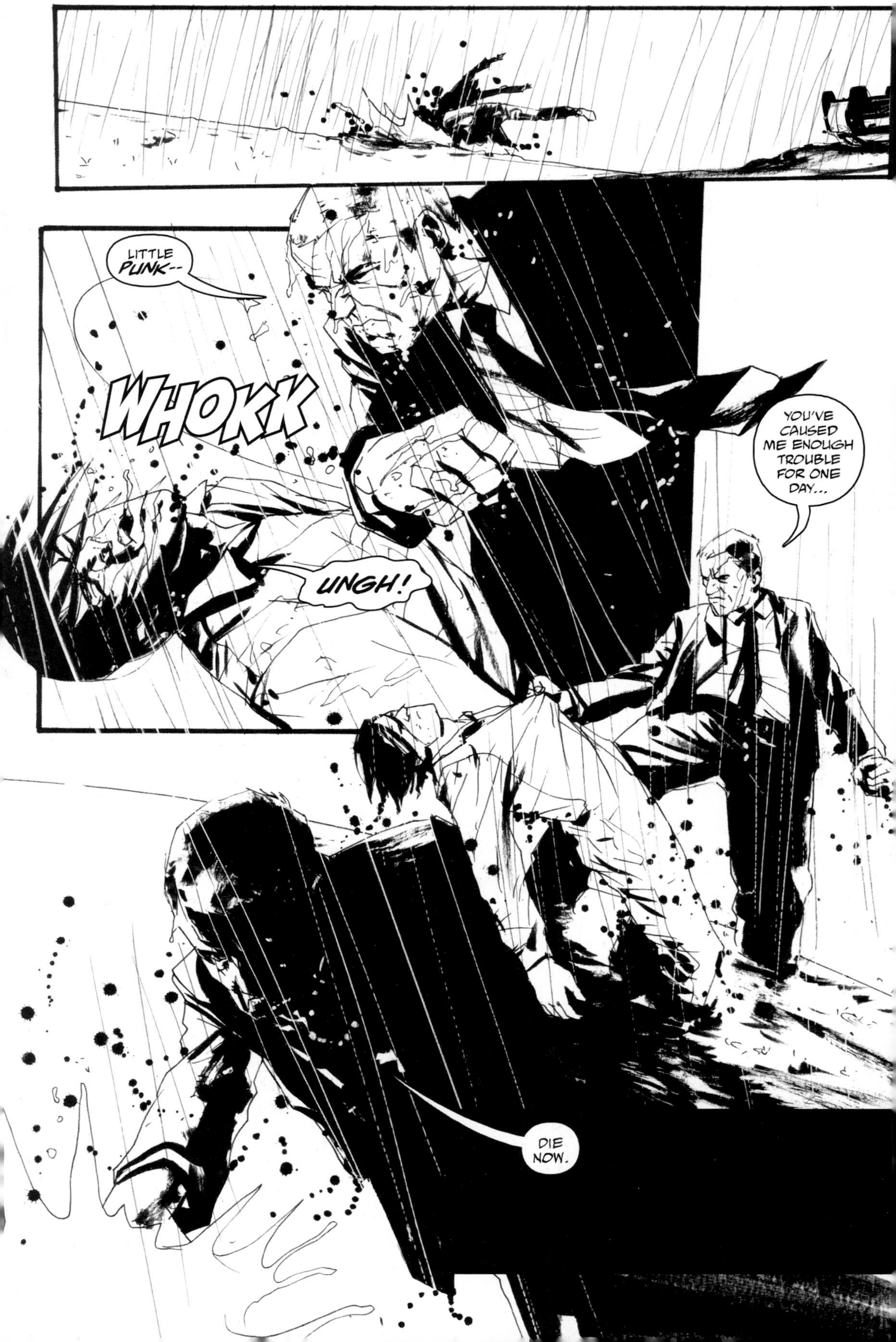
LITTLE PUNK--
WHOKK
UNGH!
YOU'VE CAUSED ME ENOUGH TROUBLE FOR ONE DAY...
DIE NOW.

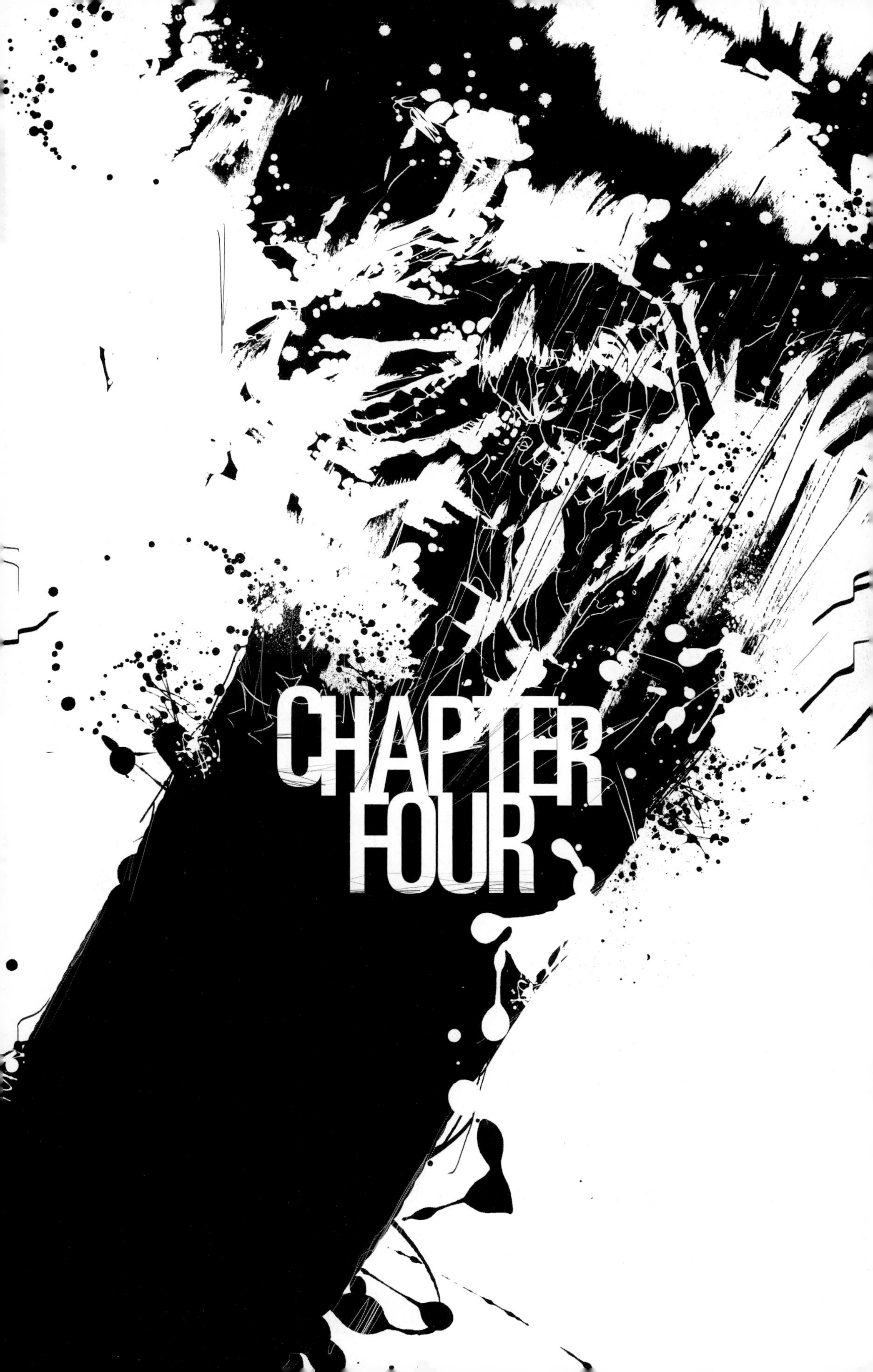
CHAPTER
FOUR

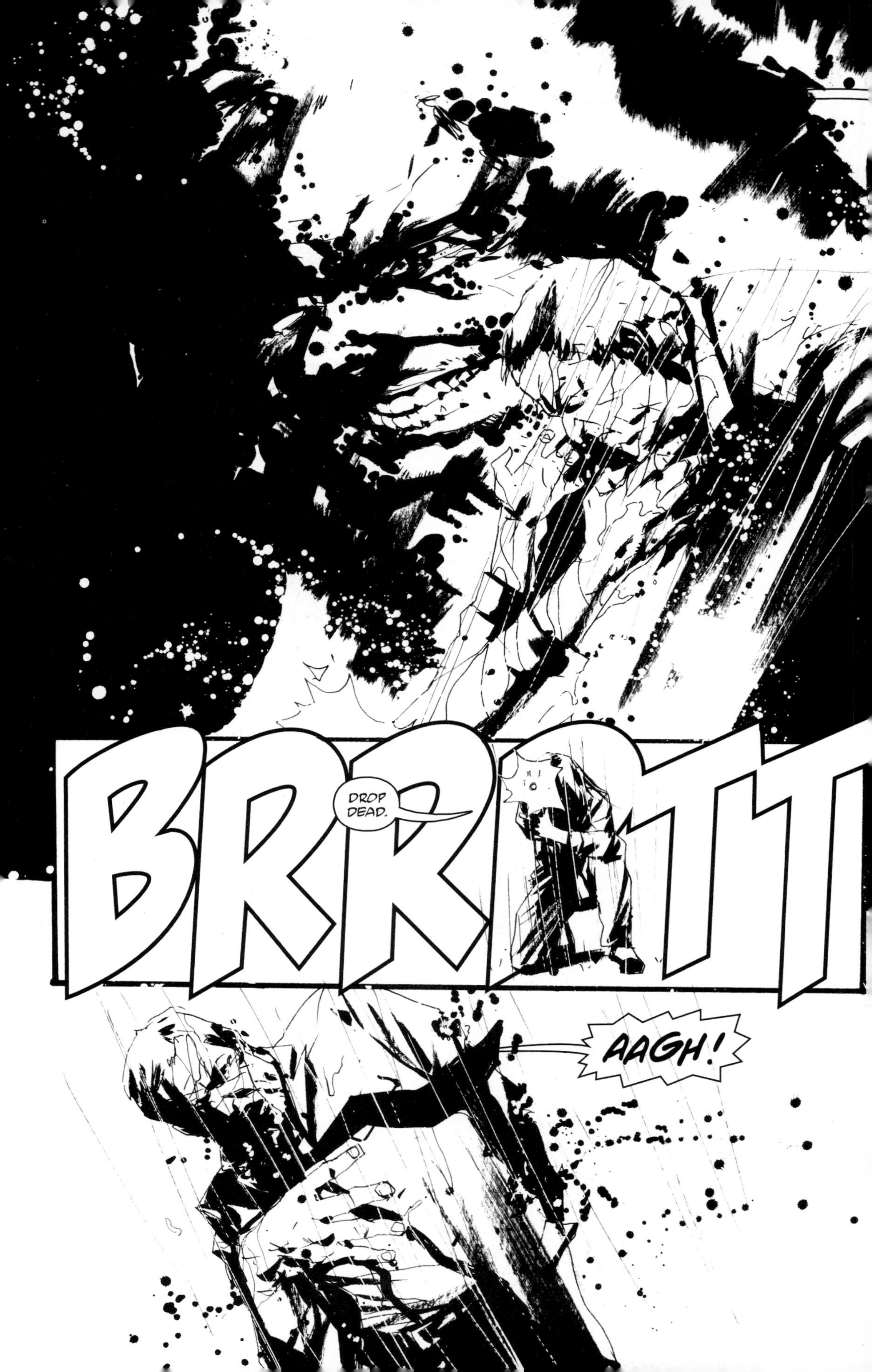
BRRATT
DROP DEAD.
AAGH!

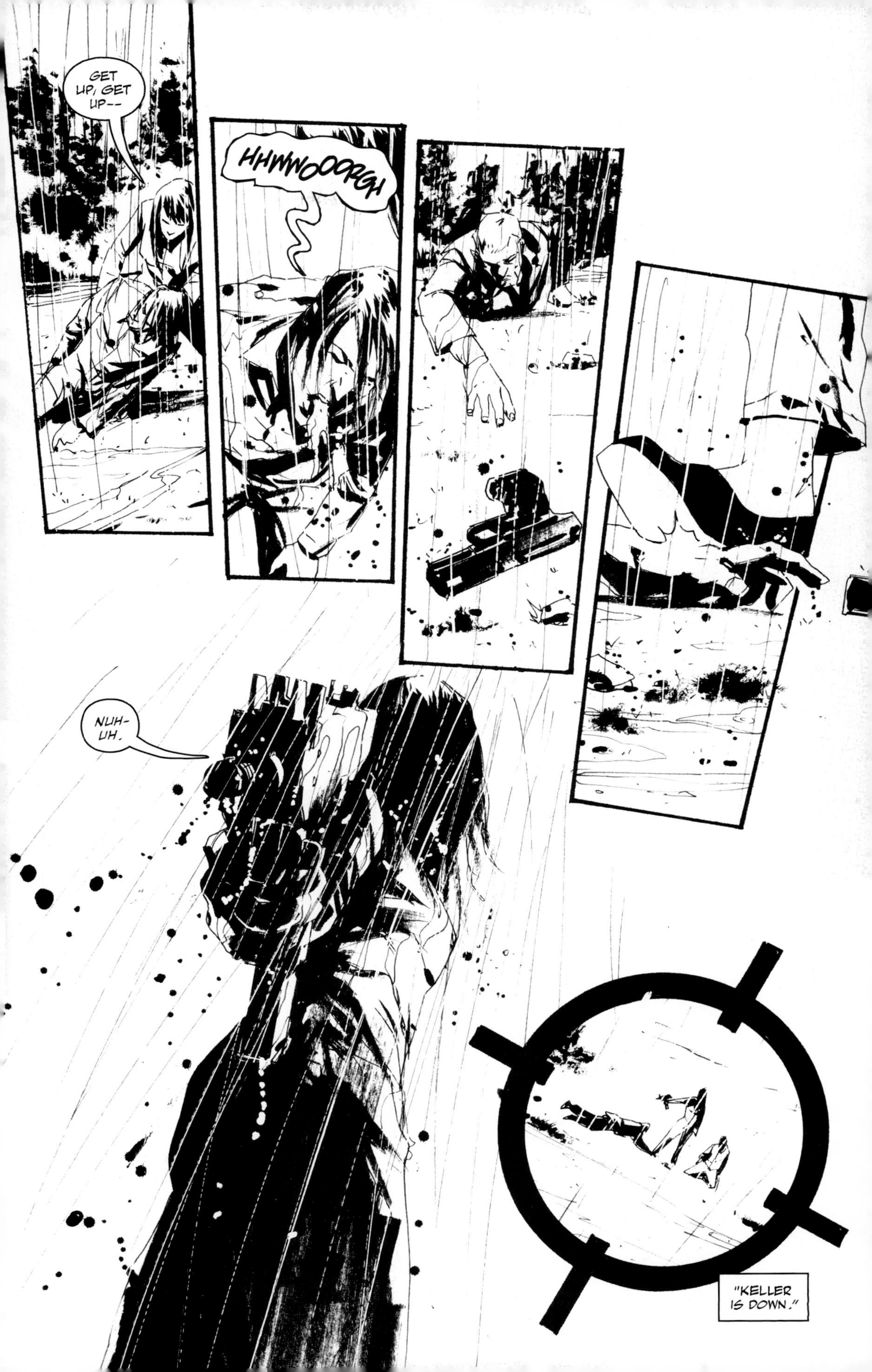
GET UP, GET UP--
HHWWOOORGH
NUH-UH.
"KELLER IS DOWN."

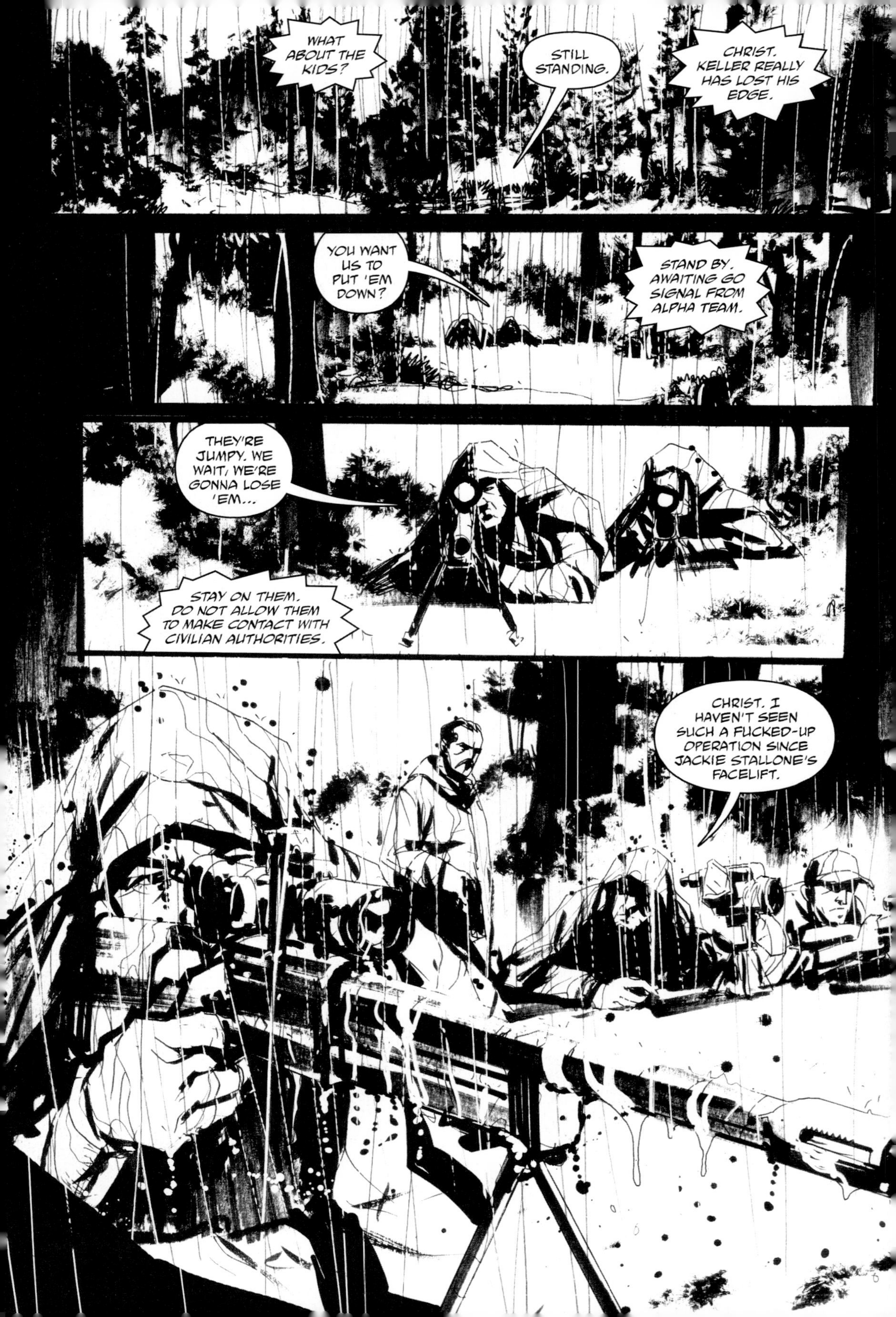
WHAT ABOUT THE KIDS?
STILL STANDING.
CHRIST. KELLER REALLY HAS LOST HIS EDGE.
YOU WANT US TO PUT 'EM DOWN?
STAND BY. AWAITING GO SIGNAL FROM ALPHA TEAM.
THEY'RE JUMPY. WE WAIT, WE'RE GONNA LOSE 'EM...
STAY ON THEM. DO NOT ALLOW THEM TO MAKE CONTACT WITH CIVILIAN AUTHORITIES.
CHRIST. I HAVEN'T SEEN SUCH A FUCKED-UP OPERATION SINCE JACKIE STALLONE'S FACELIFT.

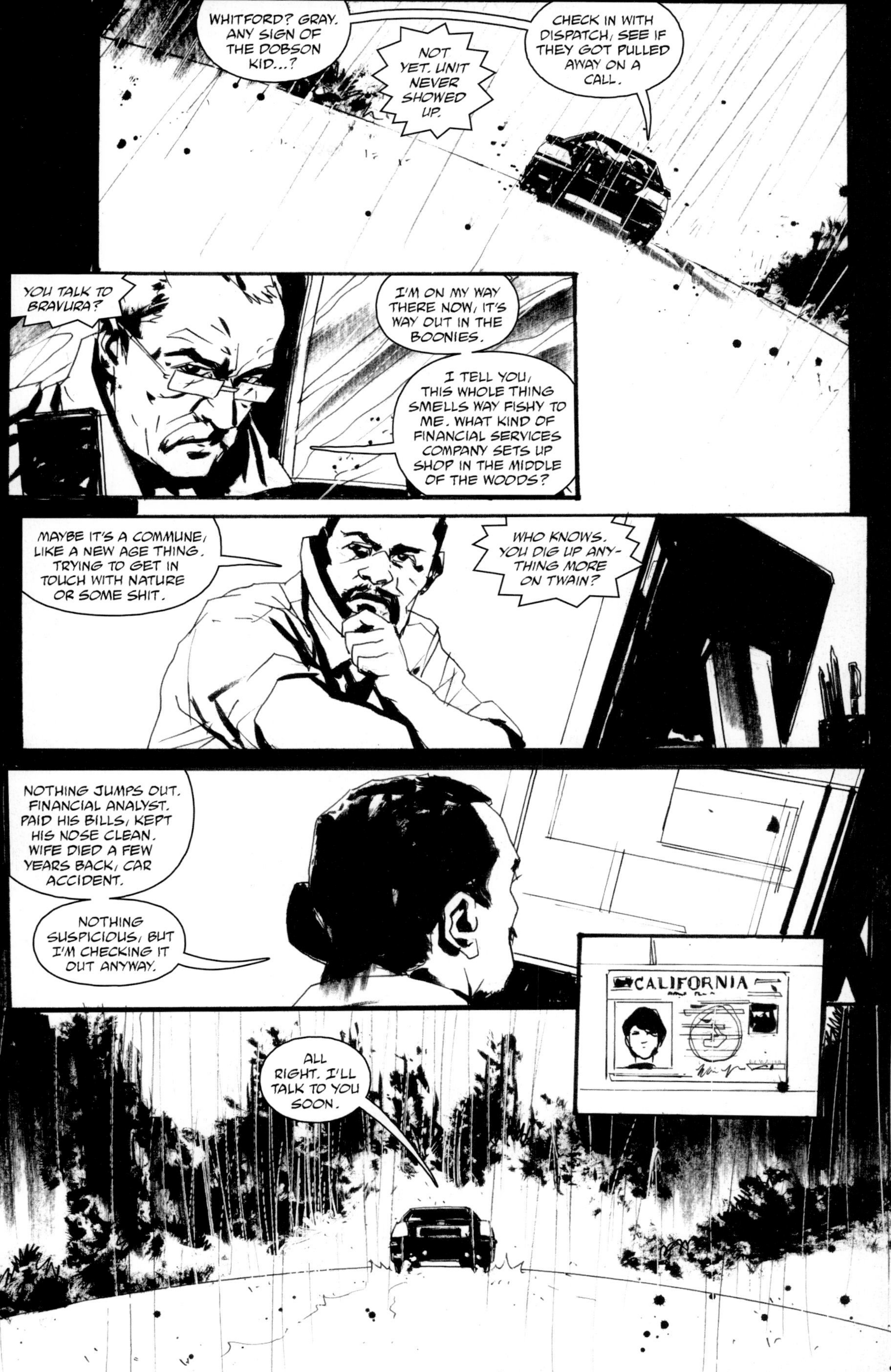
WHITFORD? GRAY. ANY SIGN OF THE DOBSON KID...?
NOT YET. UNIT NEVER SHOWED UP.
CHECK IN WITH DISPATCH, SEE IF THEY GOT PULLED AWAY ON A CALL.
YOU TALK TO BRAVURA?
I'M ON MY WAY THERE NOW, IT'S WAY OUT IN THE BOONIES.
I TELL YOU, THIS WHOLE THING SMELLS WAY FISHY TO ME. WHAT KIND OF FINANCIAL SERVICES COMPANY SETS UP SHOP IN THE MIDDLE OF THE WOODS?
MAYBE IT'S A COMMUNE, LIKE A NEW AGE THING. TRYING TO GET IN TOUCH WITH NATURE OR SOME SHIT.
WHO KNOWS. YOU DIG UP ANYTHING MORE ON TWAIN?
NOTHING JUMPS OUT. FINANCIAL ANALYST. PAID HIS BILLS, KEPT HIS NOSE CLEAN. WIFE DIED A FEW YEARS BACK, CAR ACCIDENT.
NOTHING SUSPICIOUS, BUT I'M CHECKING IT OUT ANYWAY.
CALIFORNIA
ALL RIGHT. I'LL TALK TO YOU SOON.

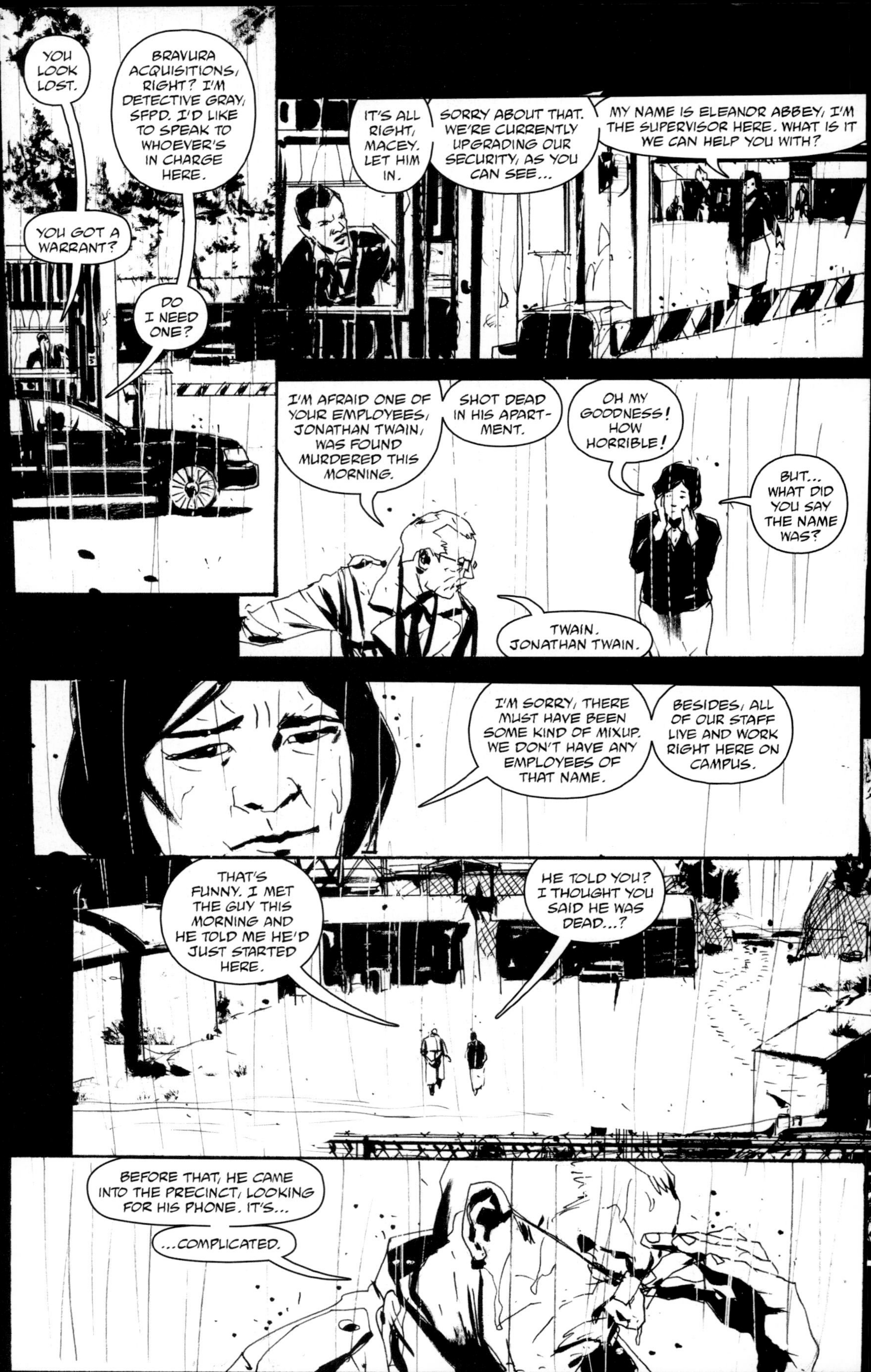
YOU LOOK LOST.
BRAVURA ACQUISITIONS, RIGHT? I'M DETECTIVE GRAY, SFPD. I'D LIKE TO SPEAK TO WHOEVER'S IN CHARGE HERE.
YOU GOT A WARRANT?
DO I NEED ONE?
IT'S ALL RIGHT, MACEY. LET HIM IN.
SORRY ABOUT THAT. WE'RE CURRENTLY UPGRADING OUR SECURITY, AS YOU CAN SEE...
MY NAME IS ELEANOR ABBEY, I'M THE SUPERVISOR HERE. WHAT IS IT WE CAN HELP YOU WITH?
I'M AFRAID ONE OF YOUR EMPLOYEES, JONATHAN TWAIN, WAS FOUND MURDERED THIS MORNING.
SHOT DEAD IN HIS APARTMENT.
OH MY GOODNESS! HOW HORRIBLE!
BUT... WHAT DID YOU SAY THE NAME WAS?
TWAIN. JONATHAN TWAIN.
I'M SORRY, THERE MUST HAVE BEEN SOME KIND OF MIXUP. WE DON'T HAVE ANY EMPLOYEES OF THAT NAME.
BESIDES, ALL OF OUR STAFF LIVE AND WORK RIGHT HERE ON CAMPUS.
THAT'S FUNNY. I MET THE GUY THIS MORNING AND HE TOLD ME HE'D JUST STARTED HERE.
HE TOLD YOU? I THOUGHT YOU SAID HE WAS DEAD...?
BEFORE THAT, HE CAME INTO THE PRECINCT, LOOKING FOR HIS PHONE. IT'S...
...COMPLICATED.

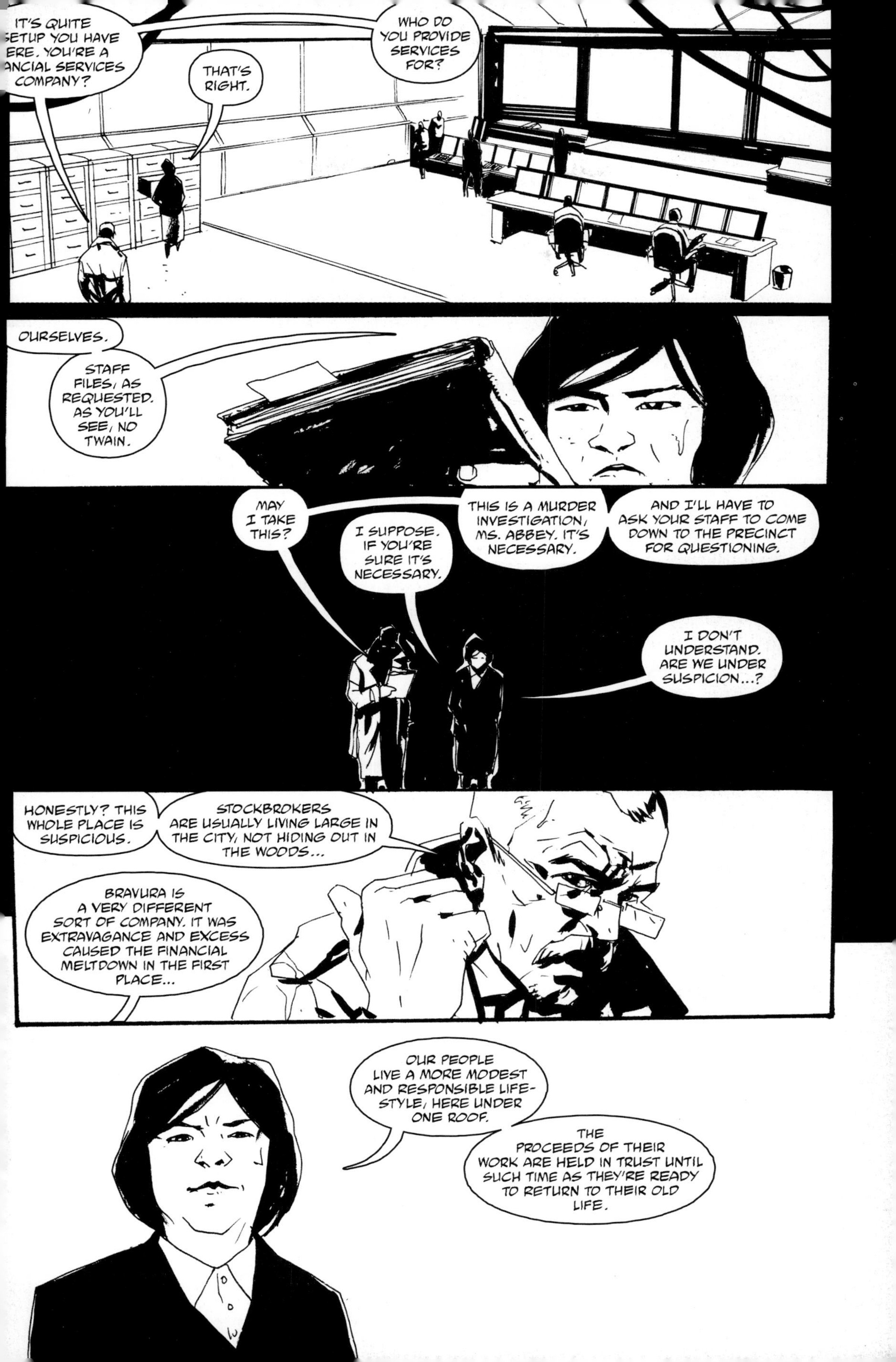
IT'S QUITE SETUP YOU HAVE ERE. YOU'RE A ANCIAL SERVICES COMPANY?
THAT'S RIGHT.
WHO DO YOU PROVIDE SERVICES FOR?
OURSELVES.
STAFF FILES, AS REQUESTED. AS YOU'LL SEE, NO TWAIN.
MAY I TAKE THIS?
I SUPPOSE. IF YOU'RE SURE IT'S NECESSARY.
THIS IS A MURDER INVESTIGATION, MS. ABBEY. IT'S NECESSARY.
AND I'LL HAVE TO ASK YOUR STAFF TO COME DOWN TO THE PRECINCT FOR QUESTIONING.
I DON'T UNDERSTAND. ARE WE UNDER SUSPICION...?
HONESTLY? THIS WHOLE PLACE IS SUSPICIOUS.
STOCKBROKERS ARE USUALLY LIVING LARGE IN THE CITY, NOT HIDING OUT IN THE WOODS...
BRAVURA IS A VERY DIFFERENT SORT OF COMPANY. IT WAS EXTRAVAGANCE AND EXCESS CAUSED THE FINANCIAL MELTDOWN IN THE FIRST PLACE...
OUR PEOPLE LIVE A MORE MODEST AND RESPONSIBLE LIFE-STYLE, HERE UNDER ONE ROOF.
THE PROCEEDS OF THEIR WORK ARE HELD IN TRUST UNTIL SUCH TIME AS THEY'RE READY TO RETURN TO THEIR OLD LIFE.

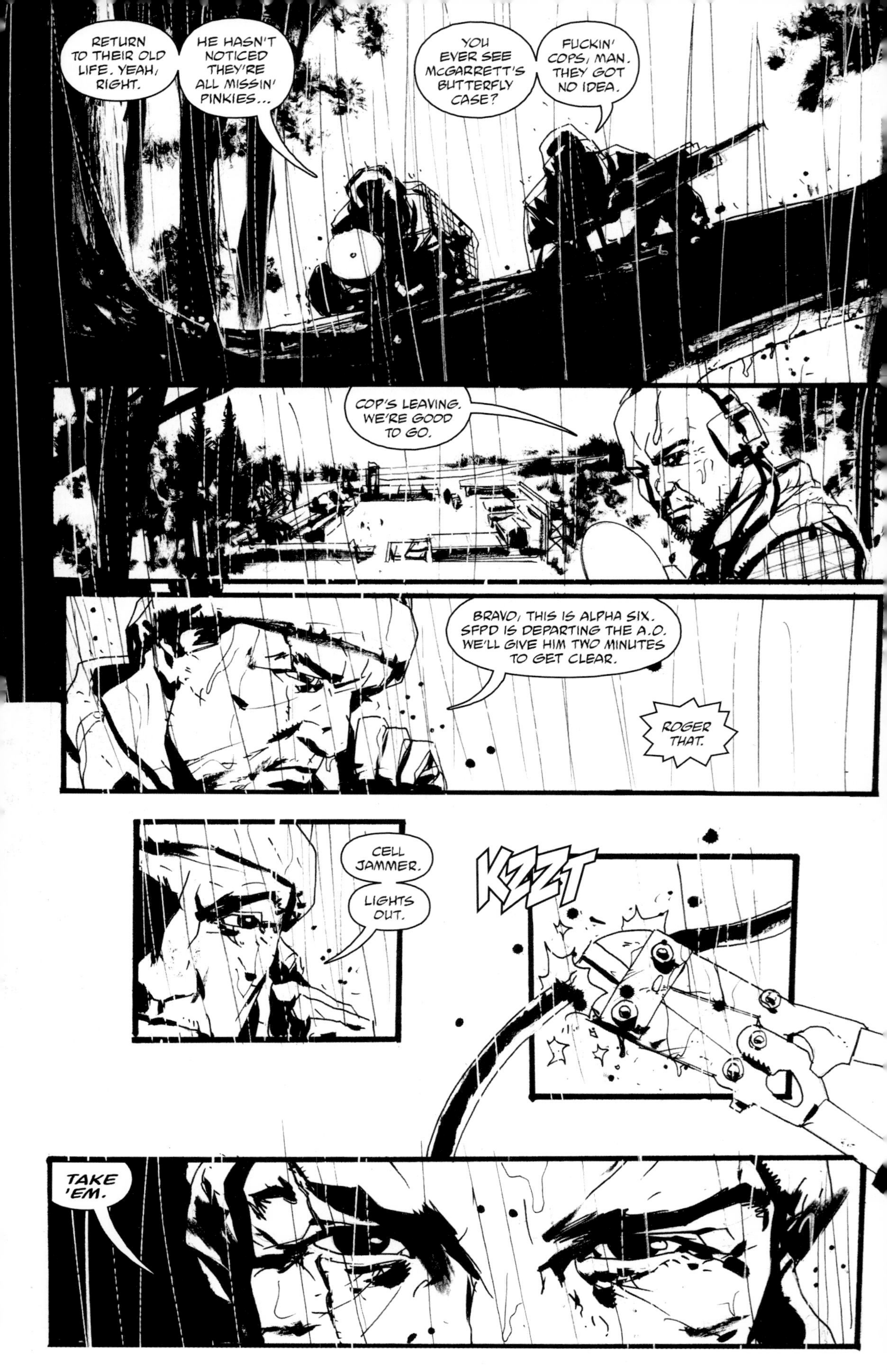
RETURN TO THEIR OLD LIFE. YEAH, RIGHT.
HE HASN'T NOTICED THEY'RE ALL MISSIN' PINKIES...
YOU EVER SEE McGARRETT'S BUTTERFLY CASE?
FUCKIN' COPS, MAN. THEY GOT NO IDEA.
COP'S LEAVING. WE'RE GOOD TO GO.
BRAVO, THIS IS ALPHA SIX. SFPD IS DEPARTING THE A.O. WE'LL GIVE HIM TWO MINUTES TO GET CLEAR.
ROGER THAT.
CELL JAMMER.
LIGHTS OUT.
KZZT
TAKE 'EM.

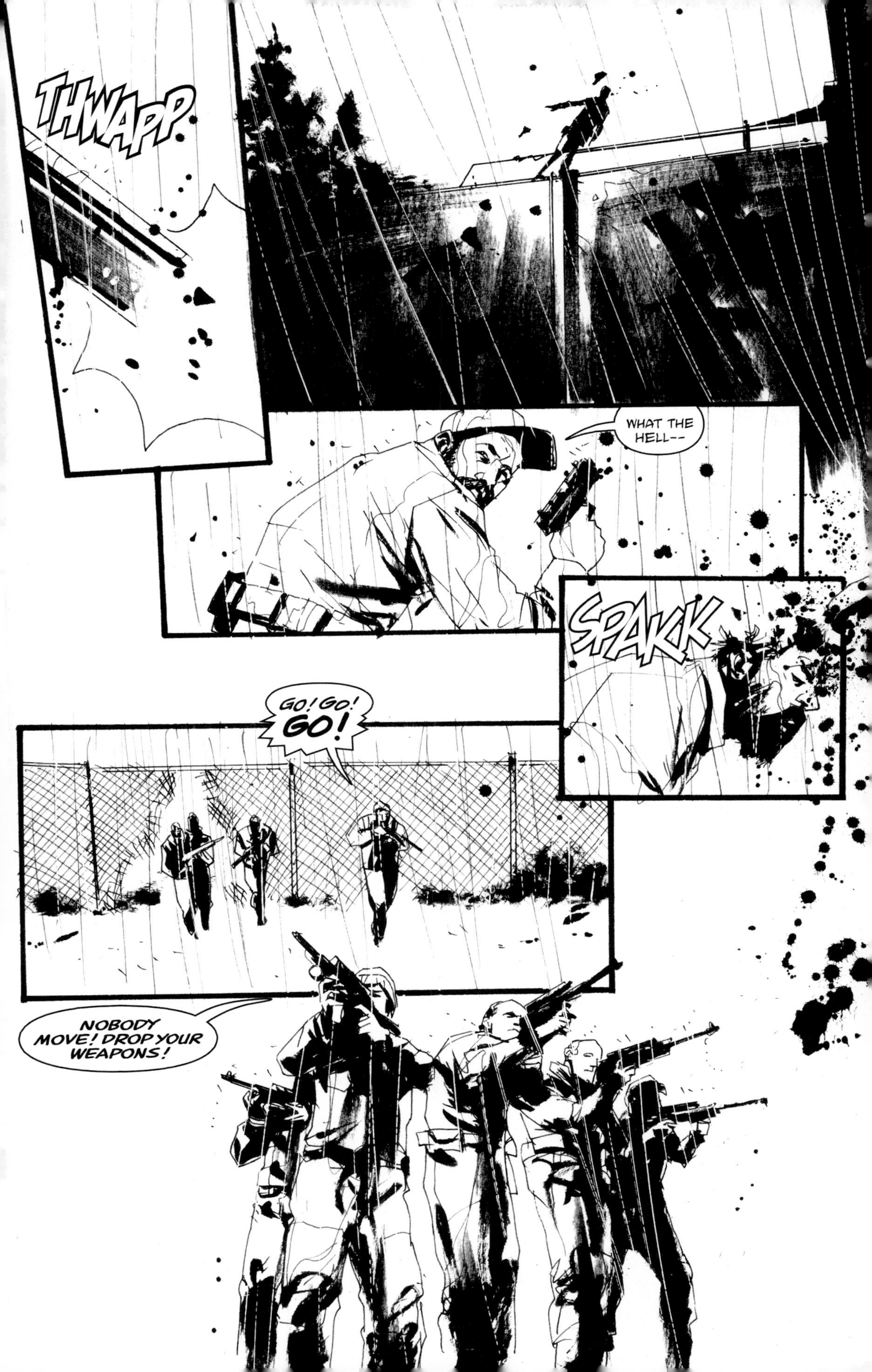
THWAPP
WHAT THE HELL--
SPAKK
GO! GO! GO!
NOBODY MOVE! DROP YOUR WEAPONS!

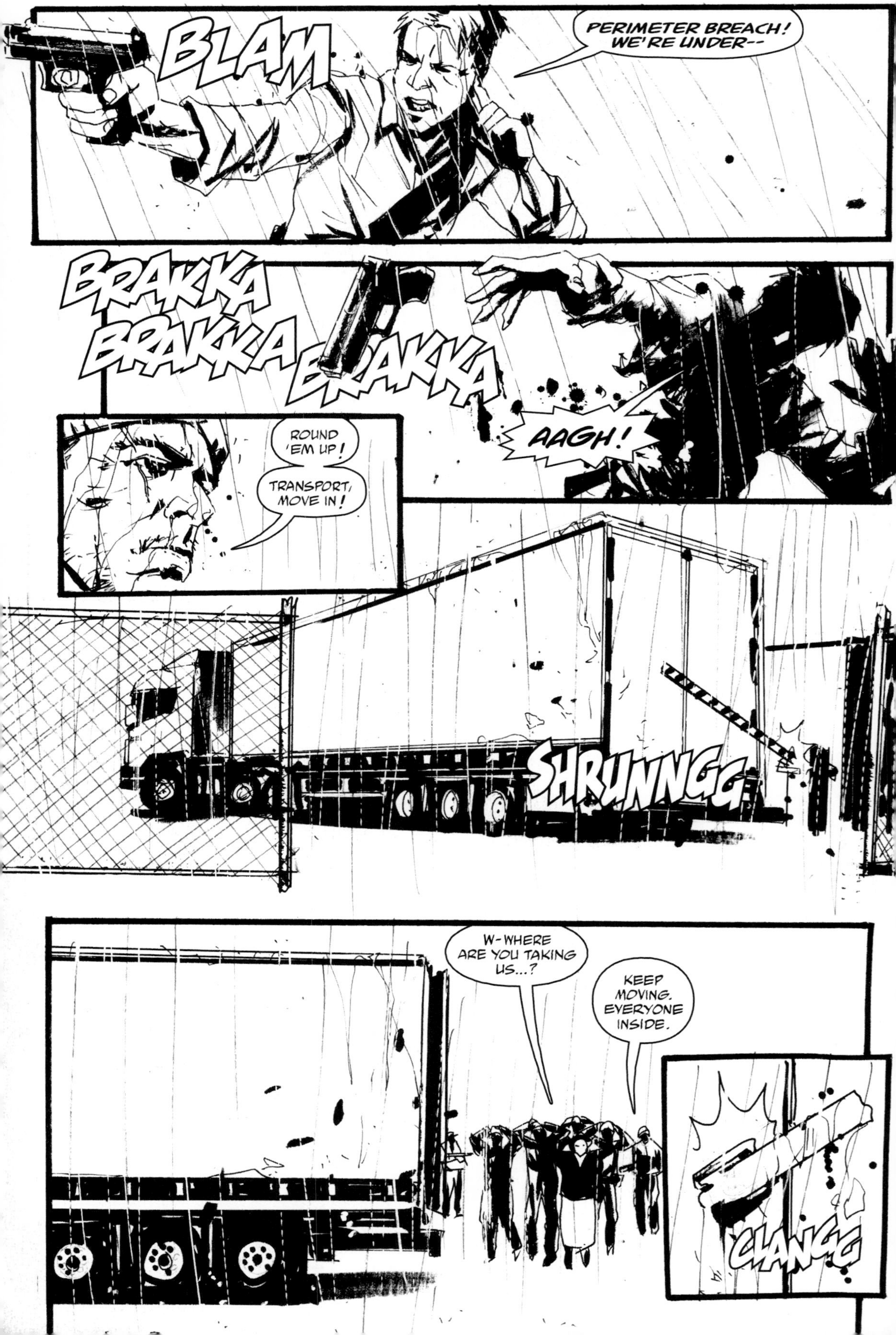
BLAM
PERIMETER BREACH! WE'RE UNDER--
BRAKKA
BRAKKA
BRAKKA
AAGH!
ROUND 'EM UP!
TRANSPORT, MOVE IN!
SHRUNNGG
W-WHERE ARE YOU TAKING US...?
KEEP MOVING. EVERYONE INSIDE.
CLANGG

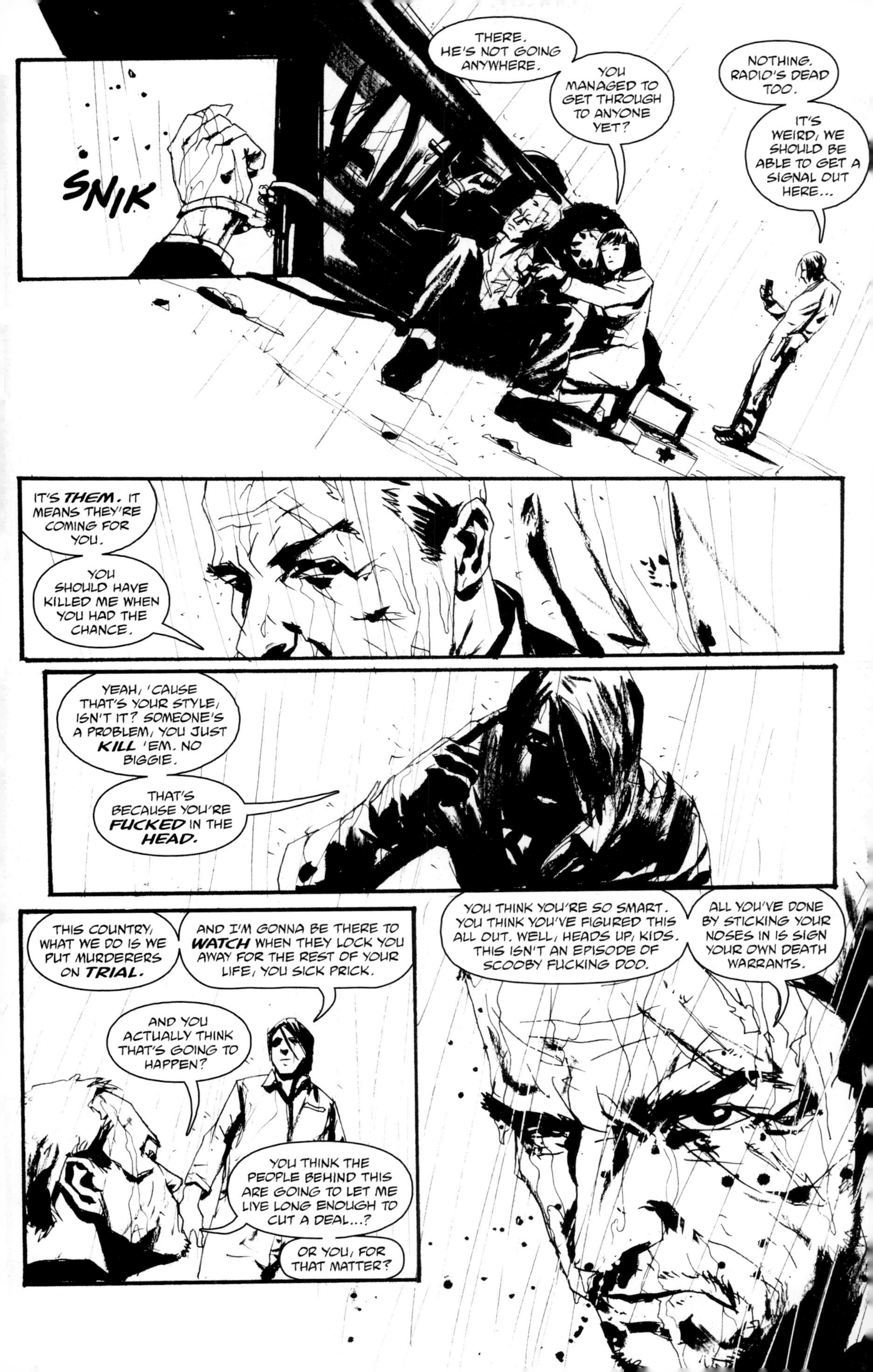

SNIK
THERE. HE'S NOT GOING ANYWHERE.
YOU MANAGED TO GET THROUGH TO ANYONE YET?
NOTHING. RADIO'S DEAD TOO.
IT'S WEIRD, WE SHOULD BE ABLE TO GET A SIGNAL OUT HERE...
IT'S THEM. IT MEANS THEY'RE COMING FOR YOU.
YOU SHOULD HAVE KILLED ME WHEN YOU HAD THE CHANCE.
YEAH, 'CAUSE THAT'S YOUR STYLE, ISN'T IT? SOMEONE'S A PROBLEM, YOU JUST KILL 'EM. NO BIGGIE.
THAT'S BECAUSE YOU'RE FUCKED IN THE HEAD.
THIS COUNTRY, WHAT WE DO IS WE PUT MURDERERS ON TRIAL.
AND I'M GONNA BE THERE TO WATCH WHEN THEY LOCK YOU AWAY FOR THE REST OF YOUR LIFE, YOU SICK PRICK.
AND YOU ACTUALLY THINK THAT'S GOING TO HAPPEN?
YOU THINK THE PEOPLE BEHIND THIS ARE GOING TO LET ME LIVE LONG ENOUGH TO CUT A DEAL...?
OR YOU, FOR THAT MATTER?
YOU THINK YOU'RE SO SMART. YOU THINK YOU'VE FIGURED THIS ALL OUT. WELL, HEADS UP, KIDS. THIS ISN'T AN EPISODE OF SCOOBY FUCKING DOO.
ALL YOU'VE DONE BY STICKING YOUR NOSES IN IS SIGN YOUR OWN DEATH WARRANTS.

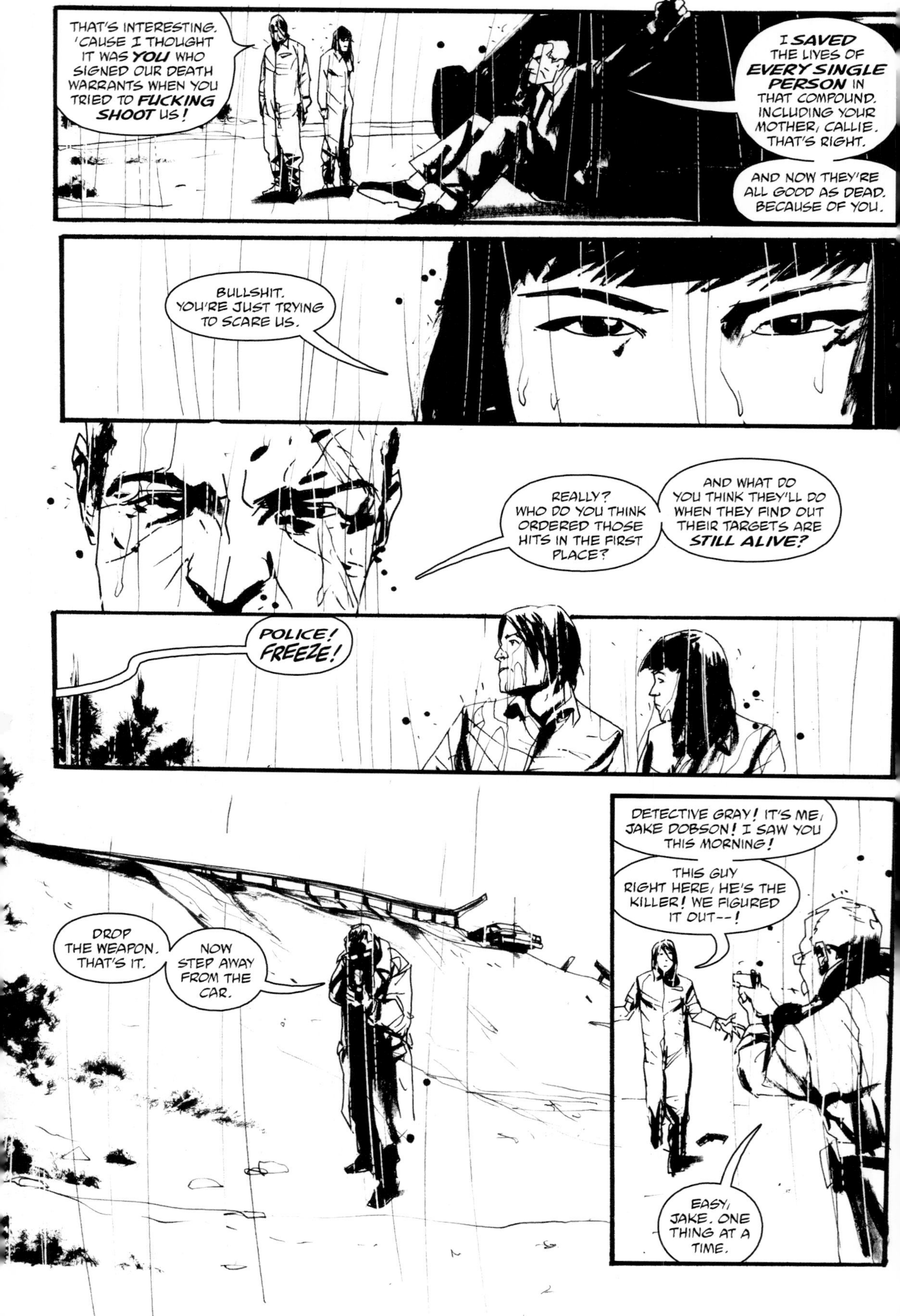
THAT'S INTERESTING. 'CAUSE I THOUGHT IT WAS YOU WHO SIGNED OUR DEATH WARRANTS WHEN YOU TRIED TO FUCKING SHOOT US!
I SAVED THE LIVES OF EVERY SINGLE PERSON IN THAT COMPOUND. INCLUDING YOUR MOTHER, CALLIE. THAT'S RIGHT.
AND NOW THEY'RE ALL GOOD AS DEAD. BECAUSE OF YOU.
BULLSHIT. YOU'RE JUST TRYING TO SCARE US.
REALLY? WHO DO YOU THINK ORDERED THOSE HITS IN THE FIRST PLACE?
AND WHAT DO YOU THINK THEY'LL DO WHEN THEY FIND OUT THEIR TARGETS ARE STILL ALIVE?
POLICE! FREEZE!
DROP THE WEAPON. THAT'S IT.
NOW STEP AWAY FROM THE CAR.
DETECTIVE GRAY! IT'S ME, JAKE DOBSON! I SAW YOU THIS MORNING!
THIS GUY RIGHT HERE, HE'S THE KILLER! WE FIGURED IT OUT--!
EASY, JAKE. ONE THING AT A TIME.

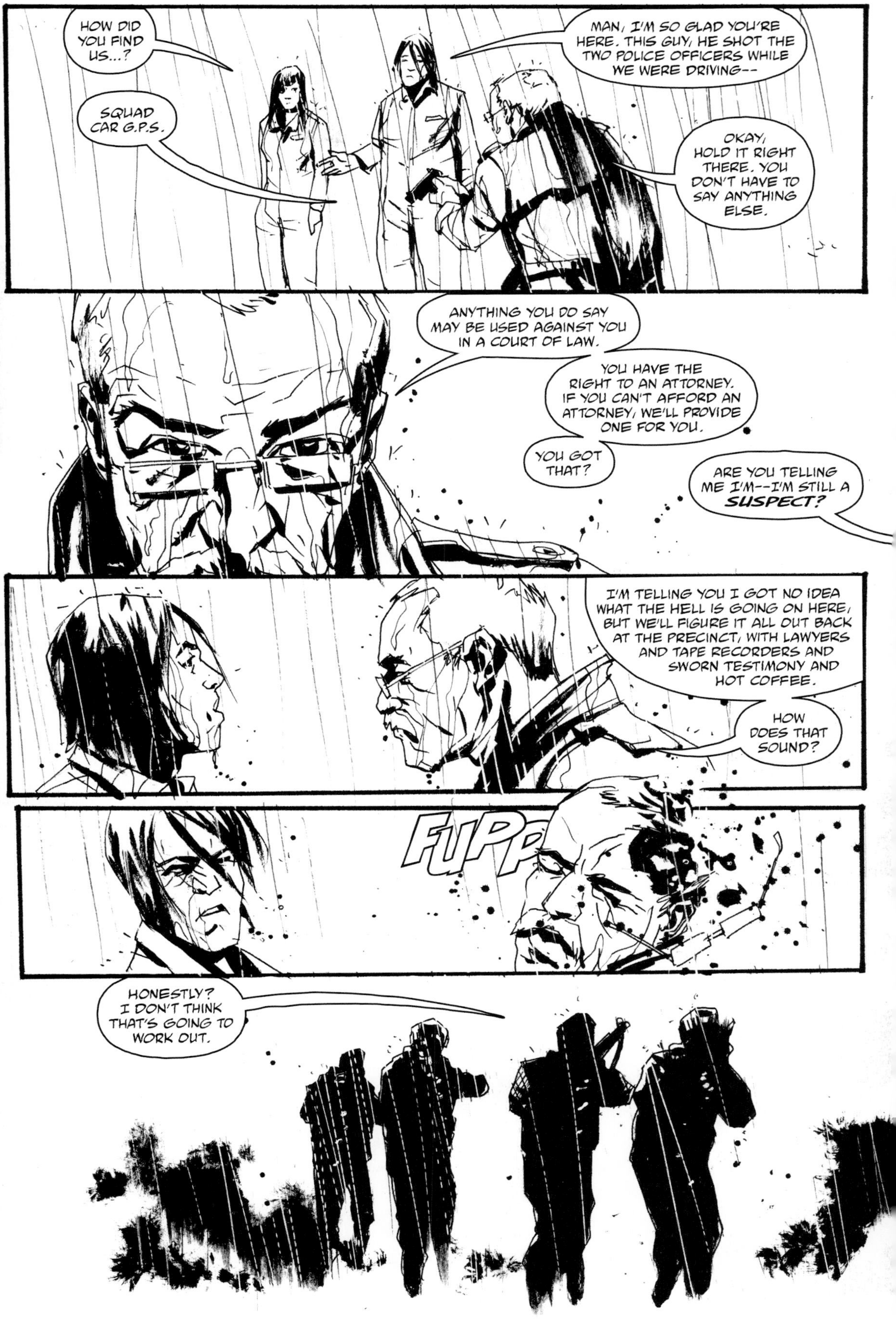

HOW DID YOU FIND US...?
SQUAD CAR G.P.S.
MAN, I'M SO GLAD YOU'RE HERE. THIS GUY, HE SHOT THE TWO POLICE OFFICERS WHILE WE WERE DRIVING--
OKAY, HOLD IT RIGHT THERE. YOU DON'T HAVE TO SAY ANYTHING ELSE.
ANYTHING YOU DO SAY MAY BE USED AGAINST YOU IN A COURT OF LAW.
YOU HAVE THE RIGHT TO AN ATTORNEY. IF YOU CAN'T AFFORD AN ATTORNEY, WE'LL PROVIDE ONE FOR YOU.
YOU GOT THAT?
ARE YOU TELLING ME I'M--I'M STILL A SUSPECT?
I'M TELLING YOU I GOT NO IDEA WHAT THE HELL IS GOING ON HERE, BUT WE'LL FIGURE IT ALL OUT BACK AT THE PRECINCT, WITH LAWYERS AND TAPE RECORDERS AND SWORN TESTIMONY AND HOT COFFEE.
HOW DOES THAT SOUND?
FUPP
HONESTLY? I DON'T THINK THAT'S GOING TO WORK OUT.

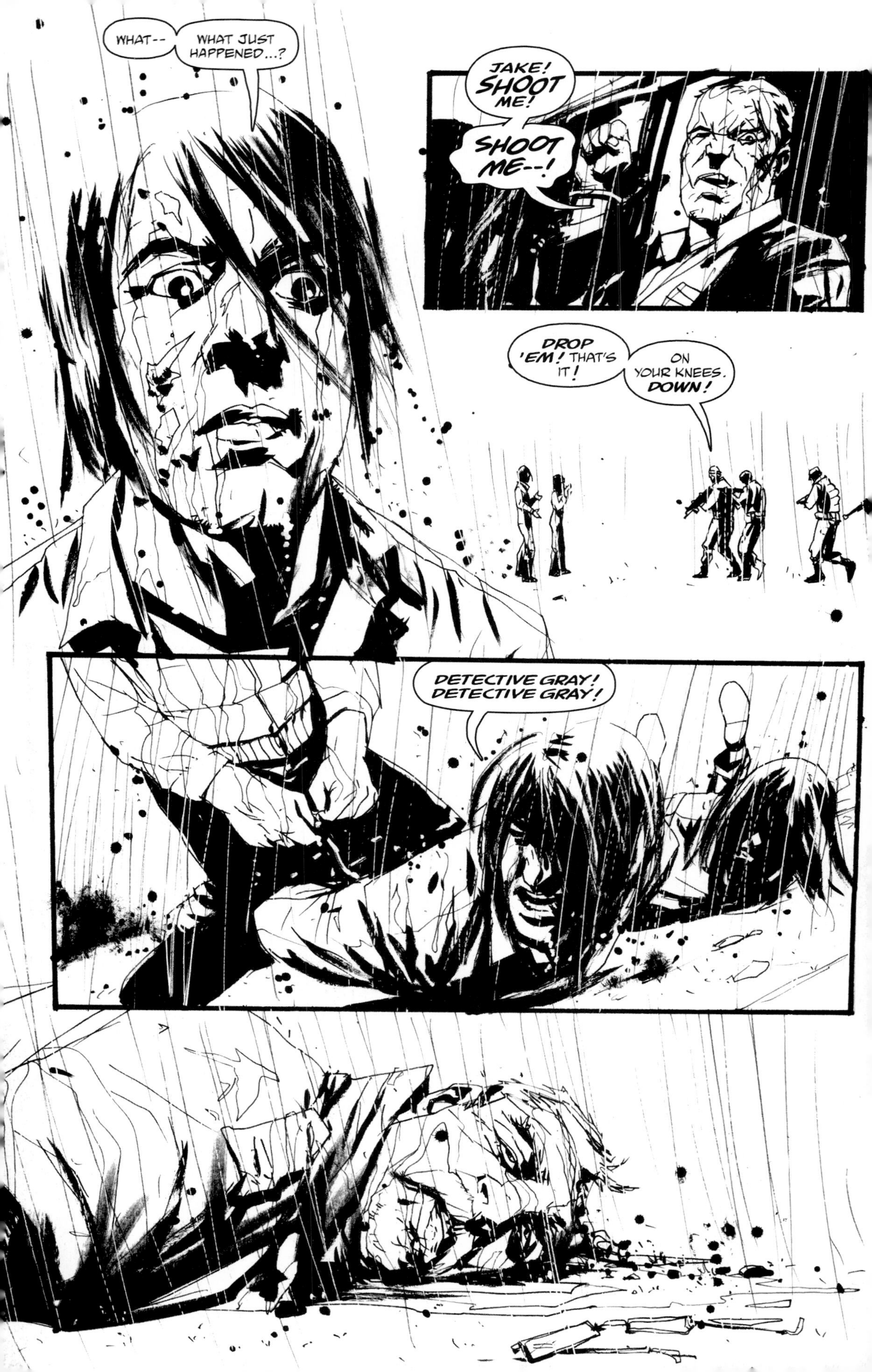
WHAT--
WHAT JUST HAPPENED...?
JAKE! SHOOT ME!
SHOOT ME--!
DROP 'EM! THAT'S IT!
ON YOUR KNEES. DOWN!
DETECTIVE GRAY! DETECTIVE GRAY!

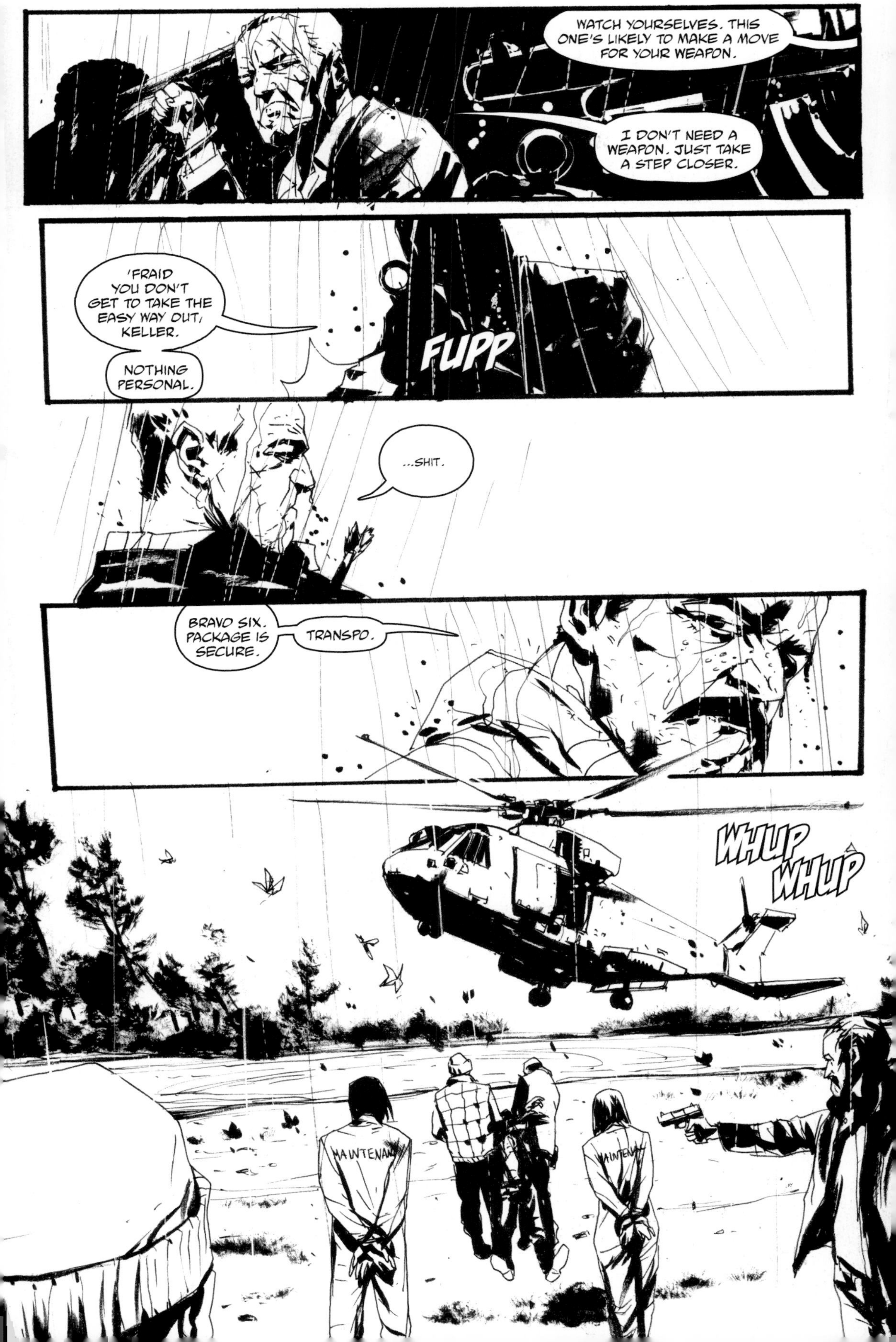
WATCH YOURSELVES. THIS ONE'S LIKELY TO MAKE A MOVE FOR YOUR WEAPON.
I DON'T NEED A WEAPON. JUST TAKE A STEP CLOSER.
'FRAID YOU DON'T GET TO TAKE THE EASY WAY OUT, KELLER.
NOTHING PERSONAL.
FUPP
...SHIT.
BRAVO SIX. PACKAGE IS SECURE.
TRANSPO.
WHUP WHUP
MAINTENAN
MAINTENA

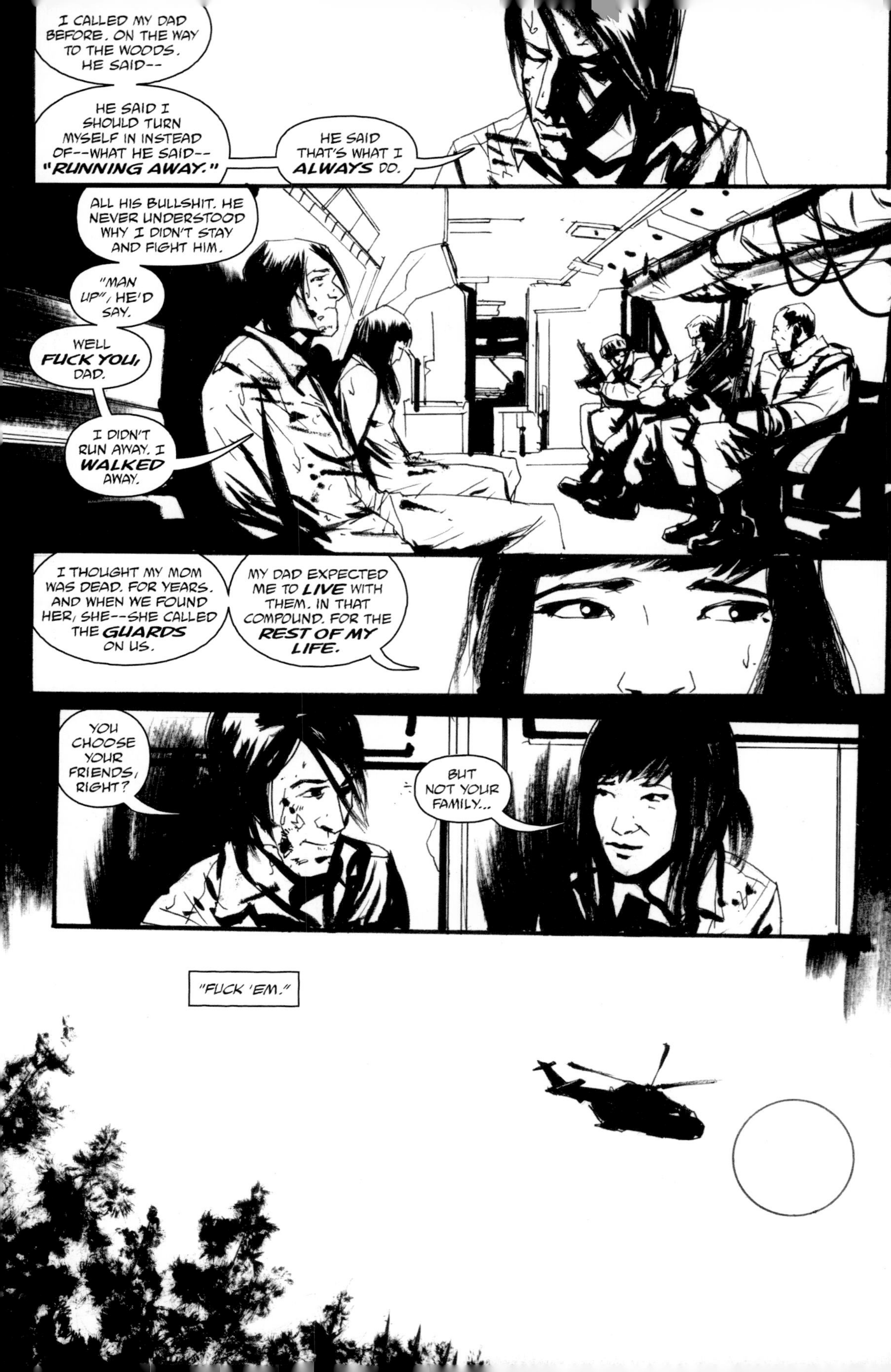
I CALLED MY DAD BEFORE. ON THE WAY TO THE WOODS. HE SAID--
HE SAID I SHOULD TURN MYSELF IN INSTEAD OF--WHAT HE SAID-- "RUNNING AWAY."
HE SAID THAT'S WHAT I ALWAYS DO.
ALL HIS BULLSHIT. HE NEVER UNDERSTOOD WHY I DIDN'T STAY AND FIGHT HIM.
"MAN UP", HE'D SAY.
WELL FUCK YOU, DAD.
I DIDN'T RUN AWAY. I WALKED AWAY.
I THOUGHT MY MOM WAS DEAD. FOR YEARS. AND WHEN WE FOUND HER, SHE--SHE CALLED THE GUARDS ON US.
MY DAD EXPECTED ME TO LIVE WITH THEM. IN THAT COMPOUND. FOR THE REST OF MY LIFE.
YOU CHOOSE YOUR FRIENDS, RIGHT?
BUT NOT YOUR FAMILY...
"FUCK 'EM."

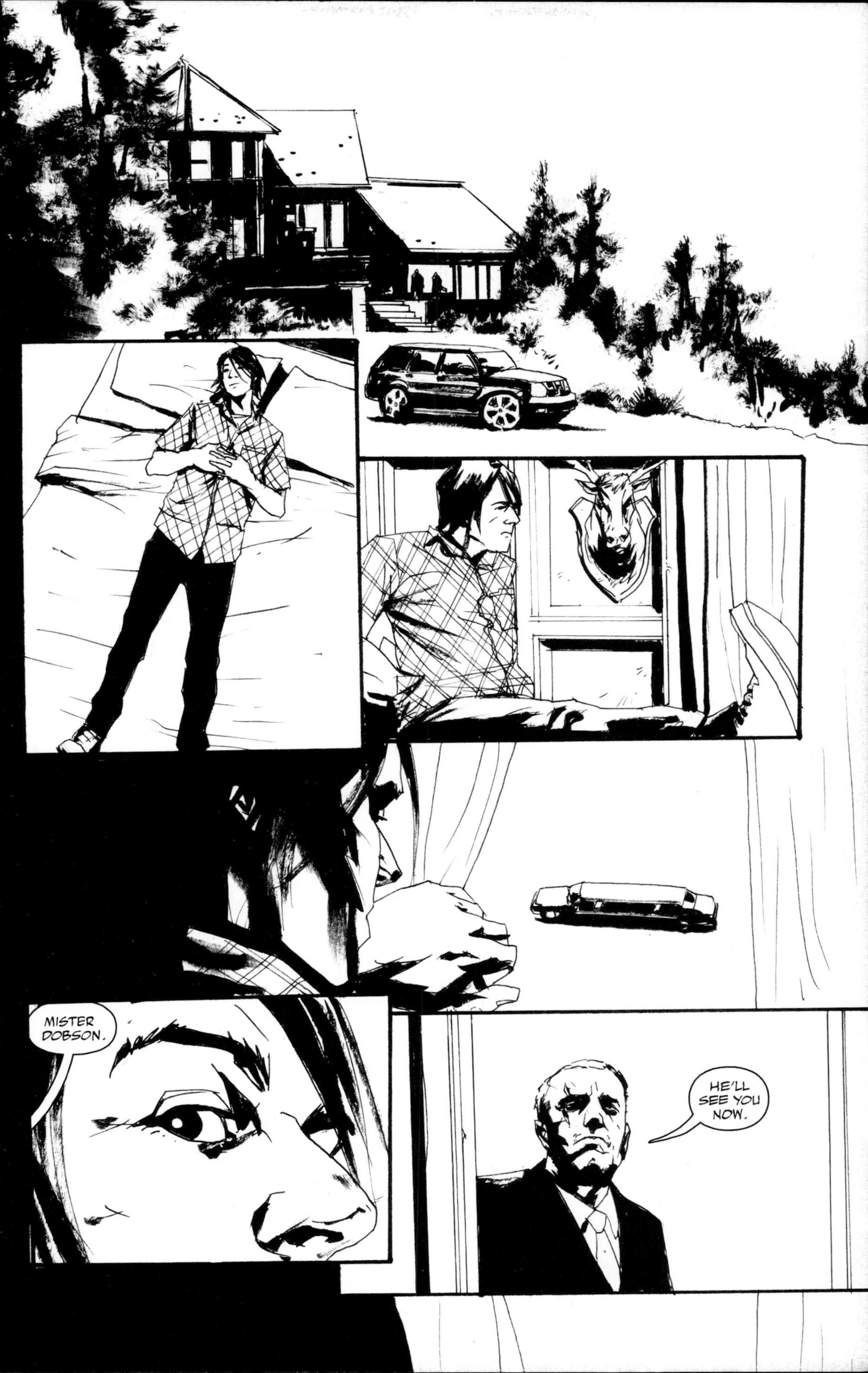
MISTER DOBSON.
HE'LL SEE YOU NOW.

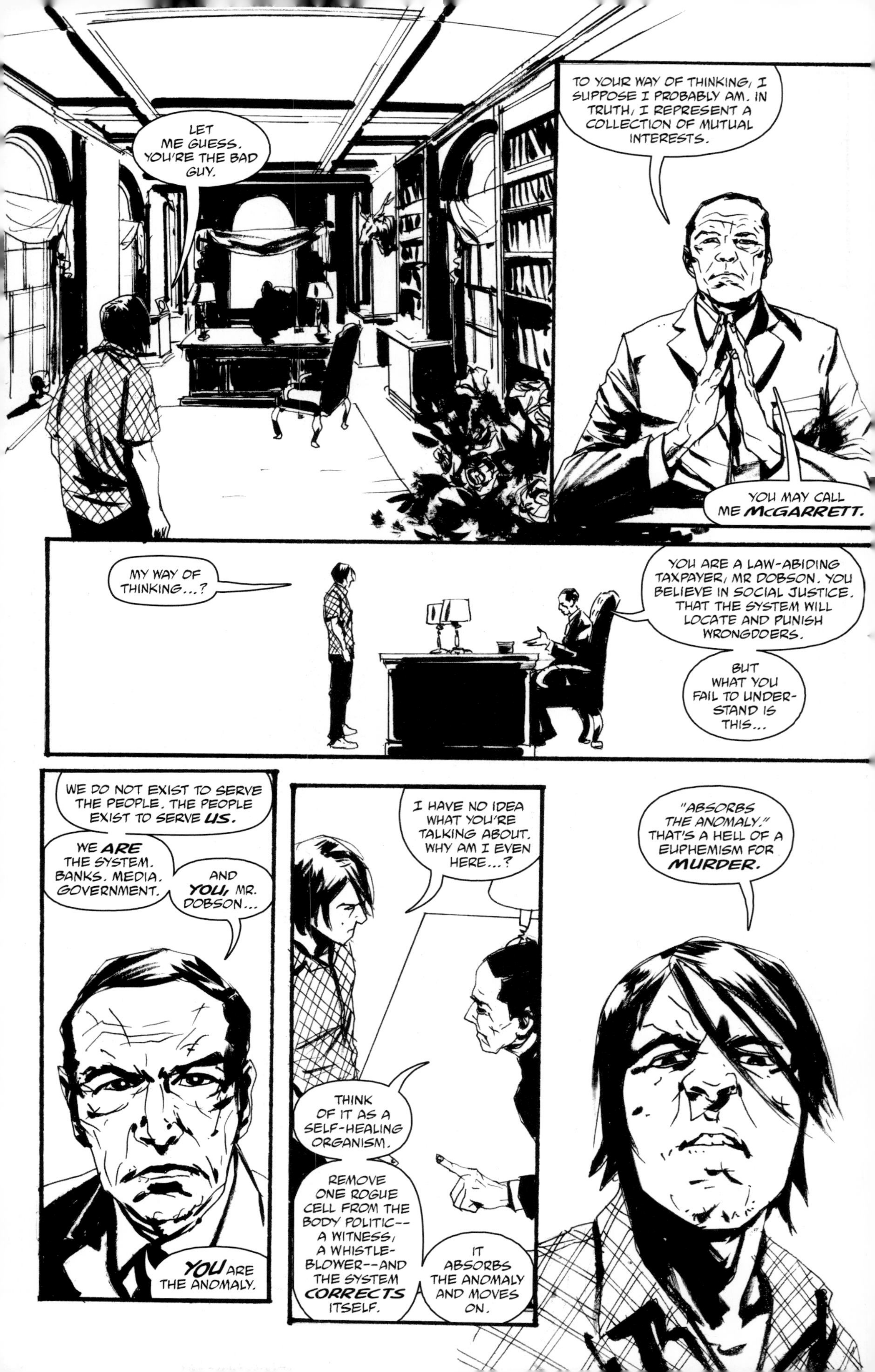
LET ME GUESS. YOU'RE THE BAD GUY.
TO YOUR WAY OF THINKING, I SUPPOSE I PROBABLY AM. IN TRUTH, I REPRESENT A COLLECTION OF MUTUAL INTERESTS.
YOU MAY CALL ME McGARRETT.
MY WAY OF THINKING...?
YOU ARE A LAW-ABIDING TAXPAYER, MR DOBSON. YOU BELIEVE IN SOCIAL JUSTICE. THAT THE SYSTEM WILL LOCATE AND PUNISH WRONGDOERS.
BUT WHAT YOU FAIL TO UNDER-STAND IS THIS...
WE DO NOT EXIST TO SERVE THE PEOPLE. THE PEOPLE EXIST TO SERVE US.
WE ARE THE SYSTEM. BANKS. MEDIA. GOVERNMENT.
AND YOU, MR. DOBSON...
YOU ARE THE ANOMALY.
I HAVE NO IDEA WHAT YOU'RE TALKING ABOUT. WHY AM I EVEN HERE...?
THINK OF IT AS A SELF-HEALING ORGANISM.
REMOVE ONE ROGUE CELL FROM THE BODY POLITIC-- A WITNESS, A WHISTLE-BLOWER--AND THE SYSTEM CORRECTS ITSELF.
IT ABSORBS THE ANOMALY AND MOVES ON.
"ABSORBS THE ANOMALY." THAT'S A HELL OF A EUPHEMISM FOR MURDER.

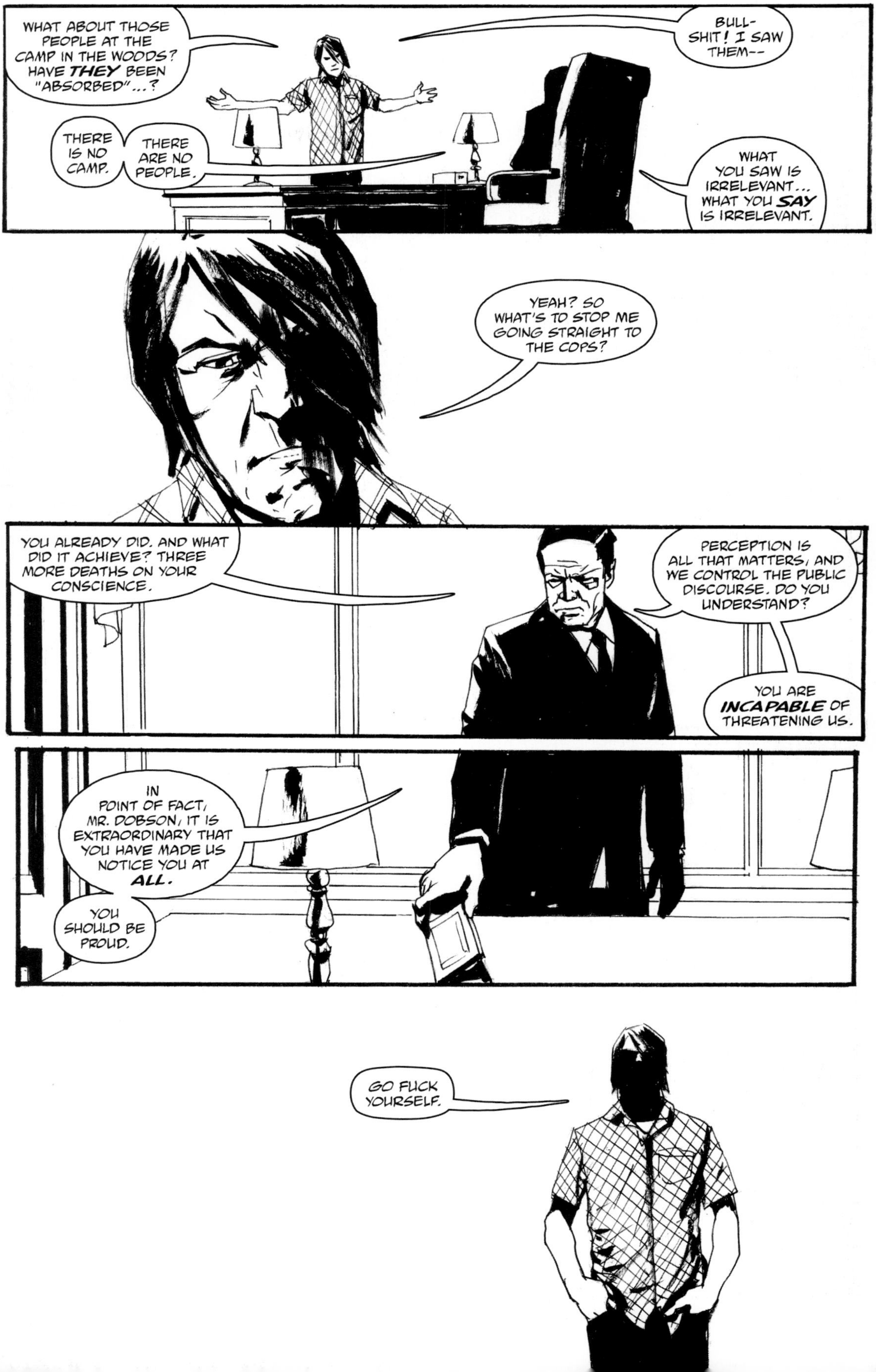
WHAT ABOUT THOSE PEOPLE AT THE CAMP IN THE WOODS? HAVE THEY BEEN "ABSORBED"...?
BULL-SHIT! I SAW THEM--
THERE IS NO CAMP.
THERE ARE NO PEOPLE.
WHAT YOU SAW IS IRRELEVANT... WHAT YOU SAY IS IRRELEVANT.
YEAH? SO WHAT'S TO STOP ME GOING STRAIGHT TO THE COPS?
YOU ALREADY DID. AND WHAT DID IT ACHIEVE? THREE MORE DEATHS ON YOUR CONSCIENCE.
PERCEPTION IS ALL THAT MATTERS, AND WE CONTROL THE PUBLIC DISCOURSE. DO YOU UNDERSTAND?
YOU ARE INCAPABLE OF THREATENING US.
IN POINT OF FACT, MR. DOBSON, IT IS EXTRAORDINARY THAT YOU HAVE MADE US NOTICE YOU AT ALL.
YOU SHOULD BE PROUD.
GO FUCK YOURSELF.

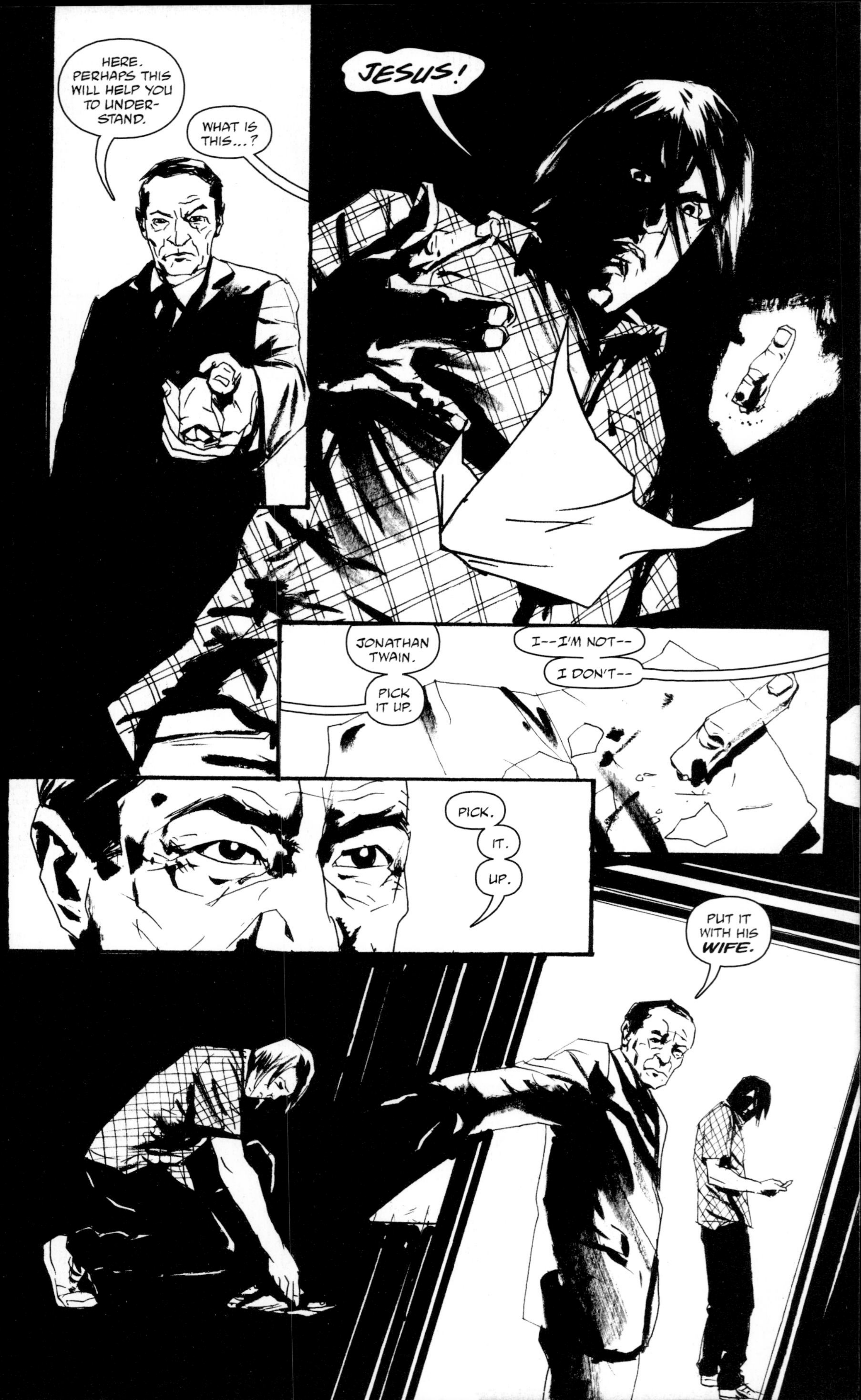
HERE. PERHAPS THIS WILL HELP YOU TO UNDER-STAND.
WHAT IS THIS...?
JESUS!
JONATHAN TWAIN.
PICK IT UP.
I--I'M NOT--
I DON'T--
PICK.
IT.
UP.
PUT IT WITH HIS WIFE.

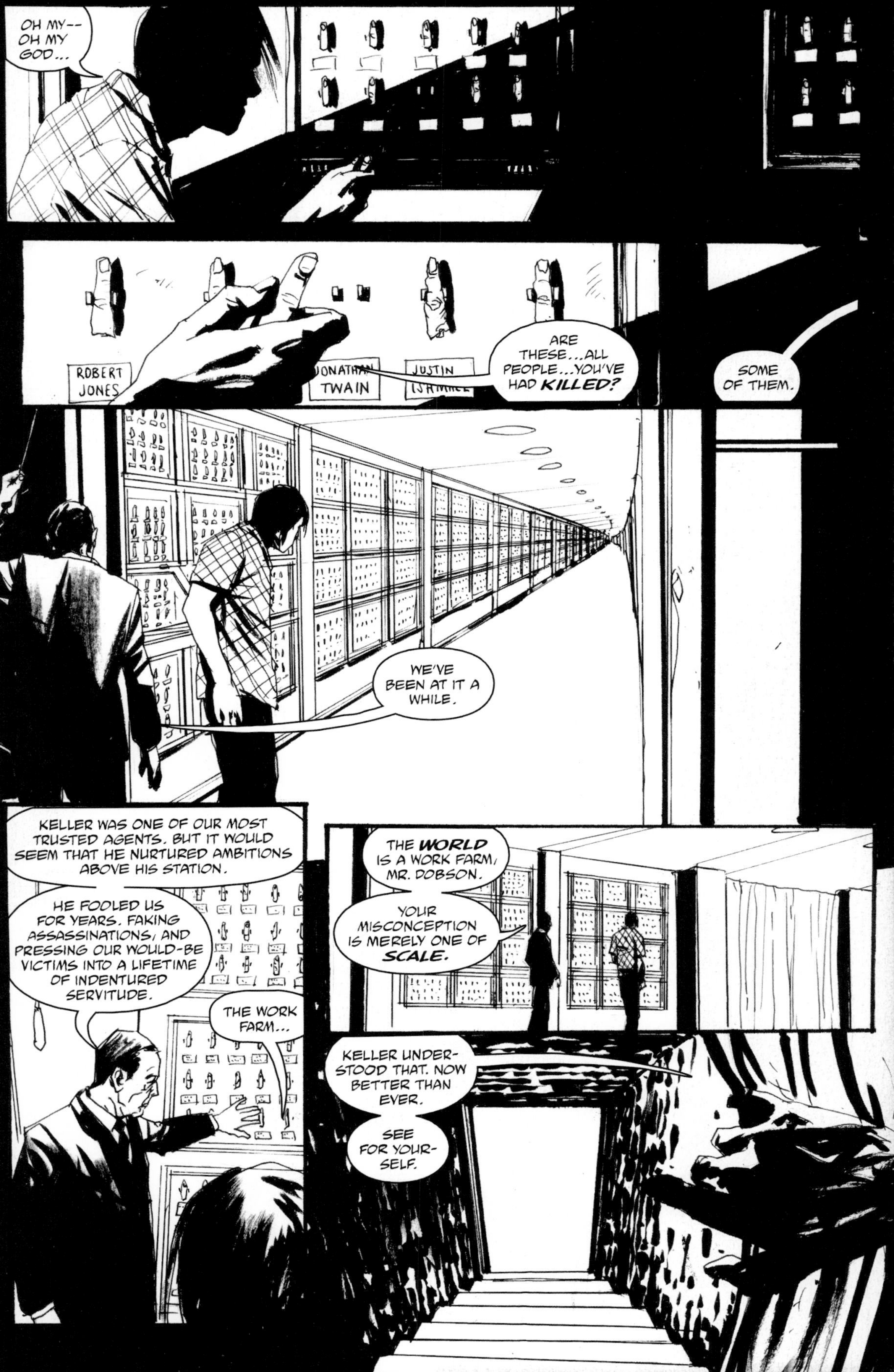
OH MY-- OH MY GOD...
ROBERT JONES
JONATHAN TWAIN
JUSTIN
ARE THESE...ALL PEOPLE...YOU'VE HAD KILLED?
SOME OF THEM.
WE'VE BEEN AT IT A WHILE.
KELLER WAS ONE OF OUR MOST TRUSTED AGENTS. BUT IT WOULD SEEM THAT HE NURTURED AMBITIONS ABOVE HIS STATION.
HE FOOLED US FOR YEARS. FAKING ASSASSINATIONS, AND PRESSING OUR WOULD-BE VICTIMS INTO A LIFETIME OF INDENTURED SERVITUDE.
THE WORK FARM...
THE WORLD IS A WORK FARM, MR. DOBSON.
YOUR MISCONCEPTION IS MERELY ONE OF SCALE.
KELLER UNDERSTOOD THAT. NOW BETTER THAN EVER.
SEE FOR YOURSELF.

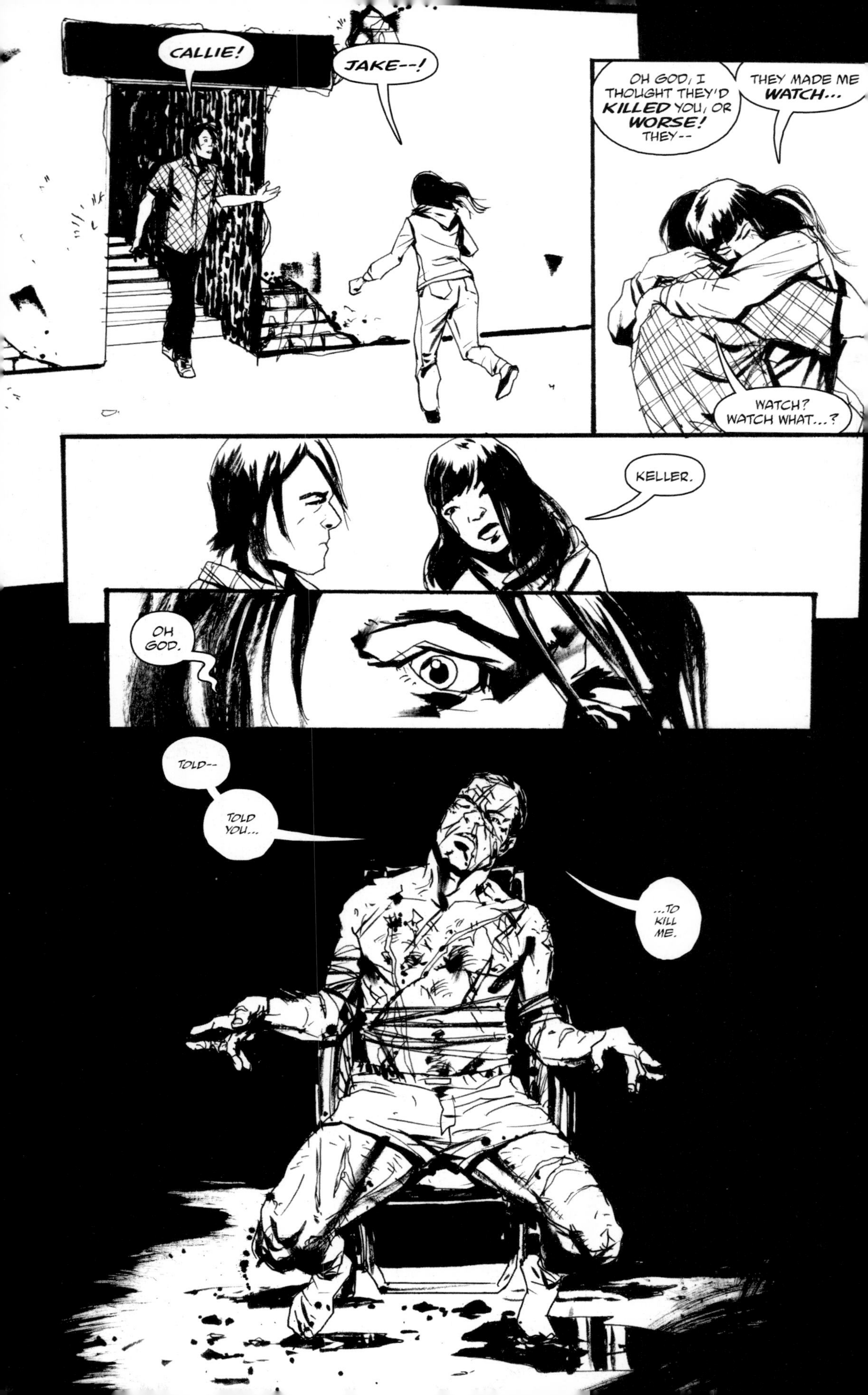
CALLIE!
JAKE--!
OH GOD, I THOUGHT THEY'D KILLED YOU, OR WORSE! THEY--
THEY MADE ME WATCH...
WATCH? WATCH WHAT...?
KELLER.
OH GOD.
TOLD--
TOLD YOU...
...TO KILL ME.

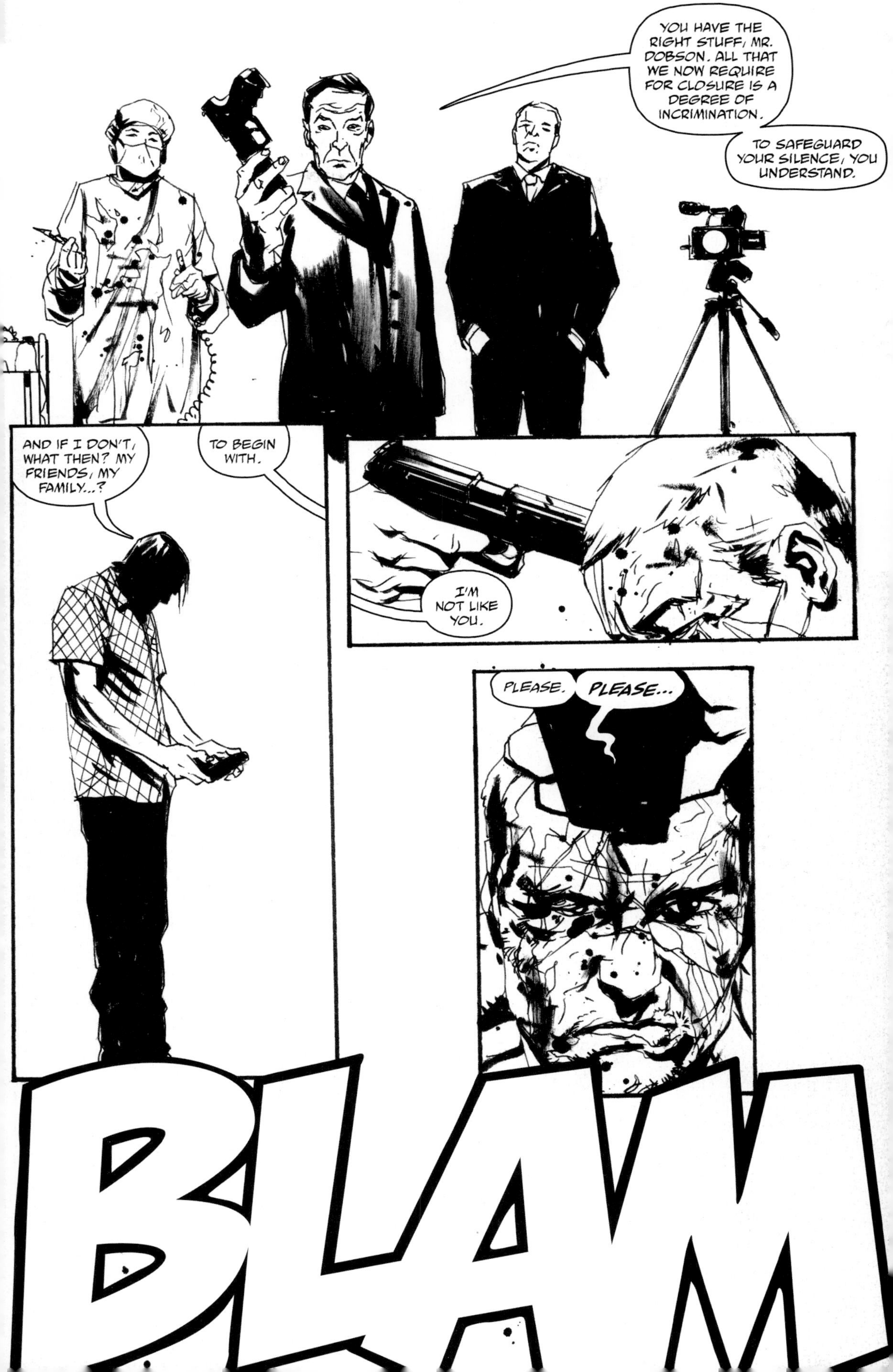

YOU HAVE THE RIGHT STUFF, MR. DOBSON. ALL THAT WE NOW REQUIRE FOR CLOSURE IS A DEGREE OF INCRIMINATION.
TO SAFEGUARD YOUR SILENCE, YOU UNDERSTAND.
AND IF I DON'T, WHAT THEN? MY FRIENDS, MY FAMILY...?
TO BEGIN WITH.
I'M NOT LIKE YOU.
PLEASE.
PLEASE...
BLAM

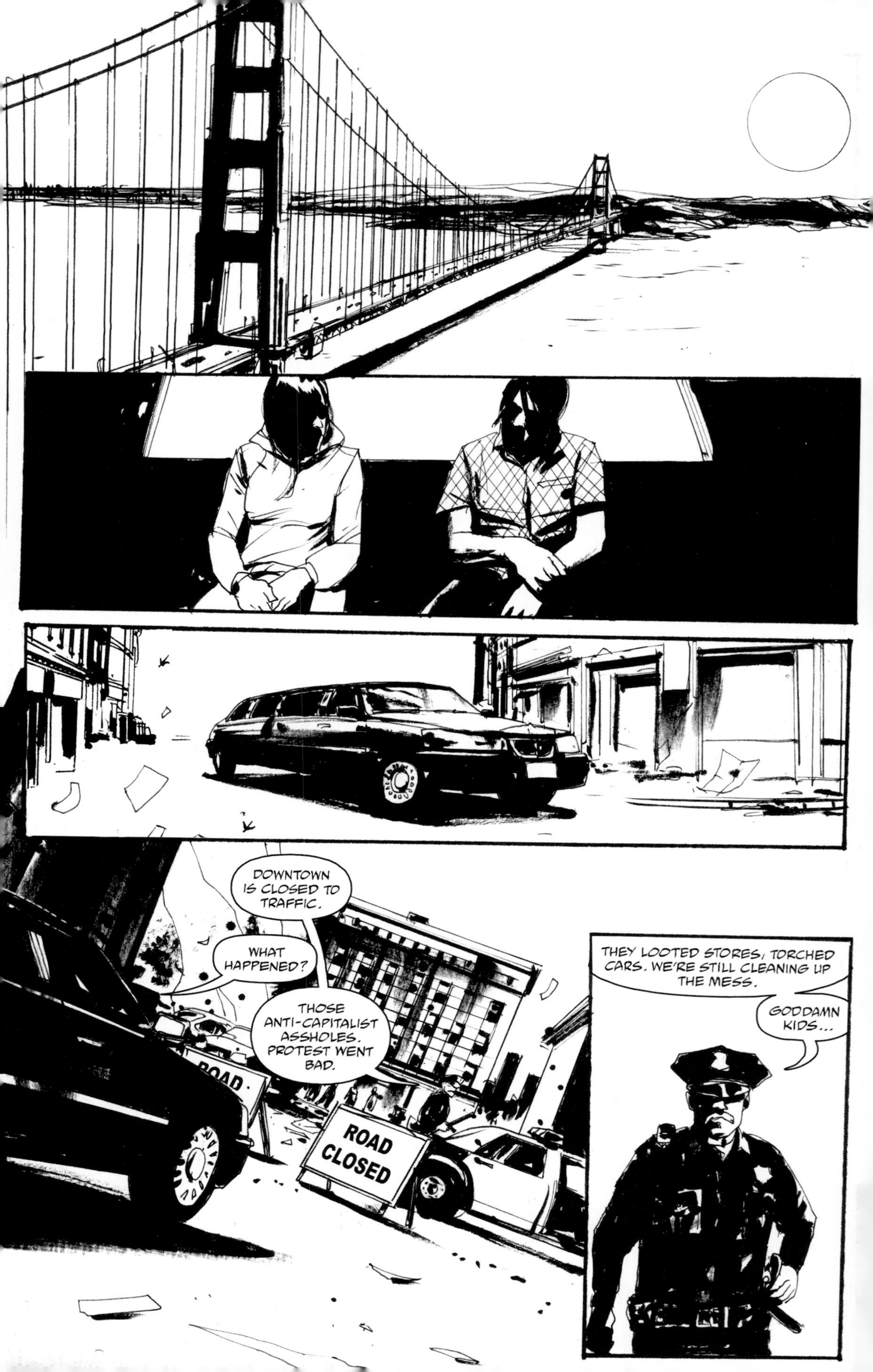
DOWNTOWN IS CLOSED TO TRAFFIC.
WHAT HAPPENED?
THOSE ANTI-CAPITALIST ASSHOLES. PROTEST WENT BAD.
ROAD CLOSED
THEY LOOTED STORES, TORCHED CARS. WE'RE STILL CLEANING UP THE MESS.
GODDAMN KIDS...

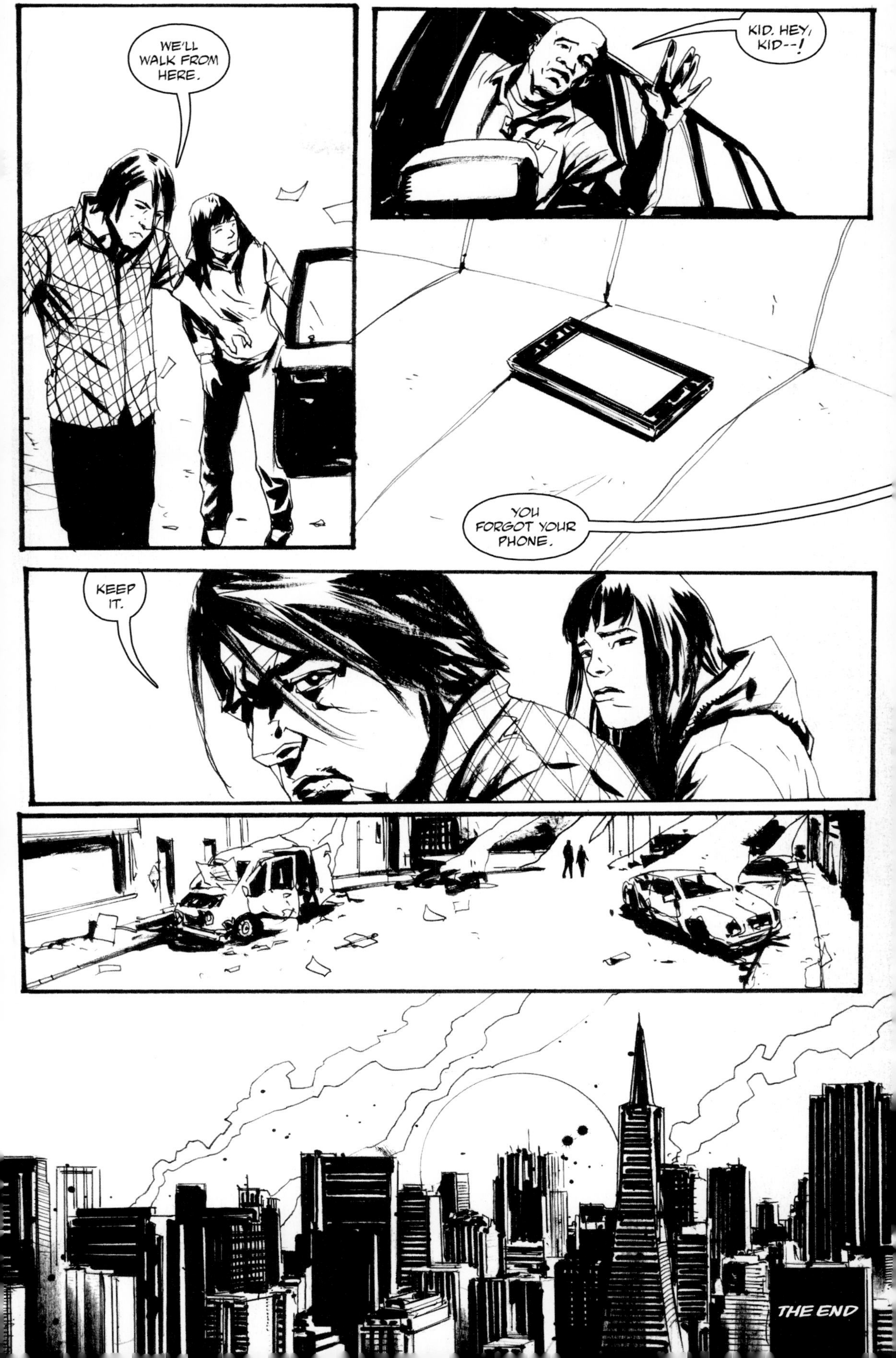
WE'LL WALK FROM HERE.
KID, HEY, KID--!
YOU FORGOT YOUR PHONE.
KEEP IT.
THE END

So that was SNAPSHOT. Maybe not the most upbeat of endings, but that that's just one of the great things about doing creator-owned work – you don't have to cop out. Jock and I would like to offer a sincere THANK YOU for reading. We hope you dug it.

SNAPSHOT's been a labor of love for us. It's slightly terrifying to think it's now eight years since I first came up with the story. I'd originally envisioned it as a screenplay, but after I told Jock about it at the Bristol comic con bar, he said, "That'd make a great comic. I'd love to draw it."

Pro tip: When Jock says he wants to draw your comic, you say YES.

It took us ages, fitting SNAPSHOT in between work-for-hire gigs. I spent a few years exclusive to DC and Marvel, and Jock's film concept design work was taking off in addition to his monthly comic art duties. There was the small matter of our Vertigo thriller THE LOSERS being turned into a movie. Our little creator-owned book kept getting nudged aside by more pressing deadlines. We both have kids to feed and mortgages to pay; but eventually there comes a time when the stories inside you just have to get out, y'know?

The final push came from another fateful conversation in another comic con bar (can you see a pattern emerging here?), this time with Matt Smith. No, not that one; I'm talking about the editor of 2000AD. We'd worked together back at the turn of the century, and I ran into him again at the Pony Bar in the wee small hours one night after New York Comic Con.

Matt had been running TANK GIRL as a back-up strip in 2000AD's sister title, the JUDGE DREDD MEGAZINE (which incidentally was where Jock and I first worked together). Seeing that he'd opened the doors to creator-owned work, I pitched him SNAPSHOT, and he said, "We could run it in the MEGAZINE if you like."

Suddenly we had a deadline. Which was exactly what we needed.

I'd designed SNAPSHOT to run as four 28-page issues, giving readers the maximum bang for their buck in a 32-page self-cover comic. And as luck would have it, the MEGAZINE slot was 14 pages per issue. So we ran it in half-issue chunks; it broke down pretty easily.

We brought in the great Clem Robins, whose lettering skills we so appreciated on THE LOSERS. And we finally finished our little creator-owned comic. We considered having it colored for the US edition, but Jock had realized part-way through that he was already drawing for black-and-white; we both love mono books, Jock's stark black-and-white artwork kicks all kinds of ass (as you can see!), and it keeps the printing costs (and therefore the cover price) down.

All we had to do then was convince Image to publish it. I showed Eric Stephenson a printout of the first issue at - hey! - a comic con bar, and we were on our way.

All it took was eight years.

We hope you think it was worth the wait.

Andy Diggle
Lancaster, UK
April 2013

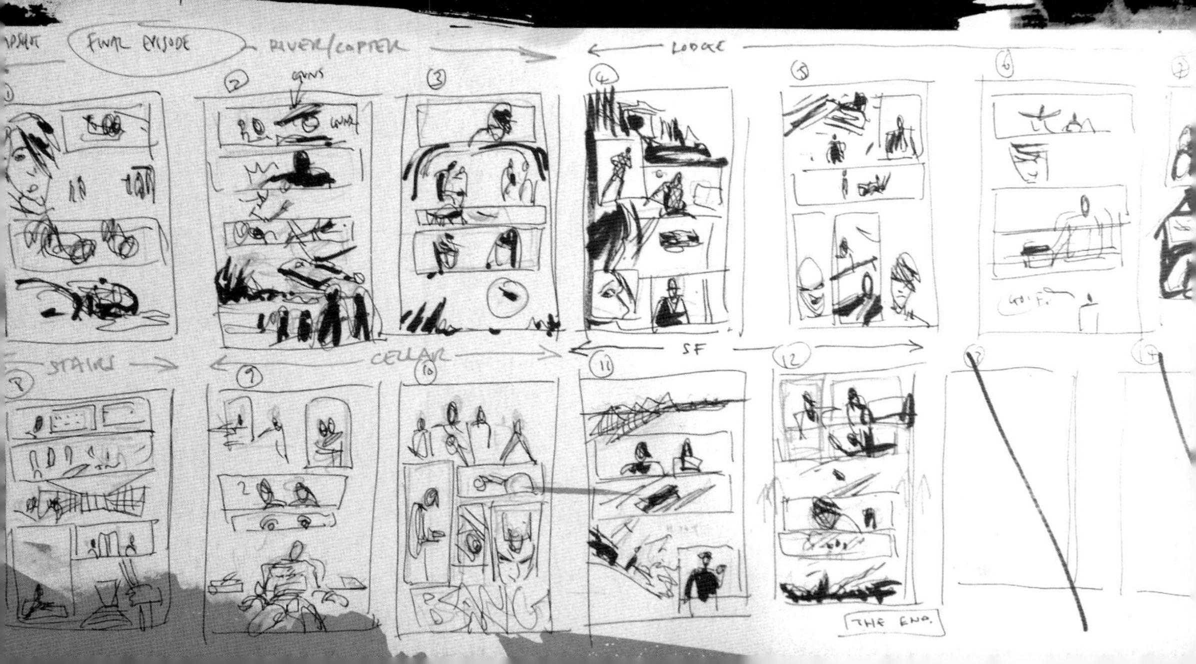
FINAL EPISODE
RIVER/COPTER
LODGE
STAIRS
CELLAR
SF
BANG
THE END

COVER GALLERY

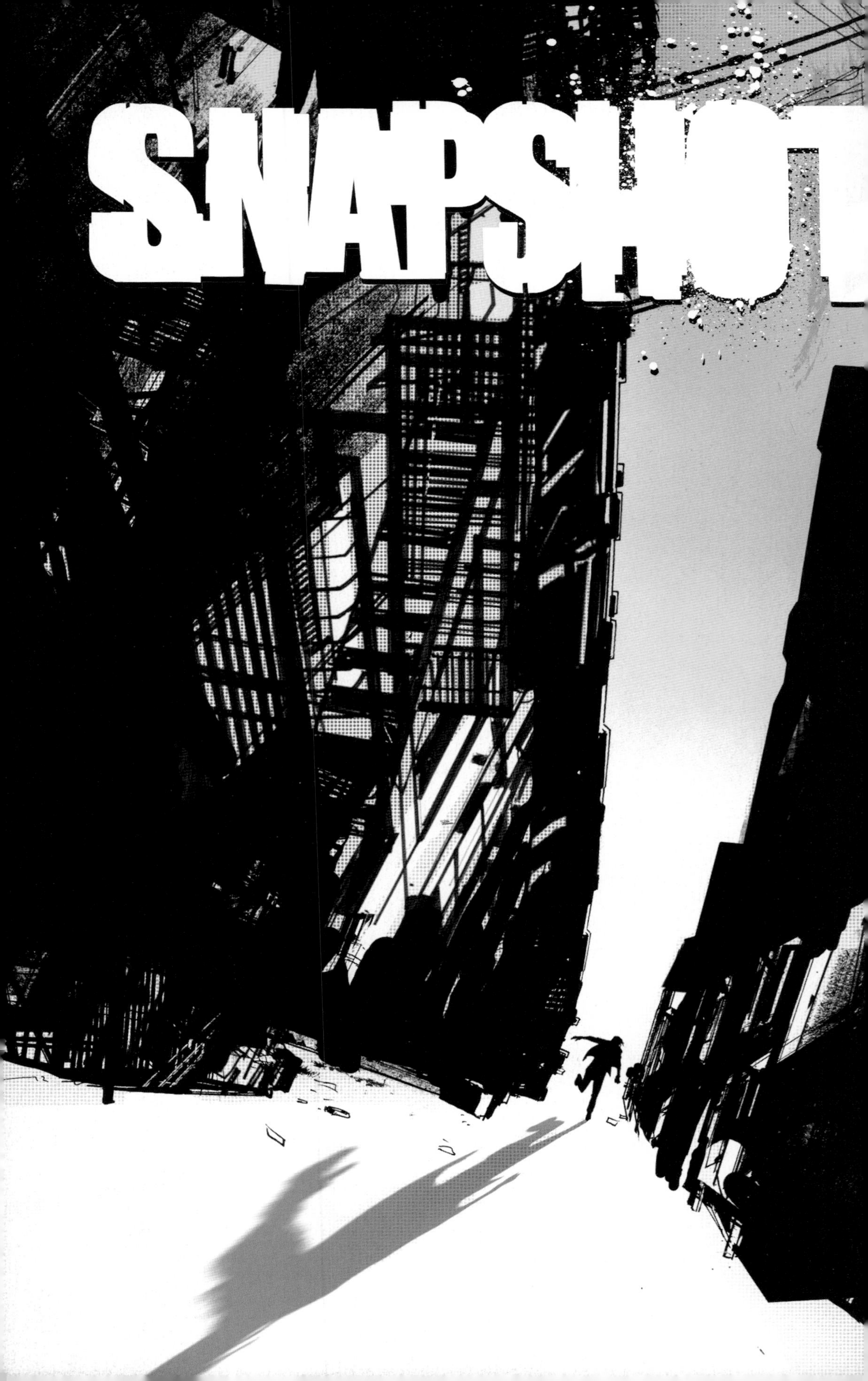
SNAPSHOT

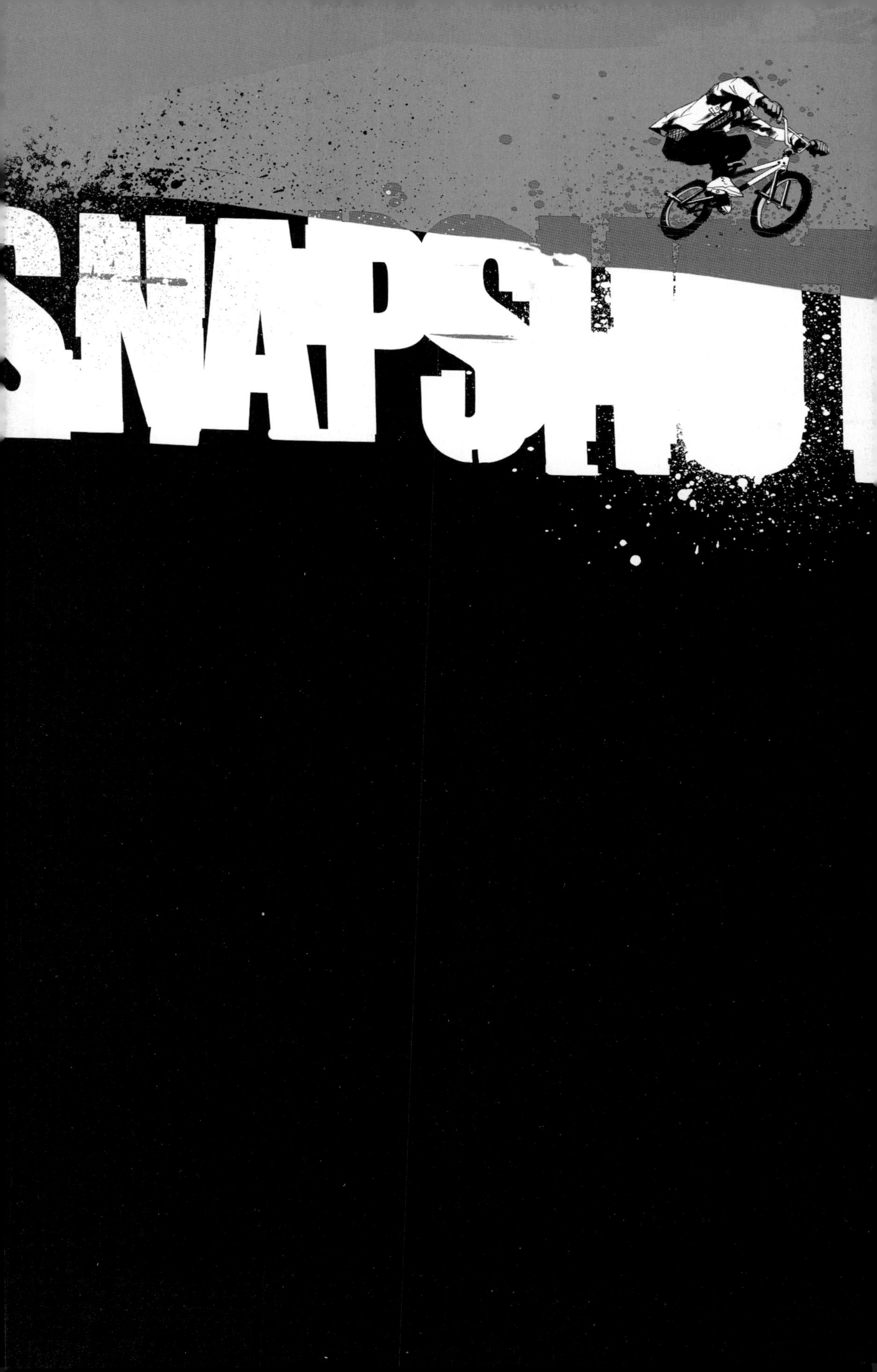
SNAPSHOT

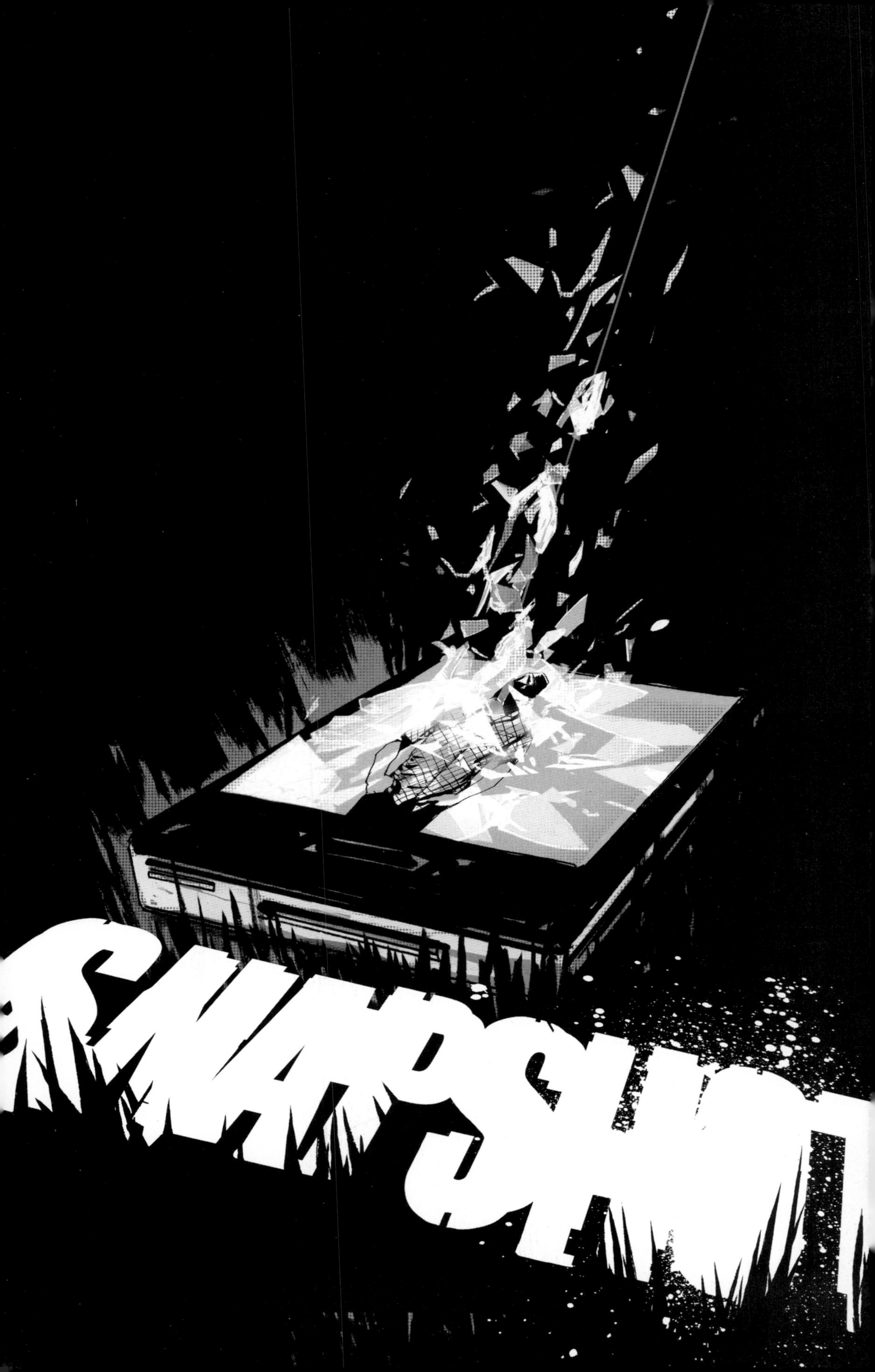
SNAPSHOT

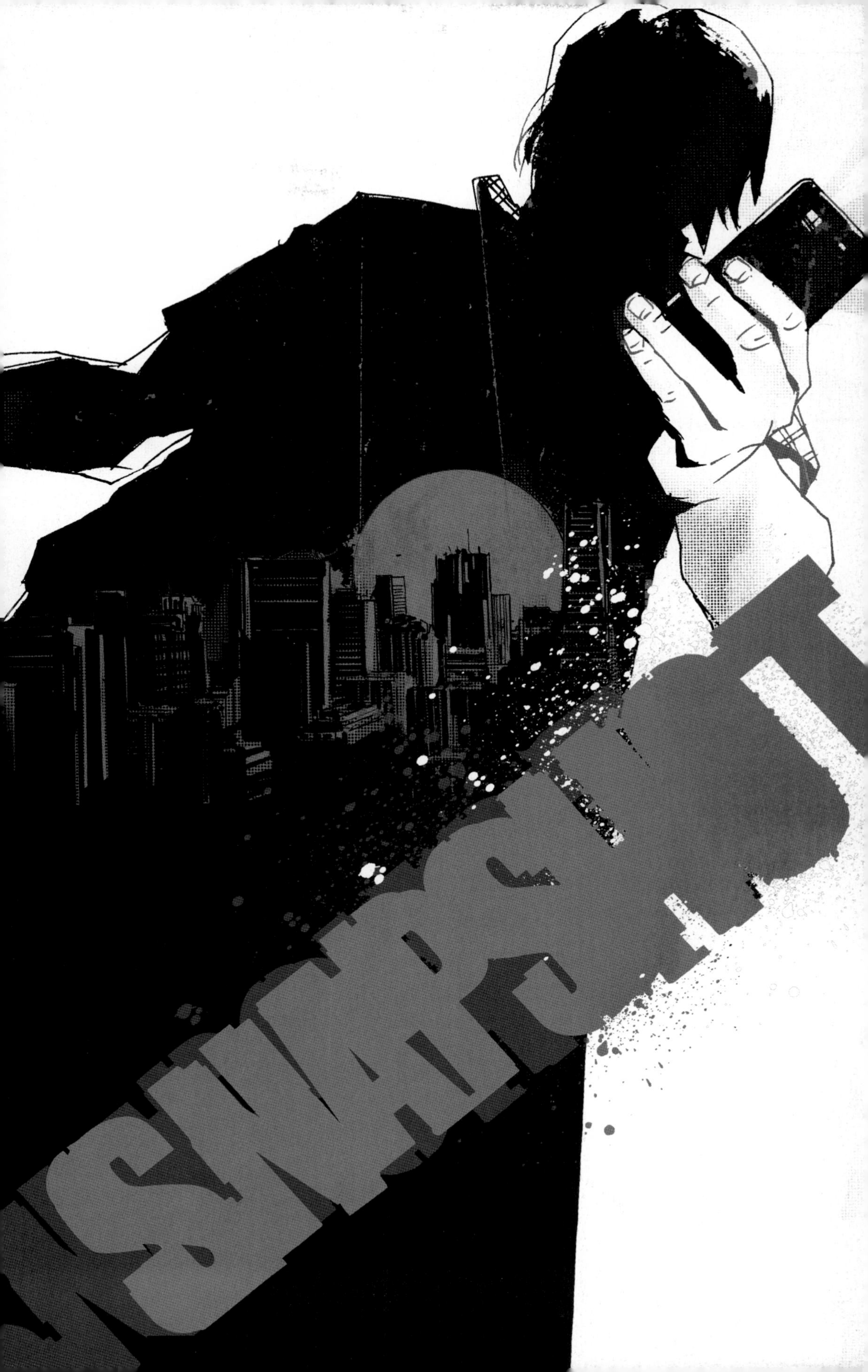

SNAPSHOT TPB.
FIRST PRINTING. DECEMBER 2013.
ISBN# 978-1-60706-842-6

PRINTED IN THE U.S.A. For information regarding the CPSIA on this printed material call: 203-595-3636 and provide reference # RICH – 536369.

FOR INTERNATIONAL RIGHTS, CONTACT : snapshot@andydiggle.com